Landmark

Intermediate **Student's Book**

Simon Haines & Barbara Stewart

OXFORD
UNIVERSITY PRESS

1 It's a pleasure

Preview

Your thoughts

1 What things do you enjoy doing? Make a list.
   - Include everyday things like drinking coffee, eating chocolate or watching TV, as well as hobbies, sports, work or studies.
   - Think about things you do alone and things you do with other people.

2 Find out whether any other students enjoy the same activities as you.

Read

1 You are going to read about what five people enjoy doing. Check that you understand the difference in meaning between these sets of words before you read.
   a *companion / friend*   c *pleasure / thrill*
   b *enjoy / love / adore*   d *intellectual / emotional*

2 a Which activities the people describe do you also enjoy?
   b Three of them feel guilty. Which ones and why?

---

1 Julio Medem, Spanish film director

I love leaving my house with some tapes and driving out of town listening to quiet music. The travelling is more important than arriving. I could drive 300 km without knowing where I'm going. It helps me to escape from myself. It's even better if I have a companion.

2 Hervé Leger, French designer

I enjoy eating enormous cream-filled cakes called Mont Blanc from Angelina's tea-room in Paris, but I feel guilty about eating them if I'm overweight.

3 Ferruccio Amendola, Italian actor

I enjoy very simple pleasures like playing card games with my partner – we both adore bridge. My work is another great enjoyment. I only feel guilty if my pleasures mean that I don't have enough time for my family and friends.

4 Sonia Rykiel, French designer

Things that give me pleasure are reading a good book, travelling first class with the man I love, eating a wonderful meal, talking to my sister on the telephone, trying on beautiful clothes which fit perfectly. I must admit, though, I feel guilty about eating too much, going to the cinema in the afternoon and having too much chocolate in my handbag.

5 Yan Pascal Tortellier, French cellist

Nothing can compare with the pleasure I get from playing to a large audience. It gives me an intellectual, emotional and technical thrill. Outdoor sports are probably my greatest pleasures away from the concert hall.

The European Magazine

3 Who enjoys … (write numbers 1–5)

a something to do with their work?
b food and eating?
c something to do with music?
d doing things with other people?

Vocabulary

Match the words in **bold** with their meanings.

a *It helps me to* **escape from** *myself.*	1 group of people who listen to music, watch a play, etc.
b *… I'm* **overweight**.	2 done in the open air, not in a building
c *… beautiful clothes which* **fit** *…*	3 get away from
d *… playing to a large* **audience**.	4 are the right shape and size
e **Outdoor** *sports …*	5 too heavy or fat

Listen

1 **1.1** You are going to hear eight people's answers to this question: *Is there anything you enjoy doing that makes you feel guilty?*

a Guess what some of the answers will be.
b Now listen and check your predictions.

2 Listen again. Make notes about each speaker under these headings.

• Enjoyable activity
• Reason for feeling guilty

Example
Speaker 1   *Smoking.*
            She takes cigarettes from other people.

Have your say

1 Tell a partner about any activities you enjoy, but feel guilty about.

2 Why do people feel guilty?

Grammar review: Frequency expressions with the Present simple

1 Listen to the speakers again and fill the gaps with the words or phrases you hear.

a *I* .... *take cigarettes from people …*
b *I* .... *spend at least half an hour in the shower …*
c *I* .... *go to sleep in front of the TV …*
d *I* .... *drive to work.*
e *… I* .... *walk, not even on warm sunny days.*
f *I* .... *buy new shoes.*
g *I don't* .... *do it. (use my Dad's computer)*
h *It's* .... *pretty cheap.*
i *I ring my boyfriend* .... *when my parents are out.*
j *I buy a bar* .... *when I'm on my way home from college.*

2 Look at the words and phrases you have written in the gaps.

a What do they tell you about the actions described in these sentences?
b Rank the words and phrases in sentences **a–g** in order, starting with *always* and finishing with *never*.
c Where do these words and phrases come
   • in sentences **a–g**?
   • in sentence **h**? Why is this different from sentence **b**?
   • in sentences **i** and **j**?

▶ **Language commentary p.124**

Check

3 Add the words and phrases in brackets to these sentences. Sometimes there is more than one correct answer.

Example
I work at the weekend. (*hardly ever*)
I **hardly ever** work at the weekend.

a She plays tennis for the college team. (*sometimes*)
b He drinks when he's driving. (*never*)
c We visit our relatives in America. (*every year*)
d She doesn't smoke in her friend's car. (*usually*)
e I'm busy in the evenings. (*always*)

4 Work in groups. Ask and answer questions about these activities. If you answer *yes* to a question, say how often you do it.

Example
Do you ever give money to beggars?
Yes, I do. I always give money to beggars.
No, I don't.

• Give money to beggars
• Speak to strangers on trains or buses
• Buy flowers for someone
• Vote in elections
• Go late-night shopping
• Hitch-hike or give a hitch-hiker a lift in your car

> ▶ Present perfect simple and adverbs   p.7
> ▶ Comparison of adjectives   p.10

Reading

In your experience

1 What activities are currently fashionable or popular among people of different ages in your country? Think about your friends and family. Think about these subjects, and add your own.

---

ways of relaxing   sports and exercise
music and dancing   night life

---

2 Compare ideas in pairs or groups.

Read

1 a Read **Part 1** of the article and decide which of these titles is the most appropriate.
  • Pleasure: the bad news
  • Eat, drink and don't be sorry
  • Guilt is good for you

b Read **Part 1** again and answer these questions.
  1 How are the Dutch different from the other nationalities mentioned?
  2 According to Jan Snell, what is the physical effect of feeling guilty?
  3 How are recent medical studies different from previous studies?
  4 What practical use(s) do you think could be made of the fact that certain smells can make people feel relaxed and happy?

2 Now read **Part 2** of the article, which describes research into the pros and cons (advantages and disadvantages) of some common activities. What information do you find surprising?

Part 1

'Let us eat and drink for tomorrow we shall die,' said a philosopher 3,000 years ago. And the Greek thinker Epicurus said, 'Pleasure is the beginning and the end of living happily.'

Unfortunately, scientists have recently found that the instinct to enjoy ourselves
5 has almost disappeared because of feelings of guilt. Apparently Germans feel bad about alcohol, Spaniards feel guilty about not going to church, and Italians feel guilty about drinking too much coffee. On the other hand, it seems that the Dutch have discovered the secret of modern living: they enjoy themselves the most and feel the least guilty. The scientists say the Dutch have got it right: guilt is bad for the body!

Jan Snell, from Amsterdam University, has some simple information for people
10 who like to enjoy themselves: 'If you enjoy what you're doing, the body produces substances which fight infection. If you feel guilty, you weaken that biological effect.'

Jan Snell has studied the connection between pleasure and guilt. To date, most medical studies have looked mainly at the negative effects of substances such as caffeine or alcohol, but neglected the positive effects. Scientists have now found
15 that even smelling coffee or whisky can affect the brain and cause chemical changes which produce feelings of relaxation and pleasure.

Part 2

Smoking tobacco
Pros: Tobacco contains nicotine which is a tranquillizer and a stimulant. It helps the body to burn food more quickly.
Cons: It is one of the main causes of cancer and heart disease.

Drinking alcohol
Pros: Studies show that a little alcohol can be better for your health than none at all. Red wine is the healthiest alcoholic drink. One or two glasses a day can reduce the risk of various illnesses.
Cons: In the short term, alcohol damages our reactions and judgement. In the long term, and if too much is consumed, it can cause liver disease and cancer.

Relaxing
Pros: Relaxing reduces blood pressure and stress hormones, which can cause disease.
Cons: It uses little or no energy, so it does nothing to reduce weight.

Drinking coffee and tea
Pros: Both drinks contain caffeine which increases alertness. Tea also contains tannin which helps to protect against heart disease.
Cons: Because they are stimulants they can interrupt sleep and relaxation. Coffee drunk at six o'clock in the evening will still be in the blood at midnight.

The European Magazine

Close up

1.3 What other *instincts* do human beings have?

1.11 *weaken* is a verb related to the adjective *weak*. Which verb, related to the adjective *strong*, means the opposite of *weaken*? Do you know any more pairs of words like this?

Understanding ideas

1 Why could it be an advantage for the body to burn food more quickly?

2 In what situations do people drink coffee in order to stay alert?

3 For which activities do the pros seem to be more important than the cons?

Have your say

Why do you think so many people enjoy doing things which are harmful to them?

Present perfect simple and adverbs

Exploring concepts

1 The verb in this sentence is in the Present perfect simple.
*Jan Snell **has studied** the connection between pleasure and guilt.*
How is this tense formed?

2 We often use the Present perfect simple to link past events with the present.

a Do you know when the events in these sentences happened?
   1 *The Dutch have discovered the secret of modern living.*
   2 *To date, most medical studies have looked at the negative effects of caffeine or alcohol.*
   3 *Scientists have found that even smelling coffee can affect the brain.*

b What are the present effects or results of the events in the sentences above? Choose one of these.
   1 We only know about the damage these substances can do to us.
   2 Our brain can be affected even if we do not drink these substances.
   3 These people are happier than other nationalities.

3 a We use certain adverbs with the Present perfect simple to stress this link with the present. Circle the adverbs or adverb phrases in these sentences.
   1 No more coffee for me, thanks. I've (already) had three cups.
   2 I've just started taking regular exercise, but I don't feel any better so far.
   3 He's been on a diet since January and he hasn't lost any weight yet.
   4 So far I've lost three kilos and I've only been on my diet for a week.
   5 She's got a terrible cough, but she still hasn't given up smoking.
   6 I've never tried whisky. What's it like?

b Which of the words or phrases you circled are used with negative verbs?

c Notice the position of the words or phrases. Which come(s)
   1 at the end of a sentence?
   2 before the auxiliary verb?
   3 at the beginning or the end of a sentence?
   4 after the auxiliary verb?

d Find *for* and *since* in the sentences. Which is followed by a point in time and which by a period of time?

▶ **Language commentary p.124**

Exploitation

1 Complete these sentences with *already, so far, yet, still* or *just*.

a A Have you had your exam result .... ?
   B No. I .... haven't heard anything.

b A *The Z Men* is on at the cinema. Shall we go and see it?
   B No, I've .... seen it.

c A How many people are coming to your party?
   B I'm not sure. I've only had seven replies ....

d A You look terrible. Are you OK?
   B I'm all right, don't worry – I've .... woken up.

e A Is Kate back?
   B Yes, she got home last week but I haven't seen her ....

2 a Complete these questions. Use a question word and the right form of one of these verbs.

buy   go to   ~~meet~~   see   sleep in

1 *Who is* the strangest person you've ever *met* ?
2 .... the most expensive thing you've ever .... ?
3 .... the most uncomfortable place you've ever .... ?
4 .... the funniest film you've ever .... ?
5 .... the most interesting place you've ever .... ?

b Ask a partner about their experiences and make a note of their answers.

c Work with another pair of students. Compare your answers. Which was the most interesting answer to each question?

Free speech

3 Work in groups.

a Choose two of these subjects, then talk about them for two minutes.
   • This month's local and national news stories
   • This year's international news
   • Recent discoveries in health, the natural world, technology, etc.
   • The latest gossip about famous people

b Make a list of important or interesting events and present them to the class as a series of radio or TV news headlines.

Skills

Write and speak

1 What is your idea of an ideal holiday? Imagine that money and time are no problem. Make notes under these headings.
- The ideal location
- The ideal time of year
- The ideal place to stay
- The ideal person to be with
- Activities you'd like to do on your ideal holiday

2 Find someone with similar ideas to yours.

Listen

1 **1.2** You are going to hear four people describing their ideal holiday. Whose ideal holiday is closest to yours?

2 Listen again and complete this table with information from the recording.

Speaker	The most important aspect(s) of the ideal holiday	Specific activities
1		
2		
3		
4		

Read

1 You are going to read about a *virtual* seaside resort. What do you think *virtual* means here? Look at the photographs and guess.

2 Now read the article quickly.
- **a** Which of the four speakers you have just listened to would be most likely to enjoy a holiday at the Ocean Dome?
- **b** Would you enjoy a holiday there? Why? Why not?

Sun, sea and roof

From Japan, the country that brought you the virtual pet and the virtual pop star, comes the latest leisure idea: the virtual seaside resort. This is the Ocean Dome at Myazaki, south-west of Tokyo, the biggest artificial indoor beach
5 in the world, where overstressed Japanese office workers can kick off their shoes and walk on the beautiful cool white sand. But it is not real sand – it's fake, made entirely from crushed stone.

In fact, everything under the dome is fake, from the 140
10 metre-long beach to the air temperature – kept at a steady 30°C by an incredible giant, ultra-modern central-heating system. If that's too hot for you, you can order an attractive plastic palm tree to provide shade. With fake waves and fake sunshine, but not fake crowds, the Ocean
15 Dome has become such a craze that the average Japanese office worker usually has to share it with about 10,000 other sunseekers.

The fake sea covers about three times the area of the beach and has 15,826 tonnes of water – that's about the
20 same as ten Olympic swimming pools. It is kept at a constant temperature of 28°C.

But why spend so much money on a man-made beach when the real thing is free? Well, bathing off the Japanese coast isn't much fun because the sea is cold, polluted
25 and full of sharks. Besides, the Ocean Dome is closer to McDonald's.

But even a fake beach holiday wouldn't be complete without some optional activities, and Ocean Dome offers an amazing choice. You can start with the 'Rocky Slider',
30 a high slide which takes you down into the water, before moving on to 'Lost World', a raft-journey on an underground lake. Here, more overstressed Japanese workers can kick off their shoes and scream with terror on a high-speed trip through white-water rapids in
35 complete darkness.

And after that, what could be better than a run on the ski-slope? Just half an hour from downtown Tokyo, there is a huge artificial ski-slope where even more overstressed workers can practise their skiing on perfect, powdery
40 snow – indoors of course. *Focus*

Guessing meanings

Guess the meanings of these words from the article. Use the other words in the sentence and these questions to help you.

a *fake* (l.7)
How are the sand, the beach and the waves at the Ocean Dome different from those at normal seaside resorts? Can you find another word in the article with a similar meaning?

b *shade* (l.13)
How can a tree help you if the sun is too hot?

c *craze* (l.15)
What does the fact that 10,000 people share the beach tell you about the Ocean Dome?

d *powdery* (l.39)
What does the noun *powder* mean?

Understanding ideas

Read the text again to find the answers to these questions.

1 Why are pets and pop stars from Japan mentioned in the first paragraph?

2 In what ways is the Ocean Dome similar to a real seaside resort?

3 In what ways is it different from a real resort?

4 In what way are the Ocean Dome and the ski-slope the same?

5 What does the article tell you about the kind of people who visit the Ocean Dome? What do you think the main reason for their visit is?

Speak

Work in groups. You are going to plan the perfect holiday resort of the future.

1 Work through these stages.
  a Decide on an ideal location.
  b Make a list of all the features and activities which the new resort should have.
  c Decide what kind of people you want to attract to the resort.
  d Plan an introductory advertising campaign. Produce one or more of these types of publicity.
    • A poster
    • A newspaper advertisement
    • A 20-second script for a radio or TV commercial

2 Using your publicity and your other notes, present your ideas and plans to the class.

3 Finally, take a class vote for the best 'ideal' resort.

Grammar extra

Comparison of adjectives

Read

1 a Many people enjoy eating and drinking. How important are they to you? Complete this survey.

Food facts

Do you agree or disagree with these statements? Write ✓, ✗ or ?

☐ The quality of the food you eat is less important than the quantity.

☐ Vegetarians are much healthier than meat-eaters.

☐ Modern production techniques mean that food is safer than it was in the past.

☐ Home-cooking is far better for you than fast food.

☐ Frozen food is just as good for you as fresh food.

Finish these sentences in your own way.

For me, the best kind of food is

....

The worst kind of food is

....

For me, the most enjoyable meal of the day is ....

and the least enjoyable is

....

The strangest food I've ever eaten is ....

The hottest or spiciest food I've ever eaten is ....

The strongest drink I've ever tasted is ....

b Compare your answers with other students. What do you agree and disagree about?

Exploring concepts

1 How much do you remember about comparative and superlative adjectives? Try this short test.

Test yourself! Finish sentences **a–h** to make the rules.

a To make the comparative of one-syllable adjectives ending in one vowel + one consonant (e.g. *hot*), ...

b To make the comparative of two-syllable adjectives ending in *-y* (e.g. *healthy*), ...

c To make the comparative of most adjectives of two or more syllables (e.g. *enjoyable*), ...

d To make the superlative of one-syllable adjectives ending in *-e* (e.g. *safe*), ...

e To make the superlative of three- or four-syllable adjectives (e.g. *uninteresting*) ....

f The comparative of *good* is ....

g *The worst* is the superlative of ....

h To compare two things which are the same, use ....

2 These words and phrases can be used with comparative adjectives.

a bit	a little	a lot	far	much	slightly

a Which refer to big differences between two things and which refer to small differences? Make two lists.

b Which word or phrase in each list is the most formal?

▶ **Language commentary p.125**

Exploitation

1 Compare different types of food. Use the adjectives from these lists. Make sentences like this:

Fruit is better for you than meat.   *Meat is the most expensive food.*

Health words	bad (for you) fattening good (for you) healthy
Taste words	bitter rich salty sour strong sweet tasty weak
Other words	cheap expensive popular safe unusual

2 a Design a sample menu for one of these people for a typical day.
  • Someone who is overweight and needs to slim.
  • Someone who has been ill and needs to put on weight.
  • Someone who eats rich food and wants a more natural diet.

b Exchange menus with a partner. Compare ideas.

Exploring words

Holidays and activities

1 a People like different types of holiday. Which of the words or phrases do you associate with these types of holiday? Write lists under these headings, adding any more words you know.

- Activity
- Beach
- Cultural

art gallery   canoeing   castle or palace   cycling   fishing   historical ruins
monument   museum   riding   rock-climbing   sailing   sand   sea   seaside resort
sightseeing   skiing   snorkelling   sunbathing   surfing   theatre
walking   water-skiing

b Which of these verbs go with the holiday words in your lists? Sometimes more than one answer is possible.

go   go round   go to   lie   play   swim   visit

Example
*People **go sightseeing**, but **visit a monument**.*

2 a Match the words from your Activity holiday list with the activities you can see in this illustration.

b Make lists of the basic equipment you need for these activities.
Example
*To go canoeing you need **a canoe, a paddle**, and **a helmet**.*

c Find out how many students in the class do or have done these activities. Ask questions like this: *Do you go canoeing?* or *Have you ever been canoeing?*

3 a Choose two of these statements about holiday activities – one you agree with and one you disagree with.

- 'Sunbathing is a pointless waste of time.'
- 'The people who visit museums are as boring as the things in them.'
- 'Art galleries are full of over-priced rubbish.'
- 'Skiing is an expensive sport for rich people.'

b Make up two more statements of the same kind.

c Now carry out a class survey to find out how many people in the class agree and disagree with your four statements. Make a note of their opinions.

d Compare your findings with the rest of the class.

Writing

Describing leisure facilities

Read

1 Read this part of a letter from friends of yours who are planning a visit to your town or city. When do they want to come?

> staying for at least a week and we were wondering if you could send us a list of interesting things to do and places to visit while we're there. It'll probably be early July. Will you be there then? It would be nice if we could meet up and go for a drink or a meal together. We've got all the tourist brochures, but we'd be really interested to hear the suggestions of someone who lives in the area.

2 Why do your friends prefer your ideas to those in the tourist brochures?

Brainstorm and notes

Work in pairs or groups.

1 Think of popular leisure facilities in your town or city (or the place where you are studying). Make notes under these headings. Follow the examples.

Leisure facilities	What to do there
Little Theatre	see plays and musicals
Rock Palace	dance to famous pop and rock bands

2 Make detailed notes about two or three of the places on your list.

Example
Rock Palace *on the outskirts of town – great atmosphere – mainly for under-25s – in old warehouse – dance to all kinds of music – live music and disco – not expensive – easy by bus and car*

3 Organize your notes in preparation for writing.

Example
Where?   *on the outskirts of town – in old warehouse*
How to get there?   *easy by public transport and car*
What happens?   *mainly under-25s – dance to all kinds of music – live music and disco – sound and lighting systems*
Your opinion   *exciting atmosphere – not expensive*

Write

1 You are going to write part of the reply to your friends. Write the first draft of your description, using the notes you have made. Write 80–100 words.

2 a Exchange descriptions with a partner from a different group.

   b Read their description. Do the places sound attractive? Make two or three suggestions for improving the descriptions.

   c Discuss the improvement ideas in pairs, then write the final version of your description.

> **Reminder**
> • Link ideas.
> • Use opinion adjectives.
> • Don't repeat nouns – use pronouns.

Language in action

Asking and answering personal questions

Introduction

1 a Read these answers someone gave in reply to questions they were asked in an interview about their personal lives and their spare time interests. Work out what the interviewer's questions were.

   1 On the 23rd of December 1976 – it was a Friday.
   2 For nearly two years, now. Before that I worked for a Japanese computer company.
   3 Yes, I do. The pay is good and the people I work with are really friendly. It's like one big happy family here.
   4 I'm sorry, but that's my business, but it's certainly better than my last job, so I'm not complaining.
   5 No, not yet, but I will be this time next year. The wedding is fixed for June 21st.
   6 She's an assistant editor on the local newspaper.
   7 She's short and slim with dark hair and she sometimes wears glasses.
   8 Sorry, I'd rather not answer that if you don't mind. It's too far in the future. Let's just say that neither of us is quite ready yet.
   9 I play the bass guitar in a rock band, I go to concerts, the cinema. I do all kinds of things, erm – I'm quite keen on sport.
  10 Yes, I do. Tennis in the summer and basketball all the year round.

b Compare your questions with another student.

2 **1.3** Listen and check.

3 a Why do you think the speaker does not want to answer questions **4** and **8**? Would people in your country answer this kind of question? Are there other questions they wouldn't answer?

  b What expressions does the speaker use when he doesn't want to answer a question?

▶ **Pronunciation p.150**

Practice

Role play

1 A well-known personality, who has a guilty secret, has agreed to give an interview to a national newspaper.

  a **Student A** Choose one of these roles, decide on what your guilty secret is, then pass this information to your partner.
- A government politician
- A famous film star
- A successful business executive
- An international sports personality

    Student B You are a reporter. You are famous for asking well-known people difficult or embarrassing questions.

  b Prepare for the interview.
    Student A Think about your life and the sort of person you are. Think about your secret in more detail. Be ready to refuse to answer difficult or embarrassing questions.
    Student B Think about your partner's character. Make up five to ten questions to find out as much as you can about their personal life. One or two questions should be directly about the guilty secret.

  c Do the interview.

  d Change roles and prepare and do the interview again.

2 a Write ten personal questions to ask other students. They must be questions you do not know the answers to. Think of questions beginning like this:
    Who …? What …? How …? Where …? When …?
    How many …? Why …? Do you …? Are you …?
    Have you ever …?

  b Go round the class asking other students your questions and answering their questions. If for any reason you do not want to answer a question, use one of the expressions from **3b**.

Unit 1 Language check

In this unit you have worked on the following language points:

- Frequency expressions with the Present simple
- Present perfect simple and adverbs
- Comparison of adjectives: comparative and superlative forms

- Vocabulary: holidays and activities
- Writing: describing leisure facilities
- Asking and answering personal questions
- Pronunciation: stressed and unstressed words

2 Traditions

Preview

Your thoughts

1 What family customs do you have? Think about meals and meal-times, holidays, weekend activities. Do you like or dislike these customs?

2 Exchange ideas with a partner. How many of your family customs are similar?

Listen

1 **2.1** You are going to hear two people talking about family customs from the past. What custom is each speaker talking about?

2 Listen again. What did each speaker like or dislike?

Read

1 Read this letter to a magazine. Is the writer describing a present or a past family custom?

Family customs

This week's star letter comes from Liz Walsh of Bolton, Lancashire. Liz wins a set of 5 CDs.

We never used to visit our relations when we were young because my mother didn't get on with most of the members of her family – except for my uncle James. He was an engineer in the merchant navy and every time he was in port my mother took my brother and me to see him. We always had lunch on the ship with the captain, which was very exciting, and we often had exotic food which I'd never tried before. In those days I loved anything to do with the sea but my brother always got sea-sick, even though the boat hardly moved. My uncle used to say he'd never make a sailor. The funny thing is now my brother's in the navy himself, whereas I work in an office and a cruise would be my idea of a holiday in hell!

Write in and tell us about your family customs. They can be about then or now, and can be amusing, sad or embarrassing.

2 a What family custom is Liz describing?
  b Do you think her story is amusing, sad, or embarrassing?

Understanding ideas

Answer these questions. Use the information in the interviews and the letter and your imagination to help you.

1 What kind of person do you think Speaker 1's father was?

2 Why do you think Speaker 2's father spoke Spanish whenever he could?

3 Why is it *funny* that the writer's brother is in the navy now and the writer hates the idea of going on a cruise?

Have your say

Has a member of your family ever done something which embarrassed you? What was it?

Vocabulary

1 What do *stiff*, *sick* and *dead* mean in these idiomatic expressions?

   a My mum, my sister and I sat in the car *bored stiff*.

   b I was *scared stiff* when the dog started growling.

   c Where have you been? I've been *worried sick*.

   d Surely you can cook an omelette? It's *dead easy*.

   e The road sign said '*Dead slow*.'

2 Tell your partner about the following in as much detail as possible.

   a Activities which are *dead easy* or *dead hard* for you.

   b An occasion when you were *worried sick* or *scared stiff*.

   c The last time you were *dead tired* or *bored stiff*.

Grammar review: *used to*

1 a Which of these sentences refer to past actions or situations that happened regularly? (Write R.) Which refer to actions or events which only happened once? (Write 1.)

   1 ☐ *My father used to drive all over the country looking for pretty views.*
   2 ☐ *How did you use to spend the summer holiday?*
   3 ☐ *… it didn't use to bother me.*
   4 ☐ *On one occasion he said something extremely rude.*
   5 ☐ *We never used to visit our relations when we were young.*
   6 ☐ *We always had lunch on the ship with the captain.*

   b What verb form or word(s) helped you decide?

2 Match these sentences with meanings 1–2 below.

   a *Andy used to smoke.*
   b *Andy didn't use to smoke.*
   1 Andy smokes now but in the past he didn't.
   2 Andy doesn't smoke now but in the past he did.

3 How is *used to* formed in questions, in affirmative sentences, and in negative sentences?

4 In which of these sentences do we know the person went skiing regularly? In which sentence did the person possibly go skiing only once?

   a *When I lived in Austria I went skiing.*
   b *When I lived in Austria I used to go skiing.*

▶ **Language commentary p.125**

Check

5 In pairs, take turns to say as many things as you can about the people in the pictures.

Example
She used to go dancing. She didn't use to have children.

6 Explain to your partner how you and your life have changed in the last five, ten, or fifteen years. Think about these topics.
   • Your character
   • Your physical appearance
   • Sports, hobbies, and interests
   • Your daily routine
   • What you do at weekends
   • Your job
   • Your likes and dislikes
   • Personal relationships
   • Habits (for example, smoking)

Example
I used to be a lot thinner. When I was 18, I weighed 58 kilos. Now I weigh about 70.

▶ Present perfect and Past simple   p.17
▶ Adjective order   p.20

Listening

In your experience

1 What special days and occasions do you celebrate every year? Make a list.

2 Compare lists with a partner. Add other events you can think of which people either celebrate regularly, or only when something special happens – for example, when someone passes their driving test.

Listen

1 **2.2** You are going to hear five people talking about birthdays. Answer these questions about each speaker.

a Who did / will they celebrate the birthday with?
b What did / will they do?

2 Tell your partner how you celebrated your last birthday or a special birthday you remember.

3 **2.3** You are now going to hear a historian talking about April Fool's Day – a day when people play tricks on each other. As you listen, answer these questions.

a When is April Fool's Day?
b Which countries celebrate April Fool's Day?
c Is the festival recent or old?
d Were people fooled by the tricks the speaker talks about?

Vocabulary

Guess the meanings of the words and phrases in **bold** from the recording.

a 'Can I start by asking you a personal question, professor?' '**By all means.**'
b That's **the whole point** of April Fool's Day.
c It's the one day in the year when you're allowed to **be silly**.
d It gives people the ideal opportunity to play a trick on their boss which they'd probably **get the sack** for any other day of the year.

Understanding ideas

1 'But isn't April Fool's Day more for children? The plastic fried egg on the breakfast plate – **that sort of thing.**' Can you think of more examples of the kind of joke the interviewer is referring to?

2 When the professor says that the documentary *showed villagers climbing up ladders and picking strings of spaghetti off the trees*, the interviewer replies '*They didn't.*' What does this mean?

3 When a Dutch newspaper announced that they had printed the paper with perfumed ink, why did many people *secretly* sniff their newspapers that day?

Have your say

1 Do you have a similar day in your country? What tricks have you played, or has someone played on you?

2 What silly day would you invent?

Present perfect and Past simple

Exploring concepts

1 a Underline the examples of the Present perfect and circle the examples of the Past simple in these sentences.

1 *When I was young I always played jokes on my parents and my teachers on April 1st.*
2 *He's 30 on Saturday so I've organized a party for him.*
3 *My last birthday was about two weeks ago and I celebrated it in France.*
4 *I've sent out the same number (of invitations) this week.*
5 *People have celebrated the festival for hundreds of years.*

b Which sentence in **1a** describes

A a completed action or event that happened at a particular time in the past?
B something which happened in the past but in an unfinished time period like *today*?
C an action that was habitual or repeated over a period of time?
D something which began in the past, is still true now and could continue into the future?
E a completed past action, activity or experience without saying when it happened?

2 Read these sentences. When is the person speaking in each case?

a *I wrote two letters this morning.* (this morning? this afternoon? this evening?)
b *I've written two letters this morning.* (this morning? this afternoon? this evening?)

▶ **Language commentary p.126**

Exploitation

1 Put the verb in brackets in the correct form – Past simple or Present perfect.

a Everybody _____ (cry) at the end of the film.
b Where _____ you _____ (go) on holiday last year?
c I _____ (order) the flowers for the wedding.
d David _____ (work) in a pub before going abroad.
e I _____ (not speak) to Philippe today.
f _____ you _____ (meet) anyone interesting at Joe's party?
g We _____ (not go) to Paris last week. We're going next week.
h _____ you _____ (finish) this exercise?
i Samantha _____ (live) in Kuala Lumpur since she was 12.

2 a In pairs, take turns to ask each other questions using these ideas.

Example

• lose something important
    Student A *Have you ever lost something important?*
    Student B *Yes, I have. / No, I haven't.*
    Student A *What was it? Why was it important? Where / How did you lose it? Did you get it back?*

• be on TV or in the newspaper
• forget somebody's birthday
• fall in love
• break something valuable
• do something you regret
• receive a fantastic present
• go abroad
• study another language (apart from English)
• have a pet
• make something to wear

b What was the most interesting piece of information? Tell the class.

Free speech

3 Imagine that you are standing for re-election in next month's government elections.

a With a partner, make a list of what your party has done about these things.

Example
We have reduced unemployment. We have encouraged investment.

• Employment
• Crime
• The environment
• Public transport
• Education
• The health service
• The elderly
• Other

b Choose four improvements from your list and add some extra information.

Example
200,000 more jobs
Last month / new factory / north-east

c Make your campaign speech.
d Decide which candidate you will vote for.

Skills

Write and speak

1 Write down two activities which you think men generally do better than women, and two activities which you think women generally do better than men.

2 Work in small groups.
   a Exchange ideas.
   b Together, make a new list of four activities for men and four for women which the majority of your group agrees about.
   c Present your ideas to the rest of the class.

Read

Do this quiz. Choose one answer only for each question.

PLAYING BY THE ROLES

Does your sex rule you? Have you ever wondered why there are so few female engineers and so few male nurses? If you have, you have probably assumed it was all to do with education and tradition. Apparently, this is not the case. It simply depends on whether your brain is male or female.

Find out for yourself what kind of brain you have. Choose one answer a, b or c.

1 You hear a cat make a sound from somewhere behind you. Without looking round, how well can you place the cat?
   a If you think about it, you can point to it.
   b You can point straight to it.
   c You don't know if you could point to it.

2 How good are you at remembering a song you've just heard?
   a You find it easy and you can sing part of it.
   b You can only do it if it's simple.
   c You find it difficult.

3 A person you've met a few times telephones you. How easy is it for you to recognize their voice in the few seconds before they tell you who they are?
   a You find it very easy to recognize people's voices.
   b You recognize most people's voices but not everyone's.
   c You find it quite difficult.

4 You're with a group of friends. Two of them are in love with each other but want to keep it a secret from the others in the group. Would you notice their relationship if no one told you about it?
   a You would notice immediately.
   b You might notice.
   c You probably wouldn't notice.

5 You're at a large social gathering. You're introduced to five strangers. If you hear their names the next day, how easily can you picture their faces?
   a You remember most of them.
   b You remember a few of them.
   c You find it difficult to remember any of them.

6 When you were nine or ten, how easy were spelling and the writing of compositions?
   a Both were quite easy.
   b One was easy.
   c Neither was easy.

7 You see a parking space: the problem is you must reverse your car into it and it's quite a small space. Do you:
   a look for another space?
   b reverse into it … carefully?
   c reverse into it quickly and easily?

8 You've spent three days in a strange village and someone asks you which direction is north.
   a You probably won't know.
   b You're not sure but you could work it out in a few moments.
   c You can point north immediately.

9 You're in a dentist's waiting room with several other people of the same sex as you. How close can you sit to one of them without feeling uncomfortable?
   a Less than 15 cm.
   b 15 cm to 60 cm.
   c Over 60 cm.

10 You're visiting your new neighbour and the two of you are talking. There's a tap dripping in the background. Apart from that, the room is quiet.
   a You notice the dripping sound immediately and try to ignore it.
   b You probably wouldn't notice it, but if you did you'd probably tell your neighbour.
   c You don't notice it.

Listen

You are going to hear three people talking about the quiz.

1 **2.4** Listen to the first part of the conversation and write in the missing scores in the box. Then work out your own score.

SCORES		
Men score	a) _____ points	
	b) _____ points	
	c) _____ points	
Women score	a) _____ points	
	b) _____ points	
	c) _____ points	

What your score means:

Most men will score between _____ and _____ points. Most women will score between _____ and _____ points. Men who score above _____ may show a _____ bias. Women who score below _____ may show a _____ bias.

Brain Sex: the Real Difference between Men and Women

2 Are these sentences True or False? Guess, then compare ideas with a partner.

a Men and women use their brains in the same way.

b Men and women use the left side of their brain for speaking.

c When two parts of our brain are used for one activity, we find the activity easier.

d Women are better than men at mathematics.

e Men are better than women at languages.

3 **2.5** Listen to the second part. Complete the section What your score means, and check your ideas about the True / False sentences. What does your score say about the kind of brain you have?

4 Turn to p.154 to find out what the answers to the quiz questions mean.

Have your say

1 Which of these theories do you think best explains why certain jobs are not usually done by women: the sex of the brain theory; the education theory; the tradition theory?

2 Think of three jobs which women traditionally do, and three jobs which men traditionally do. Would you do a job which is usually done by members of the opposite sex?

Vocabulary

1 Do you usually associate these adjectives with men, women, or both sexes? Write M, W or B next to the words.

aggressive assertive competitive imaginative practical sensible sensitive talkative

2 Compare ideas with a partner. Be prepared to justify your answers.

Pronunciation

3 **2.6** Mark the stress on the adjectives in **1**. Then listen and check your ideas.

4 Answer these questions with a partner.

a Which adjectives would you use to describe yourself?

b Do you know anyone who has any of the other characteristics?

Speak

1 Decide whether you agree or disagree with these statements.

a Men can look after babies and young children as well as women can.

b Women are as good at being bosses as men.

c Men are as good at doing housework as women.

2 Now answer these questions.

a If you had to choose someone to look after your baby or younger brother or sister for a day, would you choose a man or a woman?

b If you could choose your own boss, would you choose a man or a woman?

c If you wanted your flat cleaned and tidied, would you prefer a man or woman to do the job?

Are your opinions the same as before?

3 Compare ideas with a partner. Try to reach agreement if you can.

4 Now work with another pair and follow the same procedure.

5 Present your group's views to the class.

Grammar extra

Adjective order

1 Read this short text. Is any of it true for your country?

> Countries – and often different regions of a country – have their own traditional costumes. Nowadays, many traditional costumes are only worn by folk dance groups, at festivals or on religious occasions. But in some places in Europe, Asia and the Americas people still wear their traditional costumes every day.

2 Does your country or region have a national costume? What is it? Do people wear it?

Exploring concepts

1 Underline all the adjectives in sentences **a–d** and circle the nouns that the adjectives describe.

a Picture 1 shows a beautiful yellow silk sari.

b Picture 2 is a Sikh costume from the north of India: a smart knee-length cotton jacket over tight-fitting white cotton trousers.

c Picture 3 shows the traditional costume of Madeira. This is a full red woollen skirt with yellow, black, white or green stripes, a red woollen top over a short-sleeved white linen blouse, and white or red leather boots.

d Picture 4 shows an elegant Japanese silk kimono.

2 a Now list the adjectives from sentences 1a–d under these headings.

Where from	*Japanese*
Material	*silk*
Colour	*yellow*
Size / Age / Shape	*knee-length*
Opinion	*beautiful*

b Do **opinion** adjectives come before or after other adjectives?

c From sentences 1a–d work out rules for the correct order of adjectives before nouns.
Example
Colour comes before material.

▶ **Language commentary p.126**

Exploitation

1 Describe these objects using three adjectives for each.
Example
It's a cheap green plastic watch.

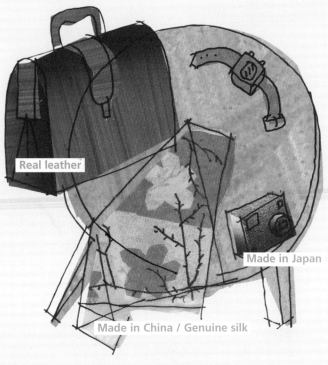

Real leather

Made in Japan

Made in China / Genuine silk

Role play

2 a Work in pairs.
Student A There has been a robbery, and some of your possessions have been stolen. (For example, an antique clock, a valuable vase, an expensive piece of jewellery.) Report your theft to the police.
Student B You are a police officer. Find out as much as possible about the missing objects by asking questions about size, age, colour, shape, etc.
Example
Student A *I'd like to report a theft. Someone's stolen my clock.*
Student B *Is it old?*
Student A *Yes, it is. It's antique.*
Student B *An antique clock. What's it made of?*
Student A *Wood.*
Student B *An antique wooden clock. How big is it?*
Student A *It's about two metres high.*
Student B *A large antique wooden clock. Did they take anything else?*

b Change roles.

3 Tell your partner about your favourite possession. Describe it in detail and say why it is special.

Exploring words

Food and cooking

1 Thanksgiving Day, a national festival in the United States, is celebrated on the fourth Thursday of November. The photograph shows a typical Thanksgiving dinner. What are the foods?

a mashed potatoes   b roast turkey   c gravy   d cranberry sauce
e boiled sweet potatoes   f peas

2 a Match these ways of cooking food with the pictures.

a bake   b barbecue   c boil   d fry   e stir-fry   f grill
g roast   h steam   i stew

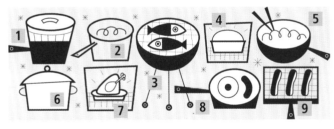

b Which of these words refer to ways of cooking and preparing potatoes? And eggs?

boiled   hard-boiled   soft-boiled   baked   fried   mashed
poached   puréed   roast   scrambled

c How do you usually cook the following foods?

beef   chicken   fish   rice   vegetables

Example
We usually stir-fry, grill or roast …

3 Complete the Thanksgiving recipe with the missing verbs from the list.

add   boil   cut   chop   decorate   drain   mash   mix   peel

Mashed potatoes with parsnips and parsley

Serves 6
Ingredients
700g potatoes
450g parsnips
1 large clove garlic (halved)
3 cups (or more) water
Can of chicken soup
50g cream
2 tablespoons butter
2 tablespoons fresh parsley

1 .... the potatoes and parsnips and .... them into pieces measuring approximately 5 cms.

2 .... the parsley.

3 Put the potatoes, parsnips and garlic into a large heavy saucepan.

4 .... the soup and enough water to cover the vegetables.

5 .... uncovered for about 25 minutes or until the vegetables are tender.

6 .... the vegetables, keeping the liquid.

7 Add the cream and butter and .... until the mixture is smooth. Add some of the cooking liquid if necessary.

8 .... in two tablespoons of parsley.

9 Put into a serving dish and .... with extra parsley.

4 Work in pairs. Describe a traditional meal in your country or region, and explain how to make it.

5 Write up your recipe. Illustrate some of the steps if you like.

Writing

Describing a public event

Listen

1 **2.7** Listen and match the descriptions of the festivals with two of the photographs.

2 **2.8** Listen to this longer description of the second festival. Complete the table.

What is the name of the festival?	Annual Sweetwater Rattlesnake Round-up
Where does it take place?	Sweetwater, _____
When does it date from?	_____
What are the origins of the festival?	To get rid of _____
When does it take place?	Second weekend in _____
What are the main events?	A parade, _____ hunting, prize-giving, snake-handling exhibitions, _____ competition
What do people eat and drink?	Chilli, _____

Brainstorm and notes

Work in pairs or small groups. Choose a popular festival. Make detailed notes in answer to the questions in the table in **2**.

Write

1 Using the notes you have made, write the first draft of an account of your festival for a tourist brochure. Write about 100 words.

2 a Exchange accounts with a student from a different group.
   b Read their account. Do you need any more information? Are the topics clear? Suggest one or two improvements.
   c Discuss the improvement ideas, then write your final version.

> **Reminder**
> * Use a new paragraph for a new topic.
> * Use a formal style.
> * Give factual information.

Language in action

Invitations

Introduction

1 Look at the illustration. In each situation the person on the left is inviting the other person to do something. The other person is accepting or refusing the invitation.

  a Work in pairs. Choose three of the situations and write what you think the people are saying.

  b What language do you already know for
    • inviting someone to do something?
    • accepting invitations?
    • refusing invitations?
  Make lists.

2 a **2.9** Now listen to five conversations and match them with the situations in the illustration.

  b Listen again. This time note down some of the language the speakers use.
  Student A Note expressions people use to invite people to do things.
  Student B Note expressions people use to accept and refuse invitations.

  c Tell each other the expressions you heard. Add these expressions to the lists you made in 1.

▶ **Pronunciation p.150**

Practice

Work in groups of four. You are going to make plans for next week.

• On some days you are free and can accept an invitation from another student.
• On some days you either have plans to do something, or you want to stay at home. You must refuse the invitation politely.
• On some days you want to do something with another person or people. You must invite another student. Write your new plans in your diary. Include the name of the person and the activity.

  Student A Turn to p.155 and look at your diary.
  Student B Turn to p.156 and look at your diary.
  Student C Turn to p.157 and look at your diary.
  Student D Turn to p.158 and look at your diary.

Unit 2 Language check

In this unit you have worked on the following language points:

• *used to*
• Present perfect and Past simple
• Adjective order

• Vocabulary: food and cooking
• Writing: describing a public event
• Invitations
• Pronunciation: sentence stress; sounding enthusiastic

3 Working practices

Preview

Your thoughts

1 a How far do you agree with these statements about work? Give each statement a number 1–5. (1 = strongly agree)

   1 *People aren't paid to enjoy themselves, they are paid to work.*

   2 *Everyone who wants to work should have a job.*

   3 *Unemployment is a fact of modern life.*

   4 *Work is much more fun than fun.*

   5 *Unemployment is one of the causes of crime.*

b What is your personal attitude to work? Write your own statement.

c Now compare ideas.

Read

1 How is work changing in the modern world? Think about your country and about people you know. These words and phrases may give you some ideas.

youth unemployment   women at work
computers   working hours   redundancy
early retirement   trade unions
multi-national companies

2 Read the four articles and match them with one of these headings.
- Presenteeism
- Child labour
- Women in management
- Multi-job holders

1 American sociologists have reported that the number of underage children in regular paid employment is rising dramatically. According to current estimates, between 300,000 and half a million children are working illegally in the United States, about half of them on commercial farms …

2 A survey into employment trends in the USA has shown that a growing number of people are doing more than one job. According to researchers, there are various reasons for this: some people are paying off debts, some are saving for the future or adding to their work experience. But the majority of people with more than one job are simply trying to earn enough money to live on.

3 A study by a leading psychologist suggests that some British managers are regularly working until 10 or 11 o'clock at night in competitive offices because no one wants to be the first to leave. As a result, their physical and mental health is suffering and the effect on their social life is acute. According to the study, managers are becoming terrified of leaving the office because they fear losing their jobs.

4 A recent study of male and female managers in over 200 organizations in the United States found that women were more effective than men in planning, communication and teamwork. Statistics show that the number of women in managerial posts is increasing rapidly. Businesses are employing them because they are essential to their success, rather than because they feel they should. But unfortunately, although women are cracking the glass ceiling, they are not actually breaking through to get the very top jobs.

Vocabulary

Find words and phrases in the articles with these meanings. The article number is in brackets.

a up to date / true at the present time (1)
b in a way which is wrong or against the law (1)
c the largest number (2)
d trying to be better than everyone else or to beat them (3)
e successful / producing the right results (4)
f people working together in a group (4)
g invisible barrier to promotion (4)

Have your say

1 How do you explain the trends described in the articles?

2 What do you think future trends might be?

Grammar review: Present continuous for trends

1 What is the difference in meaning between these sentences?
   a *I work at home on Fridays.*
   b *I'm working at home today.*

   Which sentence describes
   1 an action happening now?
   2 an action which is generally true?

2 What is the difference in meaning between these sentences? Choose one of the descriptions 1–3 below.
   a *I'm redecorating my flat at the moment.*
   b *These days, more and more people are retiring in their mid-fifties.*
   c *I'm feeding my neighbour's cat while she's on holiday.*

   Which sentence describes
   1 a repeated action happening around now?
   2 something happening now or around now?
   3 a trend or changing situation?

3 Which of the above meanings (1–3) describe the use of the Present continuous in these extracts from the articles?
   a *half a million children are working illegally in the United States …*
   b *… a growing number of people are doing more than one job.*
   c *… some British managers are regularly working until 10 or 11 o'clock …*

   ▶ **Language commentary p.127**

Check

4 Complete these sentences with the correct form of the verb in brackets.
   a These days more and more people .... (work) from home.
   b Most people .... (start) work between the ages of 16 and 20.
   c People .... (find) it increasingly difficult to get permanent jobs.
   d Companies .... (pay) their employees less and less.
   e Most weeks he .... (work) between 40 and 50 hours.
   f These days I .... (walk) to work as often as possible.

5 a Finish these sentences about trends currently taking place in your country. Think about some of these topics: work, music, clothes, shopping or politics.
      1 An increasing number of people …
      2 More and more people of my generation …
      3 Most people of my parents' age …
      4 The majority of people who live in cities …
   b Compare answers with a partner.
   c Now talk about some of the trends which are affecting you at the moment. They could be related to your family, your job or your town.

▶ Present perfect continuous   p.27
▶ Word order: time and place words and
   phrases / adverbs of manner   p.30

Listening

In your experience

1 Do you know anyone who works from home instead of going to work every day? Why do they do it?

2 What are the pros and cons of working from home?

Listen

1 a Why do you think someone who works from home is called a *teleworker*?

b Do you think you could be a teleworker? Answer these questions to find out.

		Yes	No
1	Is your job based on handling information or using computers?	☐	☐
2	Do you mostly work independently?	☐	☐
3	Is there a quiet area where you could work undisturbed at home?	☐	☐
4	Is there enough space for all the equipment you would need to use?	☐	☐
5	Are there friends nearby you could meet and chat to during the day?	☐	☐
6	Do you have a good social life outside work?	☐	☐
7	Are you good at communicating in writing and on the phone?	☐	☐
8	Are you good at solving unexpected problems on your own?	☐	☐

c If you answered *Yes* to most of the questions, you probably could be an effective teleworker.

2 **3.1** Listen to this interview with a teleworker. In what ways has his life changed since he started working at home?

Vocabulary

Match the words and phrases in **bold** from the recording with their meanings.

a ... I just **staggered** in, had a meal ...

b I can certainly **concentrate** more ...

c ... there aren't as many **distractions** at home ...

d ... I don't feel **cut off** at all.

e I'm a more **sociable** person ...

f ... there was office **gossip** ...

1 isolated

2 things that take your attention easily

3 give something all your attention

4 walk in an unsteady or shaky way

5 informal conversation about other people

6 friendly

Understanding ideas

1 Listen to the recording again and answer these questions.

a How did the teleworker use to travel to work?

b Why is he better at his job?

c When does he take a break?

d How long did he spend on the phone to colleagues in Australia and Japan?

e Who does he sometimes have lunch with?

f What little things does he miss about working in an office?

g What advice would he give to someone who was thinking about becoming a teleworker?

2 Use information from the recording and your imagination to help you answer these questions.

a Why do you think he sold his car?

b Why do you think he can concentrate better at home?

c What distractions do you think there were in his office?

d Why do you think he is a more sociable person now?

Have your say

Do you think you would enjoy being a teleworker? How would it change your life?

Present perfect continuous

Exploring concepts

1 What is the difference in meaning between the two Present perfect forms? Which extract (**a** or **b**) refers to an incomplete action and which refers to a completed action?

   a *So far this week, I've written three reports, and sent over a hundred e-mails and faxes …*

   b *… and I've been preparing for a business trip to the Far East next week.*

2 How is the Present perfect continuous formed?

3 The Present perfect continuous can refer to a single continuing activity or a repeated action. Which does it refer to in these sentences?

   a *You've been working from home for nearly a year now.*

   b *I've been seeing my friends more often.*

▶ **Language commentary p.127**

Exploitation

1 Look at the illustration. When did each person start the exercise and how long have they been doing it? Use *swim, exercise, run, cycle, row.*

Example
She started exercising five minutes ago.
She's been exercising for five minutes.

2 a Read this conversation between two friends. Choose the best verb forms.

Lynne Jo *has just called / has just been calling* **1** to say that her car *has broken down / has been breaking down* **2** on the motorway in the middle of nowhere.

Kris *Has she phoned / Has she been phoning* **3** a garage for help yet?

Lynne I don't know. *I've told her / I've been telling her* **4** to have her car fixed for ages, but she *has taken / has been taking* **5** no notice.

Kris It's not a very good car – *it's caused / it's been causing* **6** problems for ages.

Lynne I know. *She's tried / She's been trying* **7** to sell it since her accident, but now *she's given up / she's been giving up* **8** because no one's interested in buying a twenty-five-year-old pink car.

Kris That's not surprising – it's in a dreadful condition. I know *she's cleaned / she's been cleaning* **9** it several times, but *she's only taken / she's only been taking* **10** it to a garage once in the last five years.

b Compare answers with a partner. Why is the other form wrong?

c **3.2** Now listen and check your answers.

3 a This chart shows the changes in Debbie's life in the last six years. Make sentences saying what happened, what has happened and what has been happening.

Example
*Debbie **moved** to London six years ago and **she's been living** there since then. **She's spent** holidays in Poland but **she's been going to Spain** for the last three years.*

	Job	Home	Relationships	Holidays	Sports
6 years ago	Started work for IBM	Moved to a flat in London	Split up with Kris	Poland	Played tennis
5 years ago				Poland	Played tennis
4 years ago			New boyfriend – Mario	No holiday	Injured
3 years ago	Moved to SONY			Spain	Started tennis again
2 years ago		Bought a house		Spain	Took up golf
Last year				Spain	
NOW					

b Now make a chart like this for yourself. When you have finished, talk to a partner. Ask questions about their life and tell them about yours.

Skills

Speak

1 Give two more examples of each of these kinds of work.

- manual   *builder*
- office   *secretary*
- professional   *doctor*
- artistic   *designer*

2 What are the disadvantages of these different kinds of work?

3 Why might someone change from one type of work to another?

Listen

1 **3.3** You are going to hear three people describing their jobs. As you listen, guess what the jobs are.

2 Would you like to try any of these jobs? Which one(s)? Why?

Read

1 Look at the photograph and answer these questions.

a What is the man wearing? Why?

b What is the construction in front of him made of?

c What is the tool on the right-hand side? What is it normally used for?

d What do you think this man's job is?

2 a Now read the first paragraph of the article. Was your guess in 1d correct?

b Read the rest of the article. What is his attitude to the job?

odd job man

1 Duncan Hamilton's works would make an extraordinary exhibition. The problem is, they no longer exist. When you sculpt with ice, as 50-year-old Hamilton has done since the late seventies, the life of your work is about seven hours. Duncan has made more than 5,000 pieces, mostly for parties and advertisements, including a two-metre-tall Eiffel Tower, but sadly they all end up as pools of water.

2 'But watching them melt is beautiful,' he says. 'As ice sculpture continues evolving after I've finished, it can look its best about two hours later. It's brilliant!'

3 'I've been fascinated by ice since my late twenties, when I was a cookery teacher. Near where I lived there was an ice factory. I used to go there because they let me practise in their car park. It all started there. Ice sculpting had been a traditional art in the hotel business, but it had almost died out.

4 'Nowadays I do almost everything in my home studio in west London, which has special work tables and machinery to lift the blocks of ice. Ice is a scary material: cold, fragile and heavy. I wear rubber gloves and use hand-made Japanese steel tools, made specifically for the job, and costing up to £500. The ideal working temperature is two or three degrees Celsius. For storage, it's minus ten.

I use clear ice and white ice. Clear ice is made by moving the water around as it freezes. For white ice, the water is kept still, like in a normal freezer.

5 'The work, for which I charge from £400 to £2,000, has taken me all over the place, and I've met so many famous people, including Steven Spielberg. My hardest job was in the Arctic, where it was minus 28 degrees. I worked for six days, sculpting a seated lady for a vodka advert. Afterwards I was told they loved it, but that they wanted the lady standing! I didn't mind going back, though. I loved the place.'
The Sunday Express Magazine

Vocabulary

Find words in the article with these meanings. The numbers in brackets tell you the paragraphs the words are in.

a a public display or show of an artist's work (1)
b change from solid into liquid through heat (2)
c very interested (3)
d disappeared completely / come to an end (3)
e frightening (4)
f easily broken (4)
g ask people to pay (5)

Understanding ideas

1 Read the text again to find the answers to these questions.

a Why is it impossible to arrange an exhibition of Duncan Hamilton's work?
b How long has Hamilton been working as a sculptor?
c How did he learn to do ice sculpture?
d What was the difference between the two sculptures he did for the vodka advert?

2 Think of possible answers to these questions.

a Is there a connection between ice sculpture and Hamilton's first job?
b Why does the fact that ice is cold, fragile and heavy make it 'scary'?
c What does the fact that Hamilton has met so many famous people suggest?
d Why do you think he describes his work in the Arctic as his 'hardest job'?

Have your say

1 If you could choose to be an artist, what kind of art would you create?

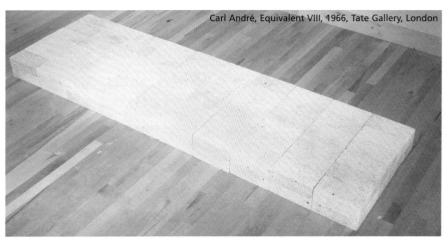

Carl André, Equivalent VIII, 1966, Tate Gallery, London

2 Duncan Hamilton works with ice. What material(s) would you work with?

Speak

Work in groups.

1 a Think of two jobs: your ideal job and the worst job you can imagine.
   b Make brief notes, describing each job and saying why you would like it or dislike it.

2 Present your ideas to the group. Talk for 1–2 minutes about each job.

3 When everyone has presented their ideas, decide as a group which are the best and the worst jobs you have heard about.

Grammar extra

Word order: time and place words and phrases / adverbs of manner

Exploring concepts

1 a Read this text and underline the eight **time** words or phrases.

Example
yesterday / since 1987

b Now circle the six **place** words or phrases.

Example
here / in the city

1 Andrew Hayton has worked at Longleat for over eight years.
2 At the moment he is an elephant keeper at the world-famous safari park.
3 He has also looked after rhinos in the past.
4 The elephants are in an 80-acre enclosure during the day and in a house at night.
5 Andrew works in the park from 8.30 a.m. to 4.00 p.m., ...
6 ... but he doesn't stay for long because it can get dangerous there after dark.

2 There are six sections in the article. Match each one with the appropriate word order pattern, as in the example.

a Subject + Verb → Place → Time

  1 *Andrew Hayton has worked* → *at Longleat* →
   for over eight years.

b Subject + Verb → Time

c Time → Subject + Verb → Place

3 a Underline all the words (adverbs) in this text which describe
1 how someone does an action, like *quickly*.
2 how often something happens, like *sometimes*.

> Brad always reads the job adverts in the weekend newspaper. Last week he saw one that looked fantastic. He read it slowly and thought about it carefully. It was the perfect job for him. So he phoned and asked for more details. He filled the application form in neatly, posted it and then waited patiently for the reply. Brad usually wore jeans, but on the day of the interview, he dressed smartly. He answered all the interviewer's questions politely. Brad knew he had done well and when he was offered the job later in the day, he accepted it gratefully.

b Look at the position of the adverbs in relation to the verbs they are with, then answer these questions.
1 Where are the *how* words?
2 Where are the *how often* words?

▶ **Language commentary p.127**

Exploitation

1 a Correct the word order in these sentences. Usually more than one answer is possible.
1 I get often early on Friday mornings to work.
2 with my boss after work go I sometimes out to a bar.
3 to the cinema last night with a couple of friends I went.
4 at the weekend to Greece I'm flying.
5 next Tuesday there my sister is meeting me.
6 until a five-star hotel in Saturday we're staying.

b Compare answers with a partner.

2 a Add an appropriate adverb from the list to each of these sentences.

angrily	never	noisily	quickly	secretly	sweetly

1 Every morning Sylvia got up early, so she was late for work.
2 She got up late this morning, so she walked to work.
3 She tried to get into the office, so that no one would see her.
4 Unfortunately the door closed behind her and everyone turned round.
5 She smiled and pretended everything was normal.
6 Her boss came up to her and said, 'Come into my office!'

b Work with a partner. Finish the story of Sylvia in no more than six sentences, using an adverb in each sentence you make up.

Exploring words

Jobs and work

1 a Match these job words **1–10** with the people in the picture.

1 vet	5 optician	9 surveyor
2 electrician	6 decorator	10 surgeon
3 farmer	7 fire-fighter	
4 mechanic	8 road-sweeper	

b Some job words end in *-er* or *-or*. A person who *farms* is a *farmer*, but a person who *decorates* is a *decorator*. What is the word for someone who
  1 looks after a large building like a school or an office block?
  2 takes photographs?
  3 cuts and styles people's hair?
  4 sails a boat or a ship?
  5 translates from one language into another?
  6 inspects hotels?
  7 collects refuse / rubbish?
  8 looks after gardens?

c Think of one or two things the people in **1a** do as a regular part of their job.
  Example
  vet   *A vet treats sick animals.*

2 a Duncan Hamilton is an ice-sculptor. He is a creative artist. What other kinds of creative artist are there? Add to these lists.

music	*composer*
literature	*poet*
film	*film star*

b Compare lists with a partner. Tell each other about your favourite composer, poet, sculptor or film star, etc.

3 a Match the verbs from **A** with as many nouns as possible from **B**.

A apply for   earn   get   go for   lose   resign from   work for

B an interview   a company   an employer   a job   a living   money   promotion   the sack   a salary   wages

b Now discuss these questions.
  1 Why might someone *lose their job*? Think of several reasons.
  2 What alternatives are there to *working for a living*?
  3 What is the best way for an employee *to get promotion*?
  4 What job would you do if you wanted *to earn a high salary*?
  5 How do people prepare when they *go for an interview*?

c Make up questions to ask a partner. Use verbs and nouns from Lists **A** and **B** above.
  Examples
  Have you ever resigned from a job?
  What is the most money you have earned for a day's work?

4 Work in groups. Discuss this statement.

THE PEOPLE WHO GET PAID THE MOST OFTEN DO THE LEAST IMPORTANT JOBS.

Writing

Letters and faxes

Read

Read these job advertisements.

1 What are the three jobs?

2 Which of these jobs could you do?

3 Which job would you least like to do?

a

Have YOU got what WE want?

We have a vacancy for a salesperson in our
Toy Department.

**You should have lots of enthusiasm and energy to
help us build up this dynamic new department. Full
training will be given to the successful candidate.**

Interested in finding out more?

Write for a full job description to:

The Personnel Manager,

Peacock and Harwell,

34 High Street, Borchester

Employment Gazette

b

WORKING CRUISES

ON-BOARD ENTERTAINER

Visit the USA, Africa, the Far East and other
wonderful places and get paid for it while meeting
people and having the adventure of a lifetime.
Earn $8000 a month tax-free.

Write for further details, sending brief career details

Fax: +31 (0) 43 327 8990

Travel Monthly

c

SCAMP FILMS

BUSY FILM PRODUCTION COMPANY URGENTLY REQUIRES ENTHUSIASTIC RECEPTIONIST.

Ability to use a computer essential.

Immediate start.   Want more info?

Write to: Sarah Mellersh
Scamp Inc. Bank Lane, London WC1 1WW
or
Fax: 0181 4568849

Cine News Weekly

Different methods of writing

The job adverts above suggest two different kinds of reply:
fax and letter. Discuss these points in pairs.

1 How are faxes and letters different? Think about the
format, layout, information and style of writing. Make a
list of points first, then check your ideas with your teacher.

2 What are the main advantages and disadvantages of each
kind of writing? When would you send a fax rather than a
letter? When might you choose not to send a fax?

Write

You are going to reply to two of the job adverts above: **a**,
and either **b** or **c**.

1 Write a 'basic letter', following this plan.

a Say why you are writing, which job you are interested
in and where you saw the advert.

b Describe your present job. OR
Say why you are interested in the advertised job.

c Ask for more information and an application form.

2 Now write first drafts of your letter and fax, adapting your
'basic letter' to suit each job and the different format.

3 a Work in groups of three. Exchange your two pieces
with two different partners.

b Read each other's writing. Are the layout and format
appropriate? Suggest one or two improvements to each
piece of writing you have read, then return them to
your partners.

c Discuss the improvement ideas, then write the
final versions.

> **Reminder**
> • Present factual details in the appropriate way.
> • Use the right style, formal or informal.

Language in action

Agreeing and disagreeing

Introduction

1 Read the story and answer these questions.
   a How many people work for PZM?
   b Why is the company closing?
   c Who will be most affected by the news?

PZM TO CLOSE! TOWN IN SHOCK

It was announced this week that PZM, one of the region's largest employers, is to close its main factory and offices, which have provided work for the town since 1965.

The majority of the three thousand employees will lose their jobs at the end of this week, leaving a small team of managers to organize the closure and finalize the sale of the property.

A PZM spokesman said that the closure was unavoidable after a year in which sales had fallen by nearly 40%. He blamed increasing pressure from foreign competition and recent changes in government policy.

The employees this will hit hardest are those who have been with the company all their working lives; most believe they are unlikely to find new work in the area. A trade union spokesman accused PZM of abandoning loyal and experienced workers at an age when most of them would not be able to find similar work.

Young people too will be affected by the closure. In recent years PZM has provided work for about a quarter of the town's school leavers, either in the factory or the offices. Most of the company's top managers started as ordinary factory workers.

2 **3.4** You are going to hear three people reacting to this story. What do they all agree about?

3 a Listen again. This time note down some of the discussion language the speakers use.
   Student A Note expressions people use to disagree.
   Student B Note expressions people use to agree.

   b Tell each other the expressions you heard. Make lists under these headings:
   • agreeing with someone
   • disagreeing with someone.

   Add any other expressions you already know to the lists.

▶ Pronunciation p.150

Practice

Work in groups.

You are going to have a meeting to discuss how the factory closure would affect your town and the people who live there.

1 Before the discussion, invent more information about the situation. For example, decide:
   • what the PZM factory makes
   • where their products are sold
   • whether there are any other employers in the area.

2 a Appoint one member of the group to be the chairperson. The chairperson should turn to p.154.

   b Everyone else in the group should turn to p.156 and choose one of the roles.

   c Get ready for the meeting by preparing a statement. This should summarize your thoughts and feelings about the closure. You can talk in general, as well as saying how you will be affected.

   d In turn, each member of the group should make their statement and give the others a brief chance to agree or disagree. Then, work through the rest of this agenda. Make a brief note of any points on which the majority agrees.

Agenda

1 Personal statements and brief reactions
2 The effect of the PZM closure on the town and people who live here:
   2.1 Immediate effects - the first 6 months
   2.2 Longer-term effects - the next 10 years
   2.3 The effects on different groups of people, especially young people, families
3 Solutions to problems
   3.1 How definite is the closure?
   3.2 What other jobs are available?

   e Decide as a group on any action you could take to help people affected by the closure. Write a brief action plan.

   f Finally, write a brief report of the meeting, including points of agreement and the action plan, to send to the local council.

Unit 3 Language check

In this unit you have worked on the following language points:

• Present continuous for trends
• Present perfect continuous
• Word order: time and place words and phrases / adverbs of manner
• Vocabulary: jobs and work
• Writing: letters and faxes
• Agreeing and disagreeing
• Pronunciation: stress and linking

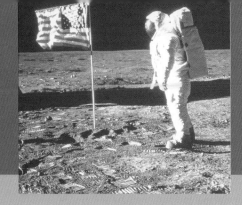

4 Journeys

Preview

Your thoughts

1 Which of these opinions do you agree with more?
   - I love travel but I hate travelling.
   - Getting to a place is more interesting than being there.

2 Work with someone who has the same opinion as you. Discuss these questions.
   What makes a journey
   - interesting or enjoyable?
   - boring?
   - uncomfortable?

Read

1 Read these texts quickly. Match each one with the best summary.

   a An embarrassing journey
   b An uncomfortable journey
   c An interesting journey

1 On Day Two we asked ourselves, 'Why are we doing this?' We could have hired a jeep and had a taste of the desert in one day – with a short ride on the camel for the photo album. Instead we decided to go on a four-day safari: four days without a wash; four nights sleeping under blankets which smelled of camels (think of wet dogs drying for an idea of the smell), and who knows how many days before we stopped walking like gorillas.
Steering my camel was about as easy as eating soup with a fork. He did exactly as he wanted. He left the path and refused to go where I wanted him to.

2 I asked my driver to stop for the umpteenth time. A shepherd wearing a red turban was walking along the road with his flock of sheep. I wanted to take his photo. I got out of the car and said in my limited Hindi, 'Apka lena photo hai?'. The shepherd agreed to my request, asking only for a copy in return. As I was climbing back into the car I wondered if the photo would ever reach its destination. The driver was probably wondering if we would ever reach ours.

3 A hot September Saturday in 1959, and we are stationary. Ahead of us a queue of cars stretches out of sight around the corner. We haven't moved for ten minutes.
 'Well, I'm not going to wait here any longer,' my father finally says. He starts the engine and pulls out into the opposite side of the road. My father does not drive particularly quickly past the stationary cars ahead. Even so it feels fast and all the occupants turn and stare as they see us coming. Some appear to be angry. Some are shouting. My sister and I hide ourselves below the seat. Our father is not with us – or rather we are not with him.

2 Read the texts again, then answer these questions.

  a Do you think the writer is pleased or sorry that she went on this trip? (Text 1)

  b Why do you think the writer wondered if the photo would ever reach its destination? (Text 2)

  c How old do you think the writer was? Why did it feel as though they were driving fast? (Text 3)

Vocabulary

Choose the correct meaning of the words in **bold**.

  a ... *steering my camel* ... (Text 1)
   1 making it go in a particular direction
   2 making it follow me

  b ... *the umpteenth time* ... (Text 2)
   1 one of very many   2 one of several

  c ... *the stationary cars ahead.* (Text 3)
   1 parked   2 not moving

  d ... *the occupants turn and stare* ... (Text 3)
   1 look in a fixed way   2 look quickly

Listen

4.1 You are going to hear three people describing journeys they went on. As you listen, answer these questions about each speaker.

1 How was the person travelling or going to travel?

2 Why was the journey memorable?

Have your say

Tell your partner about a memorable journey you have had, for example, an eventful journey, a long journey, or a journey when you met someone interesting.

Grammar review: Past simple and Past continuous

1 a Circle examples of the Past simple and underline examples of the Past continuous in these sentences.

   1 *As I was climbing back into the car ... the driver was probably wondering if we would ever reach our destination.*

   2 *When the stewardess came down to check all the passengers were on board, everybody was sitting at the back in the smoking section.*

   3 *She was hugging me and she was crying at the same time.*

   4 *When the train pulled into the station I was crying too.*

   5 *This time last year my family and I were travelling around Australia.*

  b Match each example of the Past continuous in the sentences above with one of these uses.

   A To refer to a past situation or event that was in progress at a specific time in the past.

   B To refer to a situation or event which was in progress when another event happened.

   C To refer to two past actions which were in progress at the same time.

2 What is the difference in meaning between these sentences?

  a *Carlos phoned Antonio when I arrived.*

  b *Carlos was phoning Antonio when I arrived.*

▶ **Language commentary p.128**

Check

3 Choose the most appropriate verb form – Past simple or Past continuous.

  a 'What *were you doing / did you do* when the boss came in? He looked really angry.'
   'I *was telephoning / telephoned* my boyfriend. He hates me doing that.'

  b I *was living / lived* in Sydney during the Olympics.

  c While the friends *were arguing / argued* in the kitchen, a burglar *was breaking in / broke in* and *was running away / ran away* with their video.

  d He *was standing up / stood up*, *was saying / said* goodbye and *was leaving / left*.

  e I *was waking up / woke up* and *was going / went* over to the window. Outside it *was raining / rained* and a cold wind *was blowing / blew*. I *went / was going* back to bed.

  f When I *was finishing / finished* my meal, I *was washing up / washed up*.

4 Finish these sentences.

  a At six o' clock this morning I ...

  b I looked out of the window. Someone ...

  c When the phone rang I ...

  d While I was going to work I ...

  e As you ... I ...

  f I did three things yesterday. I ...

▶ Past perfect   p.37
▶ Time clauses and sequencers   p.40

Reading

In your view

1 Why do you think some people want to be explorers? What kind of people make good explorers?

2 Would you like to explore space? the Antarctic? the Arctic? the Amazon basin? If so, why? Is there another place you would like to explore?

Read

1 You are going to read about Michael Palin, who decided to become an explorer when he was a boy. Read the information about him below and predict the answers to these questions.

a What do you think was his favourite subject at school?

b What hobby do you think he had?

c How old do you think he was when he first went abroad?

d Which do you think was more important to him after university – jobs, relationships, or travel?

Michael Palin is an actor, writer and explorer. He has appeared in several feature films, including *A Fish called Wanda*, and *American Friends*, and several TV productions: *Monty Python*, *Around the World in 80 Days* and *Pole to Pole*. He has also written books which are based on his travels around the world, and a novel.

2 a Read the article and check your ideas.

b Which is the best summary?

- The article explains why Michael Palin became an explorer.
- The article looks at the importance of exploration in Michael Palin's life.
- The article tells Michael Palin's life story.

AND NOW FOR SOMEWHERE COMPLETELY DIFFERENT

The urge to explore can be irresistible. Even the most well-travelled adventurer feels compelled to set off on new journeys of discovery. British actor and TV explorer Michael Palin looks at the origins of his own desire to explore the world.

The desire to explore is something which is inside us: we are born with it. Of course, I didn't know it at the time, but I suppose it first affected me when I was old enough to crawl behind the sofa to see what was there. Certainly, when I was eight I had already decided on my future – I wanted to be an explorer.

The desire to explore influenced every area of my early life. I collected stamps for the pictures of the waterfalls of Nyasaland and the sugar plantations of Mauritius. I went to church every Sunday, not for the hymns but in the hope that the visiting preacher might be a missionary – a tall, thin, sun-burnt man with terrifying tales of Africa and half an arm missing. Geography was my favourite subject at school.

For some reason my parents never encouraged me with talk of their own travels, though both had been to India in the 1920s. And it was not until I was at university that I had my first real taste of travel. I went to the Tirol with a university ski-party. I was excited because I had not been abroad before, but I am afraid to say that I hardly noticed the Austrian scenery. At the age of nineteen I was much more interested in girls than places.

For the next ten years after university I stayed at home exploring things like jobs and relationships. It was only when I had both of these more or less sorted out (I was married and my acting career had finally taken off) that I began to realize that I could now start looking around. Until then the world had existed only in my imagination.

With our stage show of Monty Python, and my two TV programmes 'Around the World in 80 Days' and 'Pole to Pole', I managed to see huge areas of the world. You would think that my desire to explore would be satisfied by now but exploration is not like that. Your curiosity never dies.

The Observer

Close up

1.9 Why do babies *crawl*? What does *The traffic crawled* mean?

1.29 What does *sort out* mean in *If I don't sort out my paperwork once a month, I don't know what bills I've paid*? What other things do people have to *sort out*?

1.30 What does *take off* mean in *a plane takes off*? What do you think *take off* means here? Do you know any other meanings of *take off*?

Understanding ideas

1 Why do you think the writer hoped that the missionary would have *half an arm missing*?

2 What does *I had my first real taste of travel* mean?

3 What were the most important things in Michael Palin's life when he was
 • a child?
 • a student?
 • in his 20s?
 • in his 30s and 40s?

Have your say

1 In what ways is / isn't Michael Palin a typical explorer?

2 Which do you think is better if your time for travel is limited?
 • To visit as many different countries as possible?
 • To visit fewer countries but spend longer in each one?

— Grammar —

Past perfect

Exploring concepts

1 The Past perfect tense shows the relation between two or more past events or situations. How is it formed?

2 a Read these sentences. What events or situations are described in each sentence?
 1 *When I was eight I had already decided on my future.*
 2 *I was excited because I had not been abroad before.*

 b Which tense is used:
 • to emphasize one event or situation happened before another?
 • to give an explanation?

3 What do you notice about the position of the adverbs *already*, *just*, and *never … before* in these sentences?
 a *Daniel had **already** climbed Everest and wasn't interested in climbing it again.*
 b *The scientist looked pale. He had **just** returned from six months in the Antarctic.*
 c *We had no idea which direction to take because we had **never** been there **before**.*

4 One pair of sentences below has no real difference in meaning. What is the difference in meaning in the other two?
 a *When I was eight, I decided on my future.*
  When I was eight I had (already) decided on my future.
 b *As soon as I sat down, the phone rang.*
  As soon as I had sat down, the phone rang.
 c *When the police arrived, the party finished.*
  When the police arrived, the party had finished.

 ▶ Language commentary p.128

Exploitation

1 Write down five times of day, then ask your partner questions about yesterday.

 Example
 What had you done by 10.00 a.m. yesterday? What hadn't you done?

2 Work in groups of four. Take turns to be Student A.
 Student A Ask the question and choose the best answer.
 Students B, C, D Answer the question using *because* + Past perfect.
 Example
 A *Why was Mary late?*
 B *Because she'd forgotten to set her alarm clock …*
 a Why couldn't Joseph pay the bill?
 b Why was Lola angry?
 c Why did Sasha and Polly come back from their holiday early?
 d Why wasn't Marcus tired after the journey?
 e Why did Sally fall asleep during the film?
 f Why did the party finish at midnight?
 g Why did Alan and Mandy miss the plane?

3 a Put the verbs in brackets in the correct tense – Past simple or Past perfect.

 He *had been* (be) **1** away a long time – almost a year – and it .... (be) **2** nice to be home again. He .... (get out) **3** of the taxi, ... (pay) **4** the driver and .... (walk) **5** up the path towards the front door. The house .... (look) **6** the same, although someone .... (close) **7** the living room curtains. Strange! He immediately .... (sense) **8** that something was wrong. Maybe someone .... (break in) **9**. He .... (put down) **10** his case and the parcel containing the silk sari he .... (buy) **11** just before leaving Delhi. It was difficult to leave the house empty for so long. Usually when he .... (return) **12** he .... (find) **13** that the plants .... (die) **14**, because his sister .... (forget) **15** to call round and water them. This was much worse. What would he find? …

 b Work in pairs and complete the story in no more than 50 words. Use at least two more examples of each tense.

Skills

Speak and listen

1 Answer the quiz questions. Then compare ideas with a partner.

2 **4.2** Check your answers with the cassette.

5 IMPORTANT FIRSTS

1 Who were the first two people to climb Everest, and when did they do it?
   - a Tenzing Norgay
   - b Adolf Reist
   - c Edmund Hillary
   - d 1949
   - e 1953
   - f 1960

2 Who was the first person to reach the South Pole, and when did he do it?
   - a Roald Amundsen
   - b Robert Scott
   - c Robert Peary
   - d 1911
   - e 1925
   - f 1930

3 Who was the first person to walk on the moon, and when did he do it?
   - a Edwin 'Buzz' Aldrin
   - b Charles Conrad
   - c Neil Armstrong
   - d 1969
   - e 1970
   - f 1971

4 Who was the first person to orbit the earth, and when did he do it?
   - a John Glenn
   - b Yuri Gagarin
   - c Gherman Titov
   - d 1950
   - e 1968
   - f 1961

5 Who made the first solo round-the-world flight, and when did he do it?
   - a Orville Wright
   - b Wiley Post
   - c Percy Pilcher
   - d 1908
   - e 1919
   - f 1933

Read

You are going to read an article about human achievements. As you read it, tick (✓) the achievements which were not mentioned in the listening.

Another first, but what is there left?

When Brian Jones and Bertrand Piccard touched down near the Oasis town of Mut in Egypt in March 1999, they had achieved their objective. They had established the record for the longest aerial flight in history – 20 days – and had become the first people to circle the earth non-stop in a balloon.

Of course, circumnavigation of the globe is nothing new. Magellan sailed around the world in the 16th century, and the first plane completed the journey non-stop in 1949. But the ballooning dream had become an obsession for many adventurers at the end of a millenium which had seen so many great achievements: the exploration of the South and North Poles, the conquest of Everest, the development of air flight and space travel.

The balloonists' achievement was not of historical significance. It did not signal a technological breakthrough which would benefit mankind like going to the moon or the first great aircraft journeys. But we all need achievements like this to inspire us. 'It encourages the next generation to go on to greater things,' says Richard Noble, leader of the *Thrust* team which broke the sound barrier on land in 1997.

However, once the big success is recorded in a field the public loses interest. So, for example, when Sir Chris Bonington led a brave and successful attempt on the steepest approach to Everest in 1975, it did not have the huge appeal of the first ascent in 1953. The only adventures which now truly capture public attention are the solo trips, like Reinhold Messner's solo ascent of Everest in 1981, unaided by oxygen.

Are there then any great world firsts still to be achieved? Certainly, there are still a lot of space firsts to be achieved, but what about here on earth? Richard Noble points to the following. 'Breaking the sound barrier on water, reaching 1,600 kilometres an hour on land and 800 kilometres an hour in a wheel-driven vehicle. There are still many challenges ahead.'

The Independent

Vocabulary

Match these words and phrases from the article with their meanings.

a achieve an objective (l.3)
b breakthrough (l.16)
c field (l.23)
d appeal (l.27)
e challenges (l.37)

1 attraction or interest
2 difficult tasks that test someone's ability
3 particular subject or area of interest
4 important development or discovery especially in scientific knowledge
5 do what you have aimed to do

Understanding ideas

Read the text again, then answer these questions.

1 Why do you think so many adventurers were interested in the non-stop, round-the-world balloon challenge?

2 How do you think going to the moon and the first great aircraft journeys have been useful?

3 Why do you think the 1981 ascent of Everest was more interesting to the public than the 1975 one?

Have your say

1 Can you think of any other important achievements which were not mentioned? What can you add to the list of 'firsts' still to be achieved?

2 Why do you think more men than women have been involved in achieving 'firsts'? Do you think this will change?

Speak

Work in small groups.

1 Imagine you are in the following situations. Decide exactly what to do.

a You are on a round-the-world balloon flight when some technological problems occur. You must land the balloon soon, either in the middle of a desert or in the sea. Which will you choose and why?

b You are a round-the-world solo yachtsman. During a terrible storm your boat capsizes. It will take three days for help to arrive. How will you manage to stay alive?

c You are climbing a high mountain when one of your team falls and breaks their leg. It is very cold and your radio transmitter is broken. How will you help them?

d You are camping on a snowfield. Suddenly you hear a polar bear trying to get into your tent. You do not have a gun. What will you do?

2 Present your plans to the class. Which group has the best plan for each situation?

Grammar extra

Time clauses and sequencers

1 Have you ever been on a balloon trip? What was it like?

2 You are going to hear a description of a balloon trip. Look at the drawings. What do you think happened? Number the drawings 1–8.

3 **4.3** Listen and check.

Exploring concepts

1 Read these sentences. Underline the time clauses (clauses introduced by a time expression, like *as soon as*) and circle the sequence words or expressions (which tell you the order in which something happened).

a (First of all,) we took the balloon off the lorry.

b *Then four of the women had to get into the wicker basket to balance it.*

c <u>As soon as the balloon was inflated,</u> everyone climbed in.

d *The balloon started to rise when the pilot turned on the gas burners.*

e *While the pilot was flying the balloon, he was talking to the lorry driver, who was following below.*

f *Just before we landed, he told us to crouch down and hold tight on to the ropes.*

g *After we landed, we got out and helped to deflate the balloon.*

h *After that, we put it on the back of the lorry again.*

i *Finally, we celebrated our safe return with a glass of champagne.*

2 a Where can time clauses come in a sentence? When do we need to use a comma?

b What is the difference between *when* and *as soon as*?

c Which word is used for two actions which happen at the same time?

3 a What is the usual position of sequence words in a sentence? Which sequence word doesn't need a comma after it?

b What other words do you know which mean the same as *first of all*, *then / after that* and *finally*?

▶ **Language commentary p.128**

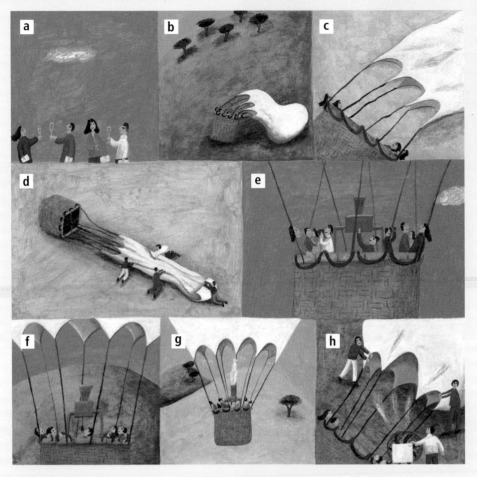

Exploitation

1 Put the sentences from this story in the correct order.

a ☐ When we went back to the canoes half an hour later, they weren't there.

b ☐ Then as soon as we had done that, we pushed off from the shore.

c ☐ They had floated away!

d ☐ We had decided to have our lunch on the island in the middle of the lake, but we were so hungry that we ate our sandwiches before we landed.

e ☐ Last week I went canoeing with some friends.

f ☐ We had forgotten to tie them up.

g ☐ The first part of the trip was very pleasant – while we paddled we chatted and told each other jokes.

h ☐ Before we got into the canoes, we put on our life-jackets.

i ☐ After we got to the island, we decided to go for a walk around.

2 Tell your partner about something adventurous, exciting or interesting which you have done.

3 Turn to p.154. Use the pictures to help you write a story.

Exploring words

Air travel

1 **a** Read this text about a flight to the USA. Then match the phrasal verbs underlined with their meanings below.

> I decided that it would be good to <u>get away</u> for a while so I booked a fortnight in Miami. I decided to fly via New York and <u>stop over</u> a couple of nights in 'The Big Apple'. It was an early flight so I was grateful when a friend offered to give me a lift to the airport. He <u>picked me up</u> at 3.00 a.m. and <u>dropped</u> me <u>off</u> just outside the terminal building. I told him not to stay to <u>see me off</u> – I hate goodbyes. A couple of hours later, the plane <u>took off</u> and I was on my way. The flight was quite uneventful. I had already seen the in-flight movie and I <u>nodded off</u> in the middle of it. I was woken up by a flight attendant telling me to fasten my seat-belt. Twenty minutes later we <u>touched down</u> at JFK airport. I was in New York at last!

1 go somewhere to collect someone in your car
2 fall into a light sleep
3 go to an airport, railway station, etc. to say goodbye to someone who is going on a journey
4 break a journey for a short stay when flying
5 (of an aircraft) leave the ground and begin to fly
6 (of an aircraft) land
7 go on holiday
8 stop a car so that someone can get out

b Discuss these questions with a partner.
1 If you could *get away* for the weekend, where would you go? What would you do?
2 If you had a round-the-world air ticket which allowed you to *stop over* in three different cities, which ones would you choose?
3 How do you feel when a plane *takes off* and *lands*? What do you do?
4 Do you like people to *see* you *off* when you go away?

2 **a** Group these words according to where you are more likely to find the people, places and things. Make three lists under these headings.
• In or on a plane
• Inside an airport terminal building
• Outside an airport terminal building

wing   air-traffic controller   aisle   arrivals hall   runway
baggage reclaim   cabin   check-in desk   cockpit
control tower   conveyor belt   customs   departure lounge
gate   hand-luggage   hold   passport control   seatbelt

b Are these sentences True or False? Correct any wrong sentences.
1 The pilot sits in the cabin to fly the plane.
2 Hand-luggage goes in the hold.
3 Your luggage is weighed at the check-in desk.
4 Your luggage may be checked at Customs.
5 Aeroplanes can park on the runway.
6 During the flight passengers can walk up and down the wing.

c Work in pairs. Write three True or False sentences of your own. Then test another pair.

d Match these words with their definitions, and answer the questions.

airline   connection   flight-attendant   jet-lag
scheduled flight   taxi

1 a feeling of tiredness you get when you travel quickly to a place where the local time is very different
   What is the adjective from this noun?
2 a company that provides regular flights
   What is the name of one from your country?
3 (of an aeroplane) move slowly along the ground
   When does an aeroplane do this?
4 a flight which follows a regular timetable
   Rearrange these letters to find the opposite. TRHACER
   (It begins with C.)
5 the next part of your journey
   What can cause you to miss this?
6 a person who looks after passengers on a plane
   What other words do you know for the same job?

3 You are going to describe to your partner a flight or another journey you have been on recently.

a Spend a few minutes preparing what to say.
b You are going to make three mistakes. Change three of the details of your story. For example, say you sat next to the window when you sat next to the aisle.
c Describe your journey to each other. Guess which information was not true.

Writing

Describing an incident

Read and write

1 Read these incomplete descriptions of incidents that happened to people while they were travelling. Which description do you like best? Why?

a I was sitting on the train reading a magazine and occasionally looking out of the window at the green fields which flashed past when the ticket inspector came down the aisle. I put my hand in my pocket. My ticket wasn't there!

b I hadn't had time to check the destination board before I jumped on the train. I was out of breath from running and my arm hurt from carrying my heavy suitcase. 'This train does go to Dublin, doesn't it?' I asked the man next to me. 'Dublin?' he said.

c Hundreds of suitcases, small and large, black and brown, grey and dark-blue went endlessly round on the conveyor belt. I watched impatiently. Was that one mine? No, similar to mine but different. Ten minutes passed, then twenty, then thirty, until finally there was one solitary case left on the belt – and it wasn't mine.

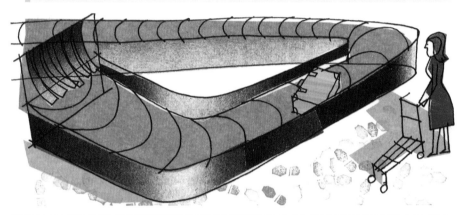

d It was late – about one o'clock in the morning and I was driving home. The road was dark and almost completely empty. I was tired – so tired that I had to sing at the top of my voice to keep myself awake. Then suddenly, in my rear-view mirror, I saw a flashing blue light.

e The car started to go slower and slower. I pulled onto the hard shoulder and stopped. There was obviously something seriously wrong. Clouds of smoke were pouring from the engine. It was dark. I was on a motorway, and stupidly I had left my mobile phone at home.

2 Work with a partner.
   a Choose three of the extracts and discuss what you think happened next.
   b Write the next **two** lines of each extract you have chosen. (Don't say which extracts they are!)
   c Exchange your lines with another pair. Which extracts have they chosen?
   d Return the lines to the other pair and tell them if they were right.
   e Now discuss how one of the extracts you chose ends, and complete it in no more than 25 words.

Brainstorm and notes

1 Work in small groups. You are going to write a similar description. Either tell the other people in your group about something that went wrong when you were on a journey, or talk about things which could go wrong. Use these questions to help you.

   • Where were you? What were you doing?
   • What went wrong?
   • How did you feel?
   • What did you do?

2 Working on your own, use the ideas from your discussion to write notes for your description.

3 Write a first draft of your description in 100 words or fewer using the notes you have made.

4 a Exchange descriptions with another person in your group.
   b Read each other's descriptions. Is the incident clearly described? Is the description interesting to read? Suggest one or two improvements.
   c Discuss the improvement ideas in pairs, then write the final version of your description.

> **Reminder**
> • Set the scene – Who? Where? When?
> • Use adjectives and adverbs.
> • Use time clauses and sequence words.

Language in action

Requests

Introduction

You are going to hear a conversation in which the woman who has just got on the train asks the other passengers to do things.

1 Work in pairs. What do you think the woman will ask them to do?

2 **4.4** Listen to the conversation. How many of your ideas are similar?

3 a Work in pairs. What request expressions do you know? Make lists under these headings:
   - making requests
   - responding to requests positively
   - responding to requests negatively.

   b Listen again.
   Student A Note any new expressions the woman uses to make requests.
   Student B Note any new expressions people use to respond to her requests.

   Tell each other the expressions you heard.

▶ **Pronunciation p.151**

Practice

Role play

Student A Follow the instructions on this page.
Student B Turn to p.155.

Student A
Situation 1
You are going to another country on a business trip. Decide which country you are going to.
Ask Student B to lend you
   - a suitcase
   - their camera
   - their … phrase book
Ask Student B to
   - pick up your flight tickets from the travel agency
   - drive you to the airport
If Student B does not want to help you, try to find another Student B who can.

Situation 2
Student B is going away on a business trip. They will ask you to lend them three things, and to do two things for them. You can agree to their requests or you can refuse them. If you refuse, be polite! (Give an excuse!)

Unit 4 Language check

In this unit you have worked on the following language points:

- Past simple and Past continuous
- Past perfect
- Time clauses and sequencers

- Vocabulary: air travel
- Writing: describing an incident
- Requests
- Pronunciation: linking; sounding polite

5 Away from it all

Preview

Your thoughts

1 Work in pairs. Talk about these alternatives. Which would you prefer in each case?

a 1 to work for a foreign company in your own country OR
  2 to work for an international company in another country

b 1 to work in an office job in a city OR
  2 to run your own bar on a peaceful small island

c 1 a holiday on an almost deserted desert island OR
  2 a holiday in a lively Mediterranean seaside resort

2 Think of an advantage and a disadvantage for each alternative.

Read

Read these extracts and match them with the situations in 1.

1 Just getting to work can be stressful. Buses, tubes and trains are usually full so you have to stand, and they often arrive late.

2 There's so much to do here. Out till late every night. I'll catch up on my sleep when I get back! See you soon. Sally XXX

3 Hi! How are you all? Very busy. More tiring than we thought but I expect things will be quieter at the end of the tourist season.

4 A spokesperson for the Japanese company said, 'We will probably have to close some of our factories in Europe.' The company has factories in Germany, Italy, France and Britain.

5 This will probably arrive after we do. We're leaving on Friday. We've done absolutely nothing since we arrived and it's been so relaxing. I recommend it. See you soon. Liz

6 Living in the country is just so different from visiting. You really get to see what people are like, how they live ...

Listen

1 **5.1** You are going to hear people talking about three of the situations. Which situations are they describing?

2 Listen again. What advantages and disadvantages do they mention?

Vocabulary

1 What do these words and phrases in **bold** from the recordings mean?

   a *… it's really* **handy** *for everywhere: it's near the beach …*

   b *There's* **loads** *to do there.*

   c *I feel a bit* **left out** *in conversations.*

   d *… my husband's always wanted to* **run** *his own business.*

2 Now answer these questions using the words above.

   a What places are your house or flat *handy* for?

   b Is there *loads* for young people to do in your town? What kind of things?

   c Think of some other occasions when a person might feel *left out*.

   d Would you like to *run* a business? What kind?

Have your say

1 Do you think it's better to go on holiday to the same place every year or a different place?

2 Have you ever felt homesick when you have been away from home? What did you miss most?

Grammar review: The future – predictions, expectations, arrangements, intentions

1 Underline the verb forms used to talk about the future in these sentences.

   a *This year … We're going back to Playa de las Americas, where we were last year.*

   b *… We're even staying in the same apartment.*

   c *I'm sure I'll feel more at home soon.*

   d *We're going to run a bar in Fiskardo on Cephalonia. … and I'm going to fly out next month.*

   e *I expect things will be quieter at the end of the tourist season.*

2 Match the verb forms with their uses.

   a *will*   1 intentions
   b *going to*   2 arrangements
   c Present continuous   3 predictions and expectations

▶ **Language commentary p.129**

Check

3 Complete these sentences with the most appropriate future form of the verb In brackets. You will need to use the negative in one sentence.

   a We .... (go) to Cyprus for three weeks in June. It's all booked.

   b Alicia says she .... (leave) school and get a job. I think she's crazy!

   c The weather forecast says it .... (be) hot and sunny in the south but cooler in the north.

   d I'm afraid I can't come with you. I .... (meet) James at seven.

   e I don't think she .... (tell) Gary.

   f I .... (invite) Paul. He's so boring!

   g He .... probably .... (phone) as soon as he arrives.

   h .... you .... (buy) Joanna a birthday present?

4 **a** Make a list of two things you have arranged to do in the next few days and two things you intend to do some time in the future. One thing in each list should be untrue.

   Example
   I'm playing tennis with Pablo tomorrow.
   I'm going to give up smoking.

   b Tell your partner your sentences. Guess which sentences are not true.

5 Work in small groups. Take turns to make predictions about life fifty years from now. Find at least six things which everyone in the group agrees about. You can talk about these topics, or your own ideas.

   • Science and technology
   • Schools and education
   • Health and medicine
   • Food and drink
   • Life expectancy
   • Space

▶ *will* and *going to:* other uses   p.47
▶ Articles   p.50

Reading

In your experience

1 Look at the photographs. Would you like to live permanently on an island like this? What do you think life would be like? Think about these topics.
   - the climate
   - jobs
   - facilities

2 What would be the main differences between living on a small island and living where you live now?

Read

1 Work in small groups. You are going to read articles about two different islands.

   Group A Read the article about Tory Island on this page and follow the instructions below.

   Group B Turn to p.159 and follow the instructions there.

2 Write brief notes about Tory Island in answer to these questions. Then check your answers with the other students in your group.

   a Where is the island? How far is it from the mainland?

   b How many people live there?

   c What language do the islanders speak?

   d How often does the ferry service operate?

   e What's the climate like?

   f What are the main problems for the islanders?

   g What important change will there soon be on the island? How will it affect the islanders?

Close up

1.4 What can make a place *inaccessible*?

1.13 *Specialize* is a verb related to the adjective *special*. What are the two related nouns?

1.13 What kinds of *seafood* do you know?

The back of beyond

Owen Bowcott speaks to Patrick Doohan, an hotelier who is preparing to offer a real 'get away from it all' holiday.

Tory Island, which lies in the stormy North Atlantic eight miles off the coast of County Donegal (Ireland), will soon be one of Europe's most inaccessible tourist
5 destinations. One guidebook warns: 'Be prepared to stay for up to a fortnight.' Patrick Doohan, who was born on the island but worked for many years in London, is building a 14-bedroom hotel there. The hotel will open in October.

Tory Island has a population of 180 people, whose first language is Irish. It has three shops and a community hall which is also the pub. There is no
10 other source of employment on the island. The inhabitants survive by fishing, growing vegetables, keeping a few sheep and painting.

'This will be the first hotel built on the island,' said Mr Doohan. 'The restaurant will specialize in seafood and the bar will be made from local stone. When it opens, I hope to be able to employ 10 people.'

15 Although links between the island and the mainland have improved in summer, when there are four or five ferries a day, it can be difficult to get to and from the island the rest of the year because of bad weather. The climate on the island is windy, stormy and wet.

Mr Doohan insisted: 'If you want to get away from it all, this is the place to
20 be. In winter you can get cut off for weeks at a time. Once it was four months. We got our Christmas mail in April.'

It certainly looks as if the hotel is going to be a success. They have already received a large number of bookings and enquiries. *The Guardian*

3 In your group, answer these questions.

   a Why do you think Patrick Doohan left the island and returned?

   b What jobs are there on the island now? What new jobs will there probably be when the hotel opens?

   c What kind of people would or wouldn't want to visit Tory Island?

4 Decide on four or five key facts about the island.

Information exchange

1 Work in pairs with someone who has read the other article. Tell your partner what you have found out about 'your' island.

2 Which of the two islands do you think has a better future?

will and *going to* : other uses

Exploring concepts

1 Read these sentences, then complete the rules below with *going to* or *will*.

a *This will be the first hotel built on the island.*

b *The restaurant will specialize in seafood, and the bar will be made from local stone.*

c *It certainly looks as if the hotel is going to be a success. They have already received a large number of bookings and enquiries.*

d *Later this year Robert Melohn will move his software business to the island.*

e *In the autumn another local boy will give up farming on the Scottish mainland.*

f *New businesses are starting up, new families are arriving and old ones are returning. It's clear that Eigg is going to have a bright future.*

• We use .... to talk about future facts.

• We use .... to make predictions which are based on what we already know or can see.

2 *Will* has three other uses. Match these examples of *will* with one of the uses 1–3 below.

a *'Are you ready to order? The fish is very good.' 'OK, I'll have the fish.'*

b *'What would you like to drink?' 'I'll just have a mineral water, please.'*

c *'How much is this?' 'That's all right. I'll get these. You bought the last round.'*

d *'I don't know what to do. There isn't any public transport.' 'I'll take you if you like.'*

e *'Let me know when you arrive.' 'Sure. I'll phone as soon as I get there.'*

f *'Are you coming or not?' 'I think I'll stay at home. It's starting to snow.'*

g *'I don't have time to do this.' 'I'll do it if you want.'*

h *'It's very important that you are at the meeting.' 'I'll be there.'*

1 an instant decision

2 an offer to do something

3 a promise

▶ **Language commentary p.129**

Exploitation

1 Give future facts about the following.

a Your age (and the ages of some other people) on your (their) next birthday.

b The year of the next election in your country.

c The year and place of important future sporting events, like the World Cup.

d The time of sunrise and sunset tomorrow.

e The time one hour from now.

2 What is going to happen in the picture? Make predictions.

Example
The people on the Big Dipper are going to scream.

3 Offer to help the people in the following situations in as many ways as you can.

Example
'I'm really tired.'   'Sit down. I'll make the dinner.'

a 'It's so hot in here!'

b 'I feel awful!'

c 'I'd love to go out with you tonight, but I'm broke.'

d 'Aren't you cold? I'm freezing!'

e 'There's something wrong with my car. It won't start.'

4 Work in pairs. Take turns to be the waiter / waitress.

Example
Student A *Are you ready to order?*
Student B *Yes. I'll have a cup of tea and a cheese roll, please. No, I've changed my mind. I'll have a chicken sandwich instead of the cheese roll. Thank you.*
Student A *I'm afraid …*

5 Work in small groups.

a Your class has decided to have a party, picnic or barbecue. Decide on the following.

• Date / time / place

• Food and drink

• Music

• Decorations

Make plans and offer to do things to help.

b Tell your plans to the other groups.

Menu

Tea	
Coffee	0.
Cola	1.
	1.0
Sandwiches (chicken, cheese, tuna)	
Rolls (cheese, tuna, egg)	2.20
Chocolate cake	2.40
Coffee cake	1.50
	1.50

Skills

Speak

1 Some people decide to take time out from work or study to do something different in their lives. Have you ever taken 'time out'? Would you like to?

2 When do you think is the best time to do this? What are the advantages or disadvantages of these times?

- Between school and university
- Between university and your first job
- After one year in a job
- After eight to ten years in a job

Read

1 You are going to read an article about two people in their twenties who took a year out to travel. First, do you think these statements are True or False?

a People who give up their jobs worry about what they will do when they return.
b Most people work while they are travelling around.
c Travel changes people's personalities.
d People lose the desire to travel after their year out.

2 Read the article. Are statements **1a–d** True or False for Fiona and Andy?

Not all companies will give people time off except for study, so taking a year out to travel can leave you homeless, jobless, and penniless. [5] Helena Pozniak talks to two people who took the plunge.

It took Fiona Brownlee a long time to decide to swap her well-paid job for a round-the-world ticket. Finally, at the [10] age of 28, she resigned and went on a trip that took her through Asia and Australia. 'I wasn't worried in the least about what I was going to do when I got back,' she said.

[15] Information technology graduate Andy Daniels left Britain at the age of 24 with £800 and a one-way ticket to Australia. 'It was a snap decision, although the idea to travel [20] had always been in the back of my mind,' he said. 'I wasn't particularly worried about what I was going to do on my return – but I should have been.'

Few can afford not to work while [25] travelling, but a change from a desk job is refreshing. Fiona wrote travel articles and worked in a ski-resort. Andy cleaned aeroplanes, decorated houses and worked as a chauffeur.

[30] Coming home, however, can be a big shock. 'After I'd got over the excitement, it was stressful,' said Fiona. 'It was as if everyone else was on the motorway and I was on a minor [35] road.'

Fiona was fortunate. She got a job immediately on her return. Andy had less luck. It took him eight months and 200 job applications to find a job.

[40] Both Fiona and Andy say the experience has changed them. 'I'm less ambitious, more laid-back, less stressed,' said Fiona. Andy is 'less concerned about money'.

[45] If taking a year out is supposed to cure you of the travel bug, it hasn't worked. Andy still plans another trip, but this time he will make sure he has a job to go back to. Fiona has [50] deliberately left a pair of skis in a resort. 'It's like leaving something at your boyfriend's flat after you've split up, so you've got an excuse to return.'

The Independent

Guessing meanings

Guess the meanings of these words from the article.

a *homeless, jobless, penniless* (l.4)
What does the suffix *-less* mean?

b *swap* (l.8)
If I have something you want, and you have something I want, we might do this.

c *snap decision* (l.18)
The next clause beginning '*although* ...' will help you.

d *laid-back* (l.42)
You can worry or you can be like this.

e *travel bug* (l.46)
bug has four meanings. Which one is used here: a small insect; an infectious disease; a keen interest; a small microphone?

Understanding ideas

1 Why do you think Fiona and Andy were not worried about what they were going to do on their return?

2 What *excitement* (l.32) is Fiona describing?

3 '*It was as if everyone else was on the motorway and I was on a minor road.*' (l.33) What does Fiona mean?

4 Do you think Andy and Fiona will go abroad again?

Have your say

Do companies in your country give people time off to do certain activities? Do you think this is a good idea? What possible benefits are there to the company?

Listen

1 **5.2** You are going to hear Lisa, an Australian, talking about her time out in France. As you listen, correct these statements.

a Lisa is going to study French and German at university.
b She went to France for five weeks.
c She stayed with other Australian girls.
d She missed her school in Australia.
e She is sorry she went to France.
f She spent a lot of money on phone calls.
g She can write French better now.
h Lisa thinks going to France was a negative experience.

2 Listen again and answer these questions.

a What problems did Lisa have at first?
b In what ways does she think the experience has changed her as a person?

3 What do you think the expressions in **bold** from the recording mean?

a *I had to **stand on my own two feet**.*
b *I can handle **what life throws at me**.*
c *I went for five months **in all**.*

Speak

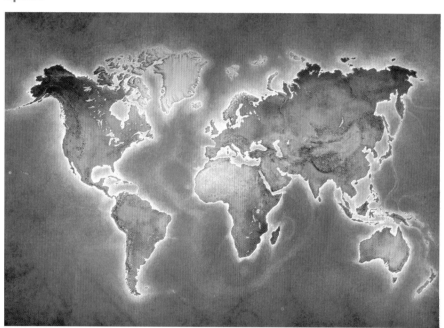

1 You are going to take a year out. Decide on your budget, then with a partner decide where to go, what to do, what plans you need to make, etc.

2 Tell the rest of the class your plans. Who has the best idea?

Grammar extra

Articles

Read

1 Read these texts about where two couples live. What advantages and disadvantages do they mention?

Anna and her husband Jake live in a block of flats in Ursynów, a district in the south of Ø Warsaw. 'We like living here,' says Anna. 'Our children can walk to Ø school, and there is an underground station nearby.'

Both Anna and Jake work in the city centre. Jake, an American from Oregon in the USA, is a university lecturer and Anna is a computer operator. 'The biggest disadvantage of living here is that I have to drive to Ø work,' says Anna. 'Jake is lucky. He can go by Ø underground. It only takes him 20 minutes to get to Ø work.'

Warsaw, which is situated on the River Vistula, is an important cultural centre with plenty to do. 'We often come into the city centre on Saturday and go to the cinema or the theatre,' adds Jake.

Joanna and Artur retired two years ago, sold their flat in Warsaw and moved to the Bieszczady mountains, where they bought a small house The house has a big garden and the couple are delighted that they decided to move. 'A colleague I used to work with gave me the idea,' says Artur. 'He kept saying how marvellous it was to live in the country.'

'It's so quiet here,' adds Joanna, 'and it's so nice to be close to Ø nature.' Not everyone would choose to live there, however. Ø Temperatures often fall below zero in Ø winter.

2 Would you prefer to live in a city suburb or in the country?

Exploring concepts

Look at the texts again and find one example in blue for each of these rules.

Indefinite article (*a / an*)

We use the indefinite article *a / an*:

1 to refer to a person or thing, but not a specific person or thing (The speaker or writer can't or doesn't want to say which person or thing they are referring to, or it doesn't matter.)
2 to refer to something or someone for the first time
3 to classify – to say what something or someone is, or what someone does.

Definite article (*the*)

We use the definite article *the*:

1 to refer to something which has been mentioned before
2 when there is only one of something (in a particular context)
3 in a superlative expression
4 with names of oceans, seas, rivers, mountain ranges
5 with the names of some countries and groups of islands
6 with certain public buildings.

No article (Ø)

We don't use an article:

1 with plural countable nouns (when we are speaking generally)
2 with uncountable nouns (when we are speaking generally)
3 with names of towns, cities and most countries
4 with nouns for certain types of places
5 with *by* and means of transport.

▶ **Language commentary p.130**

Exploitation

1 Complete these sentences with *a / an*, *the* or no article (Ø).

a Rob's mother is .... teacher; his father is .... architect.
b .... capital of .... France, ... Paris, is situated on .... River Seine.
c After she left .... school she went to .... university.
d Mount Everest is .... highest mountain in .... world. It is in .... Himalayas.
e Rebecca is in .... hospital. She had .... operation on her foot yesterday. .... doctor says .... operation went well.
f If .... sun comes out, we can go to .... beach and have .... picnic.
g .... dogs make better pets than .... cats.
h .... food keeps fresher longer if you put it in .... fridge.

2 Work in groups. Take turns to choose one of these subjects, then talk about it for two minutes. If you stop talking or hesitate the next person should take over. They must continue on the same subject but can't repeat what anyone has already said. Talk until the two minutes is up.

- Food
- Films / the cinema
- Music
- Sport
- English
- Families
- Towns / cities
- The country

Exploring words

Places

1 Match these geographical features with letters **a–l** on the map.

coast   desert   estuary   gulf   island   mountain range   ocean   peninsula   plain
plateau   sea   lake

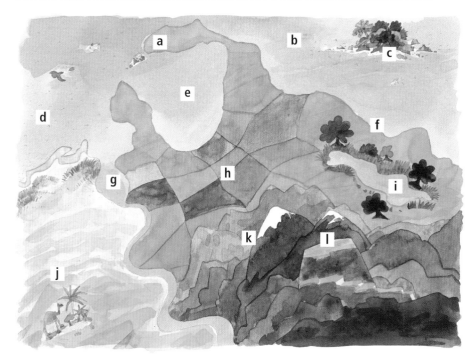

2 a Look at these sentences which describe where places are. What rules can you work out for the use of the prepositions *in* and *on*?
   1 Lisbon is on the River Tagus.
   2 Milan is in Italy.
   3 Paris is in the north-east of France.
   4 Madrid is in the centre of Spain.
   5 Tunis, the capital of Tunisia, is on the Gulf of Tunis.
   6 The island of Rhodes is in the Mediterranean Sea.
   7 Mount Everest is in the Himalayas.
   8 The island of Madeira is in the Atlantic Ocean.

  b Read these sentences. What is the difference between *on* and *off*?
   1 The island of Madeira is off the west coast of Africa.
   2 Bombay is on the west coast of India.

  c Work in groups. Take turns to think of a city, town or island in your country, or in the country where you are studying. The others in your group will ask questions to find out which place you are thinking of.
   Example
   Is it an island? Is it on the coast? Is it in the north?

3 Which is the odd one ou[...]
these groups of words?
  a harbour bay port
  b pool stream river
  c path road street
  d shore beach sand
  e boulder cliff pebble

4 a Look at this list and find the opposites of the adjectives in **bold**.

crowded **deep** deserted
fast-flowing golden **high** low
narrow palm-fringed pebbly
sandy shallow snow-capped
straight turquoise wide winding

  b Which of the adjectives in the list can be used to describe
   • a road?
   • a river?
   • a beach?
   • a mountain?
   • the sea?

5 Work in pairs. You are going to create your ideal desert island.

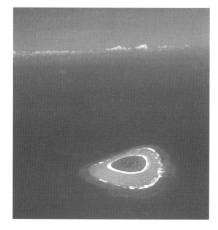

  a Draw an outline map of the island, and decide where it is located and how big it is.
  b Decide what features and amenities there will be on the island and mark them on your map.
  c Each decide where you will live.
  d Describe your design and discuss your plans with another pair. What are the main differences?

Writing

Describing places

Read

1 Read this description of Granada. What similarities and differences are there between Granada and the place where you live?

Granada is a <u>medium-sized</u> city situated in the south of Spain near the snow-capped Sierra Nevada mountains and just over an hour away from the beautiful sandy beaches of the Costa del Sol.

The old part of Granada is the most interesting. Here the streets are narrow and winding and mostly cobbled. There are small shops on both sides. Some are modern clothes shops selling the latest fashions, others are food shops. In some of these, brightly-coloured mountains of fruit and vegetables are on display. In others, freshly-caught fish or sweet-smelling hams hang from the ceiling.

The windows of the flats above the shops have dark-coloured shutters. These are open and the noise of music and people laughing or arguing comes from them. Red, pink or white geraniums cascade like waterfalls from every balcony.

2 Read the description again and underline the adjectives. How do they improve the description?

Vocabulary

Where do you usually find these features?

fields   fountains   grass   parks   pine trees   rapids   rocks
rock-pools   seaweed   shells   statues   trees   wild flowers

• In a town or city?
• At the seaside?
• In the country?
• In the mountains?

Brainstorm and notes

Work in pairs or groups.
Think of an interesting part of your town (or the place where you are studying), or somewhere in the country, by the sea or in the mountains. Use one of these checklists to help you with ideas, and make notes.

Town / City	Seaside	Country	Mountains
Size	Beach	River / stream	Height
Buildings	Sea	Other features	Other features
Shops	Other features		
Streets			
Other features			

Write

1 Write the first draft of your description in 100 words or fewer using the notes you have made. If you are describing a town or city, say where it is situated.

2 a Exchange your description with someone from another group.
   b Read their description. Is it interesting? Can you imagine the place? Suggest two or three improvements.
   c Return the description and discuss your ideas for improvements.
   d Write your final version of the description.

> **Reminder**
> • Use interesting adjectives.
> • Select interesting features.
> • Use prepositions and prepositional phrases.

Language in action

Opinions

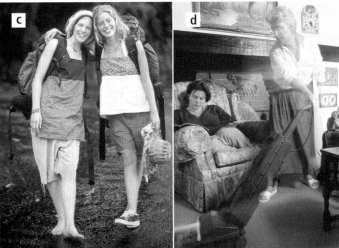

Introduction

1 You are going to hear four conversations in which people are asked for an opinion about something.

a **5.3** Listen and match the conversations to the photographs.

b Listen again. This time note down some of the language the speakers use.
Student A Note expressions they use to ask for opinions.
Student B Note expressions they use to give opinions.
Student C Note expressions they use to avoid giving opinions.

c Tell each other the expressions you heard. Make lists under these headings:
- asking for opinions
- giving opinions
- avoiding giving opinions.

2 What are your personal views on the topics?

▶ **Pronunciation p.151**

Practice

1 Work in pairs. You are going to do a class survey to find out people's opinions about a variety of topics.

a Choose one of these topics or think of one of your own.
- Advertising on television
- Smoking in the workplace
- Banning cars from city centres
- Killing animals for their fur
- Making people stay at school until they are 18

b Design your questionnaire.

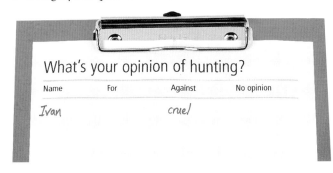

What's your opinion of hunting?

Name	For	Against	No opinion
Ivan		cruel	

c Ask five or six people in the class for their opinions. Make notes of their answers.

2 Together, write a report giving the results of your survey.
Example
We interviewed ten people. Six people think that …

Unit 5 Language check

In this unit you have worked on the following language points:

- The future – predictions, expectations, arrangements, intentions
- *will* and *going to*: other uses
- Articles

- Vocabulary: places
- Writing: describing places
- Opinions
- Pronunciation: silent letters; linking

6 Relationships

Preview

Your thoughts

1 Do you agree or disagree with these sayings about love and marriage?

- *Money can't buy me love.*
- *Happiness in marriage is entirely a matter of chance.*
- *Marriage is like a cage: one sees the birds outside desperate to get in, and those inside equally desperate to get out.*

2 Do you know any other sayings?

Listen

1 You are going to hear a song called *Where have all the cowboys gone?* by Paula Cole. Before you listen, decide where you think these words go in the song.

baby   bills (x2)   dishes   down   dress
friends   glass   TV   week

2 **6.1** Listen and check.

Oh, you get me ready in your '56 Chevy
Why don't we go sit .... in the shade?
Take shelter on my front porch
Dandelion, sun-scorched
Like a .... of cold lemonade?
I will do the laundry
If you pay all the ....
Where is my John Wayne? Where is my prairie son?
Where is my happy ending? Where have all the cowboys gone?
Why don't you stay the evening?
Kick back and watch the ....
And I'll fix a little something to eat
Oh, I know your back hurts
From working on the tractor
How do you take your coffee, my sweet?
I will raise the children
If you pay all the ....

I am wearing my new .... tonight
But you, but you don't even notice me ...

We finally sold the Chevy
When we had another ....
And you took the job in Tennessee
You made .... at the farm
And you join them at the bar
Most every single day of the ....
I will wash the ....
While you go have a beer

Where is my Marlboro man?
Where is his shiny gun?
Where is my lonely ranger?
Where have all the cowboys gone?

Chevy = Chevrolet, a make of car.

Understanding ideas

What kind of person is the woman in the song? Why isn't she happy?

Listen

1 Answer these three questions about marriage in your country.

  a What is the average age when people get married?

  b At what age can people get married without their parents' permission?

  c Can people get married in any place they like?

2 **6.2** Listen to three people talking about marriage in the USA, Britain and Japan. How do they answer questions 1a–c?

Read

Read this text about marriage in the Amish community. Does anything surprise you?

Amish weddings

Before an Amish couple can marry, both must join the Amish church and promise to follow the Ordnung, a set of rules for daily living.

After the young man asks the girl to marry him, he gives her china or a clock. The couple mustn't tell anyone their plans. They must keep them secret until July or August, when the young woman tells her family.

Amish couples can't get married any time they like. Wedding dates are limited to November and part of December, when the harvest has been completed and severe winter weather has not yet arrived. Naturally, they have to get married in church.

Blue is the most popular colour for the wedding dress, which is always new and usually made by the bride. The dress is plain and mid-calf length. After her wedding day, an Amish bride will wear her dress to church every Sunday and will be buried in the same dress when she dies.

Grammar review: Permission, obligation, prohibition

1 Complete these rules. Use sentences a–e to help you.

  • We use .... to talk about permission and .... to talk about absence of permission.

  • We use .... and .... to talk about obligation and .... to talk about absence of obligation.

  • We use .... to talk about prohibition.

  a *In Japan women* **can** *get married when they are sixteen but they* **have to** *have their parents' permission.*

  b *You* **don't have to** *get married in a church. You* **can** *get married in a registry office if you prefer.*

  c *Before an Amish couple* **can** *marry, both* **must** *join the Amish church.*

  d *The couple* **mustn't** *tell anyone their plans. They* **must** *keep them secret until July or August.*

  e *Amish couples* **can't** *get married any time they like.*

2 In which two of these pairs of sentences is there no real difference in meaning? What is the difference in meaning in the other pair?

  a *16-year-olds must have their parents' permission to get married.*
     16-year-olds have to have their parents' permission to get married.

  b *The couple mustn't tell anyone their plans.*
     The couple don't have to tell anyone their plans.

  c *In most countries you can't marry a blood relative.*
     In most countries you mustn't marry a blood relative.

▶ **Language commentary p.130**

Check

3 Choose the correct alternative in *italics* in these sentences. In one sentence there are two possible answers.

  a You *must / have to / can* get divorced in most countries these days.

  b In many countries you *must / mustn't / don't have to* be married to more than one person at a time. It's against the law.

  c In other countries men can have up to four wives at a time but they *can't / mustn't / don't have to* have more than one.

  d In some countries divorce is not recognized by the church, so a divorced person *can't / doesn't have to / mustn't* get re-married in church.

  e If you get married in a place other than a church or registry office, you *can / must / have to* be married by an authorized person.

4 Work in pairs or small groups. Make up as many sentences as you can using *can / can't / have to / don't have to / must / mustn't* about your country.

  Example
  In parks *You* **can** *walk on the grass. You* **mustn't** *pick the flowers.*

  • In zoos   • On aeroplanes   • In the countryside
  • On trains   • On motorways

5 Work in small groups. Tell each other about the place where you work or study. Talk about what you are allowed and not allowed to do, and any rules and regulations there are. What changes would you make?

▶ Permission and obligation (2)   p.57
▶ Indefinite pronouns   p.60

Reading

In your experience

1 How important to you are these things when choosing a life-partner? Rank them from **1** (very important) to **5** (not very important).

- Looks
- Intelligence
- Job (or job prospects)
- Interests
- Sense of humour
- Religion
- Personality
- Background

2 Compare answers with a partner.

Read

1 You are going to read a newspaper article. Look at the title. What do you think the article will tell you?

2 Read the article. Were your ideas in 1 right?

Arranged marriage versus love match

Jeyaben Desai, an Asian woman living in Britain, once described her views on marriage: 'You girls have no idea what it means. Marriage is not something between two individuals, but two families. It is a serious business. These instant passions soon disappear. In my day we married men carefully chosen by our
5 parents. They looked for long-term qualities like responsibility and respect.'

Most older Asian women would agree that young people simply fail to understand what is required for a life-long partnership, that to follow something as unreliable and fragile as your heart
10 when choosing a husband is foolish and dangerous. In Asian homes across Britain, mothers use these arguments to persuade (and sometimes force) their daughters not to abandon tradition.

Asha's daughter, Nimu, didn't have to get her
15 parents' permission to marry and Nimu has just announced that she is marrying a divorced Englishman. Asha thinks her daughter is 'off her head'. Nimu disagrees. 'In their day they couldn't choose who they married,' she says. 'They could
20 only marry men that their parents had chosen for them. They had to accept things, they had no choice. We have a choice and we can have the kind of relationship they could not even dream of. They were taught to pretend to be happy, to put
25 themselves last. I will not do that.'

But it seems that things may be beginning to change. Instead of fighting against an arranged marriage, more and more young Asian women who have been brought up in Britain are now
30 asking their parents to arrange their marriages for them. Mariyam, a recently graduated doctor, has been pressing her parents to do this for months. The reason she says is simple. 'I want the marriage they have. They respect each other. They are
35 partners, not competitors. They would never think of breaking up. I look around at all these unstable relationships and I am scared of ending up in one.'

However, Mariyam's mother, Suraya, refuses to arrange her daughter's marriage, saying, 'It was different in our time. That was what we grew up to expect. You have so many chances I never had. Don't throw them away.'

Close up

1.7 What does *fail to understand* mean? What other meaning of *fail* do you know?

1.9 What does *fragile* mean here? Give examples of things which are *fragile*.

1.17 What other informal expressions do you know which mean the same as *to be off your head*?

1.22 *choice* is a noun. What is the verb?

1.39 What does *throw away* mean here? What other meaning do you know? What things can you *throw away*?

Understanding ideas

1 What kind of person do you think Nimu is?

2 Why do you think more and more Asian women in Britain are asking their parents to arrange their marriages?

3 What *chances* do you think Suraya is referring to? (l.39)

4 What are the main arguments in the text for and against arranged marriages?

Have your say

Which system of marriage do you think is better? Why?

Permission and obligation (2)

Exploring concepts

1 Read sentences **a–d**.

a *Nimu didn't have to get her parents' permission to marry.*

b *In their day they couldn't choose who they married.*

c *They could only marry men that their parents had chosen for them.*

d *They had to accept things. They had no choice.*

Which sentences refer to
- obligation in the past?
- permission in the past?

2 In which of these pairs of sentences is there no real difference in meaning? What is the difference in meaning in the other pair?

a *In Asha's day women couldn't choose who they married.*
In Asha's day women didn't have to choose who they married.

b *Nimu didn't have to get her parents' permission to marry.*
Nimu could get married without her parents' permission.

3 a What are the past and future forms of *must / mustn't, can / can't, have to / don't have to*?

b How do you form questions in the past for *have to* and *can*?

▶ **Language commentary p.131**

Exploitation

1 Complete this text with an appropriate form of *have to* or *can*.

Before I got married and had a family, I lived at home with my parents. I had a lot of money because I .... ¹ pay any rent. My mother did everything for me. Although I .... ² clean my room, I .... ³ do any other housework. I .... ⁴ do any cooking either. There were one or two minor restrictions. I .... ⁵ have parties in the house – my parents didn't allow that, but I .... ⁶ invite friends round. If I was going to be late home, I .... ⁷ phone to tell them. But I .... ⁸ come home any time I wanted as long as they knew where I was.

2 Work in pairs or small groups. What **couldn't** people do in your country before that they can do now? What obligations were there then that there aren't now? Talk about these subjects and add others.

- Love and marriage
- Education
- Work
- Politics
- Clothes
- Social behaviour

Example
In England in the 18th century an unmarried woman from a wealthy family couldn't go on holiday alone with her fiancé. She had to have a chaperone.

3 Work in pairs or small groups. Talk about past times in your life when you *could / couldn't* and *had to / didn't have to* do certain things. Choose from these times.

- When you were at school
- When you lived at home with your parents
- Before you were married
- Before you had a family
- When you did military service
- When you were at university
- In a previous job

Skills

Speak

Work in small groups.

1 Have you got a car or have you ever had a car? What make, model and colour is / was it? If you haven't got a car, would you like to have one?

2 What do you look for when you buy a car? Think about these points. List your priorities.
- Price
- Size
- Colour
- Fuel consumption
- Other features

3 If you could buy any car you wanted, which make (and model) would you buy and why?

4 How do you feel about driving?

Listen

0.3 You are going to hear five people talking about their favourite cars. Listen and tick (✓) the features which they mention.

Features	Speaker 1	Speaker 2	Speaker 3	Speaker 4	Speaker 5
colour	✓				
make					
age					
reliability					
comfort					
stereo					
registration number					

Understanding ideas

Listen again and answer these questions.

1 Speaker 1 says about her car '*It's **lived** in Italy, Hungary, and travelled many miles.*' What does her choice of verb tell you about how she feels about her car?

2 How can a car *let you down*?

3 The friend said to Speaker 5, '*I didn't think of you as a red car driver. I thought of you more as a blue car driver.*' What do you think she meant? Why do you think Speaker 5 was rather upset by her comment?

Have your say

Why do you think some people are fond of their car? Do you think this only happens with old cars?

Read

1 You are going to read an article about cars. First, guess how these words from the article might relate to cars.

freedom   a piece of sculpture   ugly   a dishwasher   a luxury

Example
freedom *Driving a car gives you freedom. You can go where you like, when you like.*

2 Read the article and check your ideas.

Our romance with the car

Now that the car is a century old and its very existence is being questioned, how can anyone admit to a passion for a noisy lump of metal?

5   The answer is that the finest engines are like poems or pieces of sculpture – they should be admired for their logic, beauty, sound and performance. It is possible to admire an engine designed by people like Hassan, Royce or Porsche without even needing to see it move. If all

10 the petrol in the world was used up, car enthusiasts would still look admiringly at a Hassan V12 because they know that it represents one of the great moments in mechanical engineering history.

    The problem with the car, a century on, is that we

15 have allowed Henry Ford and not Henry Royce (of Rolls-Royce fame) to be the winner. For the most part, the car is now an ugly, commonplace form of transport rather than a beautiful toy or exquisite work of engineering. Mass-market cars may be democratic, but with a few shining

20 exceptions (the Mini; the Fiat 500; the Volkswagen 'Beetle') – the vast majority are about as inspiring as a dishwasher. They make the heart beat faster only when their drivers are about to crash into each other.

    In most European countries cars have never really

25 been a necessity. Although few car owners will admit it, they're a luxury. Owners say in defence of their Ford or Nissan that it gives them freedom; but it's a freedom (they do not admit this) to drive on crowded roads, to queue for car-parks, to develop high blood-pressure in

30 motorway traffic jams.

    Most driving in cars is, in fact, a chore, and yet we still have images of ourselves in sunglasses driving a jeep on an African safari, of beating the Formula 1 world champion in a race, or of opening the boot of a classic

35 Rolls-Royce and removing a cold-box packed with chilled champagne. Why do we make up these fantasies? Simply because the reality of motoring rarely lives up to our expectations.

Guessing meanings

Try to work out or guess the meanings of the words in **bold** from the article.

a *If all the petrol in the world was **used up** …* (l.10)
The word *up* adds a similar meaning to some other verbs, like *eat up* and *drink up*.

b *… the car is now an ugly, **commonplace** form of transport …* (l.17)
What does the word *common* mean?

c *… the majority are as **inspiring** as a dishwasher.* (l.21)
This word describes the effect of something or someone on you. The related noun is what some writers and artists need before they can start a new work.

d *… **high blood-pressure** …* (l.29)
This is what people, particularly older people, often have when they are stressed or smoke a lot.

e *Most driving in cars is … **a chore** …* (l.31)
Is *a chore* something you enjoy or something you have to do?

Understanding ideas

1 How can the first sentence of the article be expressed more simply? Choose one of these alternatives.

a People have been passionate about cars for more than a century. Why?
b How can anyone like cars? They're only pieces of metal.
c How can anyone say they like cars nowadays? Everyone knows how bad they are for the environment.

2 What is the writer's opinion of mass-market cars?

3 Do you think the writer has a car? If so, what make do you think it is?

4 How would you describe the writer? You can choose more than one description.

- an environmentalist
- a car enthusiast
- a snob
- a classic car enthusiast

Have your say

Do you agree with the writer's opinion of most modern cars? Which modern cars (if any) do you think will earn a place in automobile history?

Speak

Work in groups.

1 Design the ideal car for one or more of the following people.

- A travelling salesman
- A businessman
- A romantic
- A couple with four children, a dog and elderly parents

Think of these points.

- Shape
- Fuel consumption
- Speed
- Size
- Colour
- Special features

2 Present your group's ideas to the class. Which are the best ideas?

Grammar extra

Indefinite pronouns

Read this description of Nicholas. Are Nicholas and the writer still friends?

Friendship is important to <u>everyone</u>, and, when they are young, everybody has a best friend. When I was at school, my best friend was Nicholas. I liked him because he was very easy-going. Nothing made him angry. If someone made fun of his red hair, he just smiled and ignored them. For two years Nicholas and I were inseparable. We went everywhere together. We did everything together. Then we began to see each other less until finally we hardly saw each other at all. We didn't really have anything in common any more.

Exploring concepts

1 Underline all the indefinite pronouns and adverbs, for example, *everyone*. There are six more.

2 Use the text above and sentences a–d to help you decide the rules of use 1–3 below.

   a *Could you do something for me?*
   b *Would you like something to eat?*
   c *Why are you wearing your coat? Are you going somewhere?*
   d *Is there anybody else we should invite?*

   Choose the correct alternative.

   1 We use *some / any* in affirmative sentences.
   2 We use *some / any* in negative sentences and in questions when we don't know whether the answer will be *yes* or *no*.
   3 We use *some / any* in questions which are offers or requests, and when we expect the answer *yes*.

3 Read these sentences and answer the questions.

   a *Where I live there isn't anything for young people to do. There's absolutely nothing at all.*
   What is the difference in the verb form with *anything* and the verb form with *nothing*?

   b *Everybody needs friends.*
   What is the verb form after *everybody*?

4 Chose the correct alternative in these sentences.

   a *Everyone / Anyone can be President, if they're a US citizen.*
   b *Everyone / Anyone can win the lottery, if they buy a ticket.*
   c *Everyone / Anyone I spoke to agreed with me.*

▶ Language commentary p.131

Exploitation

1 Complete these dialogues with an appropriate indefinite pronoun or adverb.

   a Sue   What was that?
      Paul What do you mean?
      Sue   I thought I saw _____ behind that tree.
      Paul I can't see _____ but I'll have a look if you like. No, there's _____ there.

   b Mel   Has _____ seen my passport? I've looked _____ but I can't find it.
      Joe   Have you looked properly?
      Mel   Yes, but I can't find it _____.
      Eve   You've probably put it _____ safe.
      Mel   Oh, thanks a lot. That's a big help!

   c Jim   I'm sorry I'm late. I feel really bad about it. _____ is so busy. Is there _____ I can do?
      Pat   No, it's OK. We've done _____.
      Jim   Come on. There must be _____ I can do.
      Pat   No, really, there's _____.

2 Finish each of these sentences in as many ways as you can.
   Example
   Something should be done to help people who … *can't read / have been unemployed for a long time.*

   a I can't understand how anyone can …
   b Nobody knows …
   c A friend is someone who …
   d Everyone I know likes …
   e Everywhere I go …
   f There's nothing I like better on a hot summer day than …

3 Work in small groups. Take turns to think of a well-known place, a famous person or a household object. The others have to guess what you are thinking of by asking questions.
   Example
   Is it a place? Is it somewhere in Europe?
   Is it a person? Is it someone in a rock band?
   Is it an object? Is it something in the kitchen?

Exploring words

Love and marriage

1 What is the difference in meaning between the words in each pair?

a wedding / marriage
b girlfriend / fiancée
c date / appointment
d bride / groom
e husband / partner
f to like someone / to fancy someone
g father-in-law / godfather
h maiden name / married name
i relationship / relation
j half-sister / stepsister
k widow / widower
l polygamy / monogamy

2 a Match illustrations **a–h** with expressions **1–8**.

1 split up
2 get engaged
3 fall in love with someone
4 get divorced
5 have a family
6 go out with someone
7 get married
8 meet

b Complete the text with one of the expressions in **2a** in the appropriate form.

Julian _met_ **1** Emily at a friend's party. He .... **2** her the moment he saw her. She was extremely pretty. He decided to go over and speak to her. 'Haven't I seen you somewhere before?' he asked – not the most original chat-up line – but Emily liked the way he smiled, and at the end of the evening agreed to .... **3** him. They went to the cinema on their first date, and .... **4** six months later. They .... **5** in a local church the following June.

They wanted to .... **6** while they were still young. Their first child was born a year later and two others followed in quick succession. Unfortunately, though, things didn't work out, and they .... **7** just after their fifth wedding anniversary. They .... **8** two years later. Julian admitted, 'We got married too young.'

c **6.4** Listen and check.

3 Work in pairs. Ask and answer these questions.

a What are the best places to meet people?
b What is the most or least original chat-up line you have ever used or heard?
c Where do you think is the best place to go on a first date?
d What do you think is the best age to have a family?
e How important are godparents?

4 Work in pairs. You are going to write a 'love story'.

a Write one or two sentences for point **1** below, then pass your story to the pair on your left.
b Read your new story and do the same for point 2. Then pass your story on.
c Continue until you finish the story.
d Decide on the best story.
  1 Names of couple: where, when and how they met.
  2 What they said to each other.
  3 Their first date.
  4 The wedding.
  5 The end of the story.

Writing

Personal letters

Read

The sentences in this letter have been jumbled up. Put them in the correct order.

a | Her name's Anita and she's Danish.

b | Quite a lot has happened since I last wrote to you. I changed jobs two years ago.

c | Dear Tony,
How are you? It's ages since I last wrote, I know.

d | Well, I'd better sign off now. It's getting late.

e | Now I'm working for an American company called GLT Electronics.

f | I'm sorry, but as you know, I'm not the best letter-writer in the world.

g | Hope to hear from you soon.

h | Eva and I split up six months ago. I was very upset at first, but I'm over it now.

i | Yours,
Jamie

j | Anyway, I hope you are well.

k | Fortunately she speaks English, as I don't speak any Danish. We'll see how it goes – I'm not going to rush into anything.

l | In fact, I've been going out with someone else for the last six weeks.

m | Have you heard of them? The pay is quite good so I'm not complaining.

Brainstorm and notes

You are going to write a letter to a friend you haven't been in touch with for two years. Think about what has happened to you in that time and write notes. Here are some ideas.

- your studies
- family
- relationships
- future plans
- work
- friends
- purchases (flat, car, etc.)

Write

1 Write a first draft of your letter using the notes you have made.

2 a Exchange descriptions with another person.

b Read each other's letters. Is your partner's description written in an appropriate style? Is it interesting to read? Suggest one or two improvements.

c Discuss your ideas for improvements. Then write the final version of your letter.

> **Reminder**
> - Begin and end the letter in the right way.
> - Use informal language.
> - Use a new paragraph for a new topic.

Language in action

Permission

Introduction

1 How would you ask permission in these situations?
In pairs, write down what you would say. Try to use
different expressions.
  a You want to borrow a friend's CD.
  b You want to sit next to somebody in the canteen.
  c You want to borrow your friend's car.
  d You want your boss to let you leave work early.
  e You want to take a chair from another table in a
    snack bar.

2 **6.5** Listen to the conversations.
  a Tick (✓) any expressions they use which are the same
    as those you used.
  b Listen again. This time note down some of the
    language the speakers use.
    Student A Note expressions used to ask permission.
    Student B Note expressions used to give and
    refuse permission.
  c Tell each other the expressions you heard.
  d Which is the most formal expression used to ask for
    permission? Which is the most informal? Which
    expressions are used to show that the speaker is happy
    to give permission? Which expression shows that the
    speaker doesn't really want to give permission?

▶ **Pronunciation p.152**

Practice

Role play

Work in pairs.

Student A Read the information on this page.
Student B Turn to p.154.

Student A
Situation 1
You are renting out a room in your flat. Your new tenant
is going to ask you for permission to do three things. You
can give permission or not, but if you refuse, you must
give a reason.

Situation 2
You work for a very strict boss. Ask your boss for
permission to do the following.
  • Take three days off so that you can go to a wedding.
  • Make a phone call. Your mother has just had an
    operation and you want to check on her. The hospital is
    in another country.
  • Come in late tomorrow. You have to see the doctor.
Your boss will not say *yes* easily. You will need to persuade
them with good arguments.

Unit 6 Language check

In this unit you have worked on the following language points:
  • Permission, obligation, prohibition: *can, can't, must, mustn't,
    have to, don't have to*
  • Permission and obligation (2): *could, couldn't, had to, didn't
    have to*

  • Indefinite pronouns
  • Vocabulary: love and marriage
  • Writing: personal letters
  • Permission
  • Pronunciation: sounding happy to give permission

7 Seriously funny

Preview

Your thoughts

1
  a What is happening in these cartoons?

  b How funny do you find them? Rank them from **1** (the funniest) to **5** (the least funny).

  c Compare ideas with other students.

"I CAN'T BE ABSOLUTELY CERTAIN, OF COURSE, BUT YOU DO APPEAR TO BE IN SOME KIND OF TROUBLE, MR. HOWARD"

2 Work in pairs.

  a Think about some of the things that make you laugh. Think about:
- films or TV programmes
- books, magazines, adult comics
- people you know
- real-life situations or things that happen spontaneously.

  b Exchange ideas with your partner.

  c How would you describe your sense of humour? For example: *childish, ironic.*

  d Have you and your partner got a similar sense of humour?

Listen

1 **7.1** Listen to six people talking about what makes them laugh. What question were they asked?

2 Who said what? Listen again and match the six speakers with what they find funny and what they don't find funny.

Finds funny	Speaker	Doesn't find funny	Speaker
• the natural humour of friends		• slapstick, banana-skin humour	
• stand-up comedians		• comedy programmes on TV	
• black humour		• modern humour	
• people in real situations		• obvious humour	
• word humour		• the kind of jokes people tell in bars	
• ironic humour		• professional comedians	

"I'm sorry I'm not in at the moment . . . "

ross

"Your wife rang me to remind you to send me out for her birthday present from you!"

LOST PROPERTY

"No, this isn't mine—mine wasn't loaded."

Read

1 You are going to read some typical prepared jokes – the kind the first speaker doesn't find funny.

a Before you read the jokes, answer these vocabulary questions.

   1 If you are going somewhere, when do you *walk* and when do you *fly*?

   2 The phone rings, you pick it up and a voice says, '*Hello, this is Paul.*' What does it mean?

   3 What is a *bean*? What other word sounds the same?

b Now read the three jokes. Choose the one you find the funniest or the least funny, then compare ideas with a partner.

---

1 **Q**uestion *Why do birds fly south in the winter?*
Answer *Because it's too far to walk.*

2
Voice on the phone	*Hello. Is that the maternity hospital?*
Receptionist	*Yes, it is. How can I help you?*
Voice on the phone	*Can you send an ambulance, please? My wife is about to have a baby.*
Receptionist	*Is this her first baby?*
Voice on the phone	*No, this is her husband.*

---

3 '*Waiter!*'
'*Yes, sir.*'
'*What's the stuff in this bowl?*'
'*It's bean soup, sir.*'
'*I don't want to know what it's been. What is it now?*'

Have your say

1 One of the speakers says *I think humour's to do with age.* What does she mean? Do you agree with this idea?

2 People often say that you can't translate jokes from one language into another. Can you think of any examples? Try translating a joke into English.

Grammar review: *can / could*

1 a *Can* and *could* are used to talk about abilities or possibilities. Do they refer to abilities or possibilities in these sentences? (Write **A** or **P**.)

   1 ☐ *Television sit-coms can be absolutely dreadful.*

   2 ☐ *Some of my friends can make me laugh at almost anything.*

   3 ☐ *It could rain this afternoon – that's why I've got an umbrella with me.*

   4 ☐ *He can speak German, but he can't speak French.*

   5 ☐ *My sister could swim when she was three years old.*

   6   **A** *There's someone at the door.*
      ☐ **B** *It could be the postman.*

b Do the words *can / can't / could* in **1–6** above refer to the past, the present, the future or to time in general?

c What other uses do *can* and *could* have? In which sentence a–c below is the speaker

   1 making a suggestion?

   2 making a request?

   3 asking permission?

   a *Can you send an ambulance, please!*

   b *Can I use your phone, please?*

   c *We could go to Greece for our holiday. What do you think?*

▶ **Language commentary p.132**

Check

2 a Tell a partner about some of your abilities now and when you were younger.
Make sentences like this:
I can drive a car. / I could ride a horse when I was six.

b How many different ways can you think of to finish the following sentences?

   1 Watching television can …

   2 Smoking can …

   3 Eating too much can …

c Think of endings for these sentences.

   1 My car's making a strange noise. It could be …

   2 Chris and Sophie are very late. They could …

   3 What's that strange thing in the sky? It could …

3 Work in pairs. Look back at the cartoons and make suggestions in answer to these questions.

a In the first cartoon, what could the doctor do to help his patient?

b In the third cartoon, what could the secretary get the man's wife for her birthday?

▶ *can, could, may, might*   p.67
▶ Relative clauses (1)   p.70

Reading

In your experience

1 a **7.2** Listen to the recording. What are the four people you hear doing?

b Think of situations where you would *snigger*, *giggle* or *laugh*. Compare ideas with a partner.

2 How did you react to the four people? How did other students in the class react?

Read

1 You are going to read extracts from various articles related to laughter. Match each extract with one of these headlines.

- Laugh away your aches and pains
- Beware! Laughter can be catching
- Laugh your way to university
- Keep fit by laughing

Why laughter is the best medicine

1 We all do it: women do it more than men. Children do it more often than adults. Eskimos do it in competitions. Laughing, that is.
According to an American professor, laughter improves our biological fitness. Professor Weisfeld claims that what we laugh at most are topics that affect our
5 fitness. So, depressed patients are especially amused by jokes about depression, suicidal patients by jokes about death and feminists by anti-male jokes.

2 **Robert Holden**, who runs laughter therapy classes, says: 'Instinctively we all know that laughter makes us feel healthy and alive.' The idea of his classes came when he was helping people suffering from
5 depression. 'The turning point came about when people could laugh about their situation. Their perception of the problem changed and they could begin to take control of their lives.' Laughing can be highly infectious and this fact might explain why laughter classes are a
10 success. In a famous laughter epidemic in Tanzania in the 1960s, two school girls began to giggle. This spread to the rest of the class and soon the whole school and, when mothers collected their children from school, they joined in. The laughing spread to neighbouring villages
15 and continued for two weeks, affecting more than a thousand people.

3 Humour in the classroom creates a receptive frame of mind and highlights important information. The exchange of jokes between children also has important social functions. Research in British primary schools
5 suggests additional benefits. Humour can actually help children to understand mathematical concepts.

4 *Psychiatrists* have studied the effects of laughter on the body. In one experiment they got patients to watch funny films and monitored their physical responses. They discovered that laughter has a similar effect to
5 physical exercise: it speeds up the heart rate, increases blood pressure, and quickens breathing. Laughter may even relieve pain by stimulating the production of endorphins, chemicals which occur naturally in the body. Laughter can also get rid of feelings of tension
10 that might cause stress.

Close up

1.5 (Extract 1) What is the other meaning of *patient*? Is it the same kind of word as this meaning?

1.3 (Extract 2) What is the difference in meaning between *being alive* and *feeling alive*?

1.8-1.12 (Extract 2) What do these words usually describe: *infectious*, *epidemic*, *to spread*?

1.4 (Extract 3) What age of children go to *primary* schools? What school do they go to next?

2 a Read the extracts again and underline five facts about laughter.

b Choose the two most interesting pieces of information, then compare choices with a partner.

Understanding ideas

1 Why do you think women laugh more than men?

2 How do you think it helps depressed people if they can laugh at their situation?

3 How could doctors and nurses make use of the fact that laughter can relieve pain?

Have your say

What do you think of the idea of laughter classes? Can you think of anyone you know who might benefit from this kind of therapy?

Grammar

Modal verbs: *can, could, may, might*

Exploring concepts

1 Which of these sentences express definite facts? (Write **D.**) Which tense is used?
   a ☐ *Laughter improves our biological fitness.*
   b ☐ *Laughter may relieve pain.*
   c ☐ *Laughter has a similar effect to physical exercise.*
   d ☐ *Laughter can get rid of feelings of tension.*
   e ☐ *Laughing can be highly infectious.*
   f ☐ *… this fact might explain why laughter classes are a success.*

2 a Which sentences express
      1 a possibility – an idea that is true in some cases?
      2 uncertainty – an idea you cannot prove?
   b Which words tell you this?

3 Do these sentences refer to present or future time? (Write **P** or **F.**)
   a ☐ *They may be at work.*
   b ☐ *She might go to Poland.*
   c ☐ *He could be in a traffic jam.*
   d ☐ *He might be unhappy.*
   e ☐ *We could watch the film on TV.*
   f ☐ *She may retire early.*

▶ **Language commentary p.132**

Exploitation

1 a Think about the consequences of these everyday activities and make up sentences with *can, may* or *might* depending on how certain you are about the consequences. (If you are absolutely certain, use the Present simple.)
      1 Drinking coffee …   4 Watching violent films …
      2 Doing regular exercise … 5 Listening to loud music …
      3 Lack of sleep …

b Compare ideas with a partner, then together make up more sentences for each activity.

2 a Think about the next four or five months. Write down anything you know you are going to do and things that you are not quite sure about yet. Write something for each month.

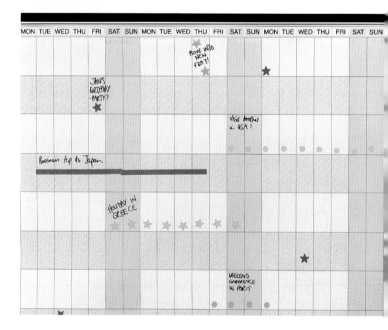

b Now compare plans with another student. Make conversations like this:
   Student A *What are you going to do in January?*
   Student B *I'm going to visit my brother in the USA.* OR *I'm not sure. I may visit my brother in the USA.*

Role play

3 Work in pairs. You and your partner are planning a short holiday. Decide on these things.
   • Where and when to go
   • How to travel
   • Where to stay
   Student A You worry about everything. You always think about all the things that could go wrong.
   Student B You are the confident type. Put your partner's mind at rest.

Skills

Listen and speak

1 Every nationality has jokes about other nationalities or about people from other regions of their own country. The jokes are often related to typical national or regional characteristics.

a Do you have jokes like this? Who are they about?

b Look at this cartoon. What do you think it shows?

c **7.3** Now listen to three nationality jokes. You will hear everything except the last lines. Guess what they will be.

d **7.4** Now listen to the complete jokes. Check the ideas you had in b–c.

2 Work in groups. Discuss these questions.

Do other people make jokes about your nationality or about people from your region? What characteristics do they laugh at?

Read

1 You are going to read an extract from *Notes from a Small Island*, by the American writer Bill Bryson, who lived in England for more than twenty years. In this extract he is writing about people from Yorkshire, a county in the north of England.

a Look at the photographs of Yorkshire. What impressions do you get of the place and the people who live there?

b Now read the extract. What does Bill Bryson think about Yorkshire people? Does he describe them positively or negatively?

They do things differently there

They do things differently in Yorkshire, you see. For one thing, people who know you come right into your house. Sometimes, they knock once and shout 'Hullo!' before sticking their head in, but often they don't even do that. It's not
5 unusual to be standing at the kitchen sink talking to yourself and then turning round to find a fresh pile of mail lying on the kitchen table. And I can't tell you the number of times I've had to dart into another room in my underpants at the sound of someone's approach and cowered breathless while
10 they've shouted, 'Hullo! Hullo! Anyone at home?' For a couple of minutes you can hear them clumping around in the kitchen, examining the messages on the fridge and holding the mail to the light. Then they come over to the pantry door and in a quiet voice they say, 'Just taking six eggs, Bill – all right?'

15   I've never understood why Yorkshire people have this terrible reputation for being mean-spirited. I've always found them to be decent and open, and, if you want to know your shortcomings, you won't find more helpful people anywhere. It's true that they don't smother you with affection,
20 which takes a little getting used to if you are from a more sociable part of the world, like anywhere else. Where I come from in America if you move into a village or a little town, everybody comes to your house to welcome you.

    In Yorkshire that would never happen. But gradually, little
25 by little, they find a corner for you in their hearts and begin to acknowledge you as you drive past with what I call the Yorkshire wave. This is an exciting day in the life of any new arrival. To make the wave, pretend that you are grasping a steering wheel. Now very slowly extend the index finger of
30 your right hand. That's it. It doesn't look like much, but it speaks volumes …

Notes from a Small Island

2 Work out (or guess) the meanings of the words in **bold** in these phrases from the extract. Use other words in the extract and the questions to help you.

  a … *I've had to **dart** into another room in my underpants* … (l.8)
How would you move if you weren't fully dressed and someone came into your house unexpectedly?

  b … *and **cowered breathless** …* (l.9)
How would you feel if you had been hurrying? What would you do if you were trying to hide?

  c … *you can hear them **clumping around** …* (l.11)
Clumping describes how someone is moving. What kind of movement does it suggest?

  d … *if you want to know your **shortcomings**, you won't find more helpful people …* (l.18)
Does *shortcomings* sound positive or negative?

3 Match these characteristics of Yorkshire people (**a–d**) with examples of behaviour (**1–4**) mentioned in the extract.

  a over-friendly / informal
  b inquisitive / nosy
  c frank / honest
  d slow to accept strangers

  1 they tell you all your shortcomings
  2 nobody welcomes you when you move to a town in Yorkshire
  3 they come into your house without being invited
  4 they hold your letters up to the light

Speak and write

Work in groups of four or five.

1 Each student in the group should follow these steps.

  a Choose a foreign country or a region of your country and think about the people who live there. (It could be somewhere you have lived or visited on holiday.)

  b Write notes under these headings.
    • Typical characteristics of these people
    • Examples of typical behaviour

2 Take turns to describe the group of people you have chosen and their behaviour. The rest of the group have to guess who you are describing.

3 Finally, use your notes to write a description of the people and their behaviour.

Grammar extra

Relative clauses (1)

Exploring concepts

1 a We use relative clauses for two reasons:

    1 to add extra, non-essential information about a person or thing.
       Woody Allen, who was born in New York in 1935, started his career as a TV scriptwriter.

    2 to give essential information which defines exactly which thing or person we are referring to.
       The film which first made Woody Allen famous was What's New Pussycat.

b Do the relative clauses in these sentences contain essential or non-essential information? Write **E** or **N**.

    1 ☐ Eddie Murphy, who started out as a TV comedian, is now a highly-paid film actor.

    2 ☐ One of the films that made him famous was *Beverly Hills Cop*.

    3 ☐ *Forrest Gump*, which was made in 1994, starred Tom Hanks.

    4 ☐ Billy Connolly, who is well-known as a brilliant comedian, is also a serious actor.

    5 ☐ There aren't many modern film actors that can make me laugh.

    6 ☐ Most of the comedians who appear on TV aren't funny at all.

c What is the difference in punctuation between the **E** sentences and the **N** sentences?

2 Which relative pronouns – *who, which, that* – refer to people, and which refer to things? Look back at the sentences in **1b**.

▶ **Language commentary p.132**

Exploitation

1 a Write simple sentences about these subjects.
    Example
    Titanic *is my favourite film.*

    1 Your favourite film
    2 Your favourite actor
    3 Your favourite song or piece of music
    4 Your favourite singer or musician
    5 Your favourite TV programme
    6 Your favourite TV personality

b Now add extra information to your sentences. Use *who, which* or *that*.
    Example
    Titanic, *which was made in 1997 and stars Leonardo DiCaprio, is my favourite film.*
    My favourite film is Titanic, *which was made in 1997 and stars Leonardo DiCaprio.*

2 a Make up your own definitions of these people and things.
    Example
    A good film is one which makes you forget your everyday life.

    1 A good film
    2 A good song or good music
    3 A good singer or musician

b Compare definitions with a partner.

c Work in pairs. Think of definitions of these people. Use *who* or *that*.
    1 A good teacher / a bad teacher
    2 A good student / a bad student
    3 A good boss / a bad boss

3 a Each student thinks of five words, then thinks of questions about the definitions of the words.
    Example
    What's the word for a special actor who does dangerous actions in place of a more famous actor in a film?

b Now work in groups. Take turns to ask the other students in the group your questions.

4 a Read these extracts from an article by the writer Miles Kington.
    • Which kind of person are you?
    • Do you know anyone who is the other kind of person?

There are two kinds of people.

• There are those who wave frantically at taxis which already contain passengers and there are those who patiently wait for an empty one to come along.

• There are those who cannot bear to be in a room where a TV set is on without watching whatever is on the screen and those who can be in a room without even being aware that the TV set is on.

• There are those who get undressed to go to bed, and those who first get undressed and then dress up again for bed in pyjamas, night-shirts or similar.

b Work in pairs. Think of some more examples of pairs of people who are opposites. Make up sentences using this structure.
There are those who … and there are those who …

Exploring words

Body language; extreme adjectives

1 a Match these *face* and *voice* verbs with the right photographs.

| **1** cry | **2** frown | **3** giggle | **4** laugh | **5** smile | **6** wink | **7** yawn |

b Work in pairs. Think of explanations for the expressions or the actions of the people in the photographs.
Example
Student A *Why do you think he's crying?*
Student B *Maybe he can't have what he wants.*

2 a Read this conversation. Who was most amused and who was least amused by the TV programme?

b Here are some more sets of adjectives with similar meanings. Find the strongest adjective in each group. Is there a difference between the others?
Example
hot   boiling   warm
Boiling is the strongest. Hot is stronger than warm.

1 angry   annoyed   furious
2 surprising   astonishing   unexpected
3 starving   hungry   peckish
4 freezing   cool   cold
5 afraid   terrified   frightened
6 unique   rare   unusual
7 intelligent   brilliant   clever

c Most adjectives can be used with *very*, and in the comparative and superlative form.
Example
*Yesterday was **very hot**, but today is even **hotter**.*
But strong or 'extreme' adjectives cannot be used like this. If you want to emphasize them, you must use *absolutely* or *really*.
Example
*The water in the pool is usually quite warm, but today it's **absolutely boiling**.*

d Complete these conversations. Liz is always extreme.
1 Gill   It's very cold in here, isn't it?
  Liz   Too right, it …
2 Gill   Did you see the horror film on TV last night? I was quite frightened.
  Liz   Frightened? I …
3 Gill   Weren't you annoyed about the train being late?
  Liz   Annoyed? …

e Choose some more sets of adjectives and make your own conversations like these.

f Work in pairs or groups. Choose three or four of these subjects and talk about each of them for no more than two minutes.
1 A person or a TV programme you find absolutely hilarious.
2 The last time you were absolutely furious about something.
3 Things you like to eat when you're absolutely starving.
4 Someone you know who is absolutely brilliant at something.
5 The last time you were absolutely terrified.
6 A place you have been to that was absolutely unique.

Writing

Short stories

Read

1 Read these short texts.

   a Which is a complete story?

   b Which is the beginning of a personal anecdote?

   c Which is part of a new version of an old story?

1 One day her mother asked her to take some organically grown fruit and mineral water across the forest to her grandmother's house.

As she was walking through the forest, which was full of endangered animals and rare plants, she met a wolf, who said, 'You know, my dear, it isn't safe for a little girl to walk through these woods alone.'

The girl said, 'I find your sexist remark offensive, but I will ignore it because of your traditional position as a social outcast. Now, please excuse me, I must be on my way.'

2 When I was at university, a friend on the same course, Phil, decided not to come to the early morning classes because he was too lazy. I went to all the classes and then lent Phil my notes to copy. Unfortunately he kept losing my notes, so I started photocopying them for him. Then I thought – why should I go to the early lectures so Phil gets the notes? So, as I photocopied the notes, I left out important details, or changed them to make them wrong. Eventually, Phil had over 200 pages of work that was completely wrong.

2 Discuss these questions in pairs.

   a How do you think the personal anecdote will continue and end?

   b Why do you think the old story has been changed?

Brainstorm and notes

Work in groups.

1 Think of your own ideas for short stories. Choose one of these types of story.

   • A personal anecdote.

   • A well-known story, which you could bring up to date or change in another way.

   • A complete story which could be written in 100 words or fewer.

2 Briefly, tell each other the basic outline of your story.

3 Write notes under these headings. Follow the example.

   • Type of story   *Personal anecdote*

   • When it took place *Last summer*

   • Who was involved   *Me, a friend, a taxi driver*

   • The beginning   *Got into a taxi after a party*

   • The middle   *Found we had no money*

   • The end   *Taxi to hospital*

3 The phone rang.

'Hello,' she whispered.

'Victoria, it's me. Meet me by the dock at midnight.'

'I'll be there, sweetheart.'

'And don't forget the bubbly, babe,' he said.

'I won't darling. I must see you tonight.'

'I can't wait!' he said, and hung up.

She sighed, then smiled.

'I wonder who that was,' she said.

Write

1 Write a first draft of your story, in 100 words or fewer, using the notes you have made.

2 **a** Exchange stories with a partner who has not already heard your story.

   b As you read each other's stories, think about these questions.

     • Is the story complete? If it is not, are you interested in finding out how it ends?

     • Are the ideas or events in the story well linked?

     • Does the dialogue sound natural?

3 Discuss your ideas with your partner. Suggest one or two improvements your partner could make to their story.

4 Write the final versions of your stories.

> **Reminder**
> • Use the correct past tenses.
> • Mark the different stages of the story clearly.
> • Dialogue can make stories more lively.

Language in action

Making suggestions

Introduction

1 a Read this short extract from a newspaper article.
    1 What routine activity or situation is it about?
    2 What ideas are mentioned for making this
       activity / situation less boring?

In the past companies relieved boredom by serving overcooked, unwanted meals. Now they try to entertain. In addition to films, electronic games and gambling, one company teaches its staff how to use humour to entertain weary business travellers. A company representative says: 'We want to have a more friendly service, so we've trained our staff to be themselves more. They don't tell jokes but we've asked them to have fun with the passengers.

'For instance, as they touch down in Berlin, someone might say, "Welcome to New York." Or an attendant might warn passengers to turn off their "mobile phones, computers and washing machines" to avoid interfering with the controls. We even have a steward who has become famous for juggling with oranges.'

b Work in pairs. Think of other ways of making this situation less boring. Make a list of your suggestions.
c Discuss your suggestions with another pair. Accept or reject each others' suggestions.

2 a **7.5** Now listen to a group of passengers discussing their suggestions for solving this problem with a company representative. Do the speakers mention any of your ideas?

b Listen again. This time note down some of the language the speakers use.
Student A Note expressions speakers use to make suggestions.
Student B Note expressions speakers use to accept or reject suggestions.

c Tell each other the expressions you heard. Make lists under these headings:
- making suggestions
- accepting suggestions
- rejecting suggestions.
Add any expressions you used in **1** to your lists.

▶ **Pronunciation p.152**

Problem-solving

Work in groups. You are going to discuss ways of making another routine activity / situation less boring.

1 Choose one of these subjects to talk about.
- Journeys to work by train or bus
- Being a hospital patient
- Waiting in a queue, for example in a supermarket or at the bank
- Being held up in a traffic jam

2 Each member of the group starts by suggesting an idea. The other members of the group discuss the ideas and accept or reject the suggestions.

3 a Make a list of all the suggestions that the group agrees about.
b Read other groups' lists of suggestions, and choose the best ideas.

Unit 7 Language check

In this unit you have worked on the following language points:
- *can* and *could*: abilities, possibilities, permission, requests, suggestions
- *can*, *could*, *may* and *might*: possibilities, degrees of uncertainty
- Relative clauses (1): *who, which, that*

- Vocabulary: body language, extreme (gradable) adjectives
- Writing: short stories
- Making suggestions
- Pronunciation: silent letters; sounding enthusiastic

8 Making contact

Preview

Your thoughts

1 Work in pairs or groups. Which of these methods of communication do you use regularly? Which method do you use most frequently? Which could you do without?
   - telephone
   - fax
   - mobile phone
   - snail mail (a traditional letter)
   - e-mail

2 Think of times when you use each method. Are there some people you only write to, or people you only phone?

Read

1 What are the main advantages of e-mail? Make a list with your partner.

2 a Read this text. Are any of the advantages of e-mail from your list mentioned?

> It once seemed that the telephone had made writing to people, and especially to friends, unnecessary. E-mail has allowed us to find its benefits again. Phone calls are intrusive; they always interrupt something, even if it is only thought. E-mail, like the letter, has better manners. It respects the demands of more urgent business and allows for differences in time zones. It waits to be read in a so-called 'mailbox'.
>
> E-mails are usually more informal than letters – they allow writers to put down present thoughts and even changes of mind. This informality also means that it seems OK to write a two-line message to someone on another continent, or to send a joke or an unimportant piece of gossip to someone in the next office.

b How does the text compare e-mails to phone calls and to traditional letters?

Listen

1 a **8.1** You are going to listen to seven people talking about mobile phones. How many of them have one?

b Listen again. Are these statements True or False?
1 All the people who don't have a mobile phone would like one.
2 Most people said mobile phones were useful when travelling by car.
3 Two people said they used a mobile phone in their jobs.
4 One speaker said he had never used his mobile phone.

2 a You are now going to listen to people saying what annoys them about mobile phones. What do you think they will say?

b **8.2** Listen and check which of your ideas are mentioned by the speakers.

Vocabulary

1 Here are some everyday expressions used by the speakers. What do you think they mean? Compare ideas with a partner.
a *I might **get stuck** in a car somewhere.*
b *I don't use it very often, just when I'm **out and about** …*
c *… for getting emergency help **in the middle of nowhere**.*
d *I think they're **a real pain in the neck**.*
e *… they don't have any respect for your privacy or their privacy, **funnily enough**.*

2 Now answer these questions.
a Have you ever *got stuck* somewhere in a car? What did you do?
b Why do some people choose to live *in the middle of nowhere*?
c What kind of people do you find *a pain in the neck*?

Have your say

Discuss these statements.

1 Mobile phones should be banned in public places.

2 Traditional letters are an out-of-date means of communication.

Grammar review: Reported speech (1)

1 Read these pairs of sentences. In each case, the first sentence is direct speech and the second is reported speech.
a Underline the words that are different in the second sentence in each pair.
1 *'I don't have a mobile phone.'*
She said she didn't have a mobile phone.
2 *'I've never used my mobile phone.'*
He said he had never used his mobile phone.
3 *'I'll get myself a mobile phone next week.'*
She said she would get herself a mobile phone the following week.

b What are the main differences between direct and reported speech? Think about:
- the verbs
- the pronouns (*I / he*, etc.)
- references to time (*today / next year*, etc.).

2 Compare these sets of sentences. What are the differences between the two sentences in reported speech? What does that tell you?
a *'I used my phone yesterday.'*
She said she'd used her phone the day before.
She said she used her phone yesterday.
b *'I'll phone you tomorrow.'*
She said she'd phone me the next day.
She says she'll phone me tomorrow.

▶ **Language commentary p.133**

Check

3 Here are some sentences in reported speech. What were the speakers' words?
a He said he preferred to write an ordinary letter.
b Sylvia said she'd phoned me two or three times the day before.
c She said she thought e-mail was fantastic.
d He said he'd send us a postcard the following week.
e They say they won't be late home this evening.
f Mark says he's buying a new computer later this week.

4 Here are some sentences in direct speech. Turn them into reported speech.
a 'I think they're a real pain in the neck,' she said.
b She said, 'I get annoyed when mobile phones go off in church.'
c 'I'll see you tomorrow,' he said.
d She said, 'I can't pay you. I've lost all my money.'
e 'I'm starting my new job today,' he said.
f 'I finished my exams yesterday,' he said.

5 a Work in groups of four.
Tell the student on your left three pieces of information. (Whisper!)
- Say something you have done recently.
- Say what you did last Sunday morning.
- Say what you're doing tomorrow evening.

b Now tell the student on your left what the student on your right has just told you.

▶ Reported speech (2): questions   p.77
▶ Expressing quantities   p.80

Listening

In your experience

Discuss these questions in pairs or groups.

1 When and why do people feel shy?

2 Here are some of the physical symptoms of shyness. Which ones have you suffered from?

---
blushing   butterflies in the stomach   dry throat   inability to speak   shaky knees
stammering   sweating

Listen

1 **8.3** Listen to someone talking about being shy. Which of the symptoms in the list above are not mentioned?

2 What can someone like this do about their problem? Could you give this young man some advice? Think of two or three suggestions.

3 Now listen to an expert giving advice to shy people.
   a **8.4** What do you think are the best suggestions for the speaker you have just heard?
   b Compare ideas with a partner.

Understanding ideas

Listen to the extract again. Why do you think the speaker makes these suggestions?

a Focus on other people.
b Think about successful past experiences.
c Imagine the worst thing that could happen.
d Breathe deeply.

Vocabulary

1 Check the meanings of the words and phrases in **bold** from the recording. Then answer the questions.

a *In the end most people learn to cope with these feelings ... not let them ruin their lives.*
  How might being shy *ruin someone's life*?

b *Stop yourself worrying what other people are thinking about you – especially in social situations.*
  What *social situations* are you often in?

c *If ... there's someone you'd like to talk to, focus on that person.*
  How do you *focus on* particular people or things?

d *Improve your small talk.*
  What are your favourite and least favourite subjects of *small talk*?

e *Use well-practised lines if you suddenly feel shy ...*
  In what everyday situations do you use *well-practised lines*?

2 Think of alternative words or phrases that could be used instead of these adjectives from the recording.

a *I start feeling tense before I get there.*
b *I just stand around feeling uncomfortable.*
c *It's hard being shy.*
d *... to form positive relationships ...*

Have your say

Do you have any fears? Do you agree that *bringing a fear out in the open* takes away its power to worry you?

Reported speech (2): questions

Exploring concepts

1 What are the main differences between direct and reported questions? Read these direct and reported questions and think about:

- verb tenses
- pronouns (*I*, *her*, etc.)
- question words
- word order.

a '*Where do you work?' I asked.*
I asked her where she worked.

b '*Have we met somewhere before?'*
I asked.
I asked her if we'd met somewhere before.

c '*Do you know anyone else in the room?' I asked.*
I asked her if she knew anyone else in the room.

d '*Can you introduce me to someone?'*
I asked her if she could introduce me to someone.

e '*When will you ring me?' she asked.*
She asked me when I would ring her.

f '*Does you father work locally?'*
she asked.
She asked whether my father worked locally.

2 How are *Yes / No* questions changed into reported questions?
Look at the examples in **1a–f** and write a rule for

a *Yes / No* questions.

b *Yes / No* questions which include the auxiliary verb *do* or *does*.

▶ **Language commentary p.133**

Exploitation

1 a **8.5** Listen to this telephone conversation and note down the questions the telesales assistant asks the customer.
Example
What's your name, please?

b Now change the questions into reported speech.
Example
She asked him what his name was.

2 a In pairs, discuss and then act out the conversations which might be taking place in these situations.

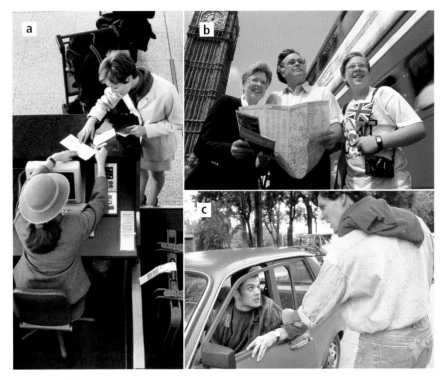

b Now write short reports of two of the conversations without using direct speech.

c Exchange your reports with other students. How similar are they?

Role play

3 a Work in groups.
You are the first arrivals at a party. You don't know each other.

  1 Choose one of the roles listed on p.158, but don't tell the others in your group which one you have chosen.

  2 Make up three or four questions you might ask people you had never met before.

  3 Now make polite conversations to find out as much as you can about each other in five minutes.

b Work with a partner from another group. Tell each other what you found out about the other guests at your party.

Skills

Write and speak

1 Complete this questionnaire.

> **1** Which languages do you speak?
>
> 1 .... 3 ....
>
> 2 .... 4 ....
>
> **2** How well can you speak these languages?
> (F = fluently / Q = quite well / L = A little)
>
> 1 .... 2 .... 3 .... 4 ....
>
> **3** At what age did you start to learn each language?
>
> 1 .... 3 ....
>
> 2 .... 4 ....
>
> **4** Are you bilingual*?   YES / NO
>
> **5** Do you know anyone who is bilingual?   YES / NO
>
> *   *bilingual* = able to speak two languages

2 Compare answers with other students.

Speak and read

1 How much do you know about being *bilingual*? How many of these common questions about bilingualism can you answer? Work through the questions with a partner. If you are not certain, make a sensible guess.

  a When should children start learning a second language in order to become bilingual?

  b Will a child be confused by two languages?

  c Should parents always speak their own language?

  d How many different languages can a child cope with?

  e Will using two languages affect how well a child does at school?

  f Will the child become equally fluent in two languages?

2 Read this article to find the answers to the six questions. Then write the question number next to the correct answer.

How to increase

Are there right and wrong ways for a child to acquire an extra language? Specialist Colin Baker answers some basic questions about bilingualism.

☐ No experiments have ever been done, but it is now known that the brain has a huge capacity for processing and storing language. Trilingualism is not uncommon in parts of Scandinavia.

☐ No. Monolingual people assume that being bilingual means being just as able in two languages as the monolingual is in one language. But for a bilingual, each language tends to have different functions and uses. Most bilinguals are stronger in one language than another, even where each parent speaks a different language.

☐ As soon as possible. Children learn best before the age of three and should start learning before they are taught to read, if possible.

☐ There is no evidence for this. Where both languages are well developed, there is some evidence to suggest that their performance may even be improved.

☐ It is usually recommended that where the parents are of different nationalities, they only use their own language with the child. It is not unusual for children to become fluent in a language other than their parents' through using it at kindergarten and in the street. Because they want to fit in, children are highly motivated to learn and are much less likely than adults to forget vocabulary and constructions they learn outside the home.

☐ Not if the two languages are kept separate initially. Experts recommend that parents and teachers use only one language at a time, even though the child may decide to mix the languages later.

The European Magazine

your word power

Let's talk
Let's talk
Let's talk
Let's talk
Let's talk

Understanding ideas

1 What two pieces of advice does the writer of the article give to parents who want their children to be bilingual?

2 What different functions and uses could the two different languages have for a bilingual person?

3 Why do you think it is better for children to learn languages before they are taught to read?

4 Why are children so keen to fit in that they are prepared to learn a new language?

Have your say

Are many people in your country bilingual? Is it particularly useful or necessary to be bilingual?

Listen

8.6 You are going to hear two people talking about being bilingual. As you listen, think about these questions.

1 Do they both feel positive about their ability?

2 Which languages do the two speakers know? What about the second speaker's son?

Understanding ideas

1 Listen again. How did each speaker learn other languages?

2 What information do they give about their attitude to being bilingual?

Have your say

1 When should children start learning a second language at school?

2 How do you think learning a second language at school is different from learning a language from your parents? Make a list of differences.

Speak and write

Work with someone whose language is the same as yours.

1 You are going to design a 45-minute lesson to teach some of your language to a class of beginners. Write notes as you work through these stages.
   a Decide whether your lesson is for children or adults.
   b Decide what to teach. Choose five to ten words and three to four useful expressions.
   c Decide how to teach. Think of several different activities which students will find useful and interesting. Make this a memorable lesson.
   d Think of ways to start and finish the lesson.

2 Present your ideas to the rest of the class. If there are students of other nationalities in your class, teach them part of your lesson.

Grammar extra

Expressing quantities

Exploring concepts

1 Underline all the words and phrases in this text which refer to quantities. The first one has been done for you.

- Although <u>lots of</u> adults talk regularly to answerphones, few people actually feel comfortable doing it.
- Many people say they feel stupid talking to machines and a few callers even blush or stammer when they leave messages.
- It is quite common for people to spend some time preparing a message if they think there is likely to be an answerphone.
- Plenty of children seem quite happy to talk to answerphones, even those who don't have much experience of telephones.
- What annoys some callers is the thought that the people they are phoning are actually listening to their message instead of picking up the phone.
- A lot of elderly people are afraid they won't have much time to speak. In fact there is always plenty of time for messages.
- In spite of these worries, there is little evidence that sales of answerphones are decreasing.

2 Look at the words you have underlined and answer these questions.

a What kind(s) of nouns follow these sets of words or phrases: plural countable nouns (like *people*) or uncountable nouns (like *time*)?

1 *few / many / a few*
2 *much / little*
3 *some / a lot of / lots of*

b Look at the verbs that are before *much* in the text. What have they got in common?

3 One sentence in each pair sounds more negative. Which one?
a *We've got little money left.*
We've got a little money left.
b *Few people came to the match.*
A few people came to the match.

4 a What kind of nouns can follow *plenty of*?
*… there is always **plenty of** time for messages.*
***Plenty of** children seem quite happy to talk to answerphones.*

b What does *plenty of* mean? Choose the best meaning.
- not enough
- lots or as much / many as you need
- too much / many

▶ **Language commentary p.134**

Exploitation

1 Make sentences about these people and these subjects, using as many of the quantity words and phrases as you can.

Examples
Many friends of mine speak two or three languages.
Few people in my family use the Internet.

People	Subjects
• Your friends	• Using the Internet
• People in your family	• Speaking different languages
• Students in your class	• Being friendly to strangers
• Colleagues you work with	• Spending or wasting time
• People in your country	• Television watching habits
• People in my town	• Using computers

2 Describe what you can see in the pictures below using quantity expressions.

Exploring words

Telephone language; *say, speak, tell*; adjectives

1 a Have you ever heard an unusual or amusing answerphone message in your own language or in English? Tell your partner.

> This is not an answerphone – it is a telepathic thought-recording device. After the tone, think about your name, your phone number and your reasons for calling. I'll think about returning your call.

b `8.7` You are going to listen to five answerphone messages. Which words or phrases mean:
1 the noise after which the caller speaks (two words)?
2 put the phone down?
3 make a return phone call (two expressions)?
4 another name for an answerphone?
5 say and record words you want the other person to hear?

c Compare answers with a partner, then check with Tapescript **8.7** on p.146.

d Work with a partner. Make up your own answerphone message.

2 Complete these sentences with the correct part of one of these 'telephone' phrasal verbs. If there is a pronoun in brackets, put it in the right place.

---
cut someone off   get through   hold on   pick something up
put someone through   ring off
---

a I've been trying to phone him all morning but I can't ....
b I was talking to Layla, then for no apparent reason she just ....
c Hello. Mr Johnson is expecting your call. I'll just .... (you).
d To make a phone call, ... the receiver and dial the number you want.
e In the middle of our conversation we .... quite suddenly. (Use the passive.)
f He's in the office somewhere. Can you just .... while I try to find him?

3 The verbs *speak*, *say* and *tell* have similar meanings but are used with different nouns.

Example
She can speak three languages. (NOT *say* or *tell*)

a Which verbs, *say, speak* or *tell*, go with these expressions?

---
someone's *fortune*   *goodbye* to someone
a *joke*   a *lie*   your *mind*   a *prayer* (for somebody)
Russian   someone a *secret*   someone a *story*
'Thank you' to someone   someone *the truth*
---

b Complete these questions with the correct form of *say, speak* or *tell*, then discuss the questions with a partner.
1 Is it always wrong to .... lies? When is it OK not to .... the truth?
2 Do you find it easy to .... your mind?
3 If people .... you a secret, do you ever pass the information on to someone else?
4 Have you ever had your fortune .... ? Who was the fortune- .... ? What did they say?
5 Why do some people .... prayers? When do you or might you .... a prayer?

4 Complete these sentences with one of the adjectives from the list.

---
mobile   public   quiet   small
---

a Parking is expensive, so I go to work by .... transport.
b Their house was flooded, so they're living in a .... home now.
c You'll have to speak a bit louder. You've got a very .... voice.
d In a democracy, politicians should always listen to .... opinion.
e If I'm not in, you can call me on my .... phone.
f I hate parties – I'm not very good at .... talk.
g We're staying at home and having a .... weekend.
h Most .... businesses have fewer than twenty employees.

Writing

E-mails

Read

1 Read these e-mails. Which one is a reply? a reminder? a request?

> **1**
>
> Subject: Nothing in particular
> Sent: 27/5/99 12:56 am
> Received: 27/5/99 5:53 pm
> From: Morris Door, 9897.0769@compuserve.com
> To: pol156@dial.pipex.com
>
> Hi Paul!
> Thanks for the e-mail. It had me laughing out loud – great to hear from you. It's really busy here at the moment, for 96 different reasons, including the fact that I'm here on my own – everyone's on holiday or out of the office, so I'd better get on. I'll be in touch in a few days.
> Bye for now
> Morris

> **2**
>
> Subject: Spain
> Sent: 12/5/99 11:33 am
> Received: 12/5/99 6:56 pm
> From: Jo Blackman, BlackmanJ@bbp.co.uk
> To: pol56@dial.pipex.com
>
> Dear Paul
> The Spanish office has asked if you would be free to go to conferences in Madrid and Barcelona in June next year. They would like you to give presentations in both places. If you would like more information, please get back to me.
> Best wishes
> Jo

> **3**
>
> Subject: Your daughter
> Sent: 29/5/99 12:36 pm
> Received: 1/6/99 4:45 pm
> From: ab0u60@liverpool.ac.uk
> To: pol56@dial.pipex.com
>
> Dad
> I've just done my next to last exam and i will do the last one in just under 2 hour. I'm not very confident so I will go and rivise. Wish me luck. Don't foget to fone me at the weekend.
> Becky XXXXX

2 Now work with a partner. How many mistakes can you find in 3? Why do you think the writer has made these mistakes and why hasn't she corrected them?

Read

Read **a** and **b**. You are going to write two e-mail replies.

> **a**
>
> Subject: Long time no see
> Sent: 3/3/99 10:55 am
> Received: 3/3/99 15:32 am
> From: charlie@compuserve.com
> To: lou@apple.demon.co.uk
>
> Hi,
> Someone's just given me your e-mail address, so I thought I'd get in touch. Hope you don't mind. I'd love to hear what you've been up to. I was working it out – it must be nearly 3 years since we last saw each other. I'm travelling around a lot so it's best to e-mail me.
> Luv
> Charlie

> **b**
>
> ### Be a Freelance Editor
>
> Seen something interesting on TV or the Net, read something in a newspaper, magazine?
> If so we want to hear from you. Contact Mediabest with your info. If we print it, you'll get a bottle of Champagne. Write to:
>
> fe@mediabest.co.uk

Preparation

Before you write, think about these points.
1 Style – how formal or informal should each e-mail be?
2 Content – what information do you want to include?
3 Length – how much do you need to write?

Write

1 Write your replies.

2 Exchange e-mails with a partner.

3 Read each other's replies. Are the content and style appropriate? Suggest one or two improvements, then discuss your ideas with your partner.

4 Write an improved version of one of your replies.

> **Reminder**
> • Present factual details in the right way.
> • Choose a suitable style.
> • Don't use unnecessary language.

Language in action

On the telephone

Introduction

1 Read these advertisements.

  a What is being advertised in each case?

  b Which advertisement do you find more interesting?

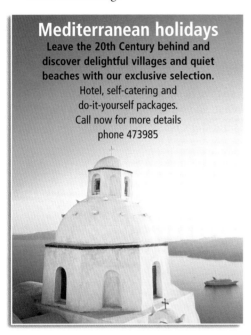

Mediterranean holidays
Leave the 20th Century behind and
discover delightful villages and quiet
beaches with our exclusive selection.
Hotel, self-catering and
do-it-yourself packages.
Call now for more details
phone 473985

ORIGINAL
DAILY NEWSPAPERS
1850–2000

To celebrate birthdates and other occasions

Pay by credit card

Details from Olden Days News
Tel. 4532621

2 a **8.8** Now listen to five people telephoning the two organizations. What happens in the third conversation? What do the callers want in the other conversations?

  b Listen again. This time note down some of the telephone language the speakers use under these headings:

    • expressions used by the callers

    • expressions used by the person answering the calls.

  c Add any other common telephone expressions you already know.

▶ **Pronunciation p.152**

Practice

Work in pairs. You are going to take turns to phone each other to ask for information about two more advertisements. Sit back to back with your partner.

Student A Turn to p.155.
Student B Turn to p.156.

Unit 8 Language check

In this unit you have worked on the following language points:

- Reported speech (1): statements
- Reported speech (2): questions
- Expressing quantities

- Vocabulary: telephone language; *say*, *speak*, *tell*; adjectives
- Writing: e-mails
- Making and answering telephone calls
- Pronunciation: strong and weak forms

9 Laws

Preview

Your thoughts

1 Read these stories about people who have taken individuals or companies to court. Which story do you find the craziest?

Dance damage
A 59-year-old New Jersey woman sued* a man she danced with at a wedding six years earlier, claiming that he had made her fall and break her leg.

Wrong toilet
In San Diego a man sued* the city authorities for $5.4 million because he was 'extremely upset' when he found a woman using the men's toilet at a rock concert.

$2.7 million for burns
A woman in America won $2.7 million in damages after suffering burns from a cup of hot coffee which she had bought from McDonalds.

Teenagers sue school
Two British teenagers are suing* their old school after they failed an important exam. The boys say that their teachers did not make them work hard enough for the exam.

* *to sue* is to go to a court of law and ask for money from somebody because they have done something bad to you.

2 Discuss these questions.
   a Can you imagine a situation in which **you** would take someone to court like this?
   b Are stories like these common in your country? Do you know of any particular cases?

Read and listen

1 Read these newspaper headlines and look at the photographs. What do you think each story is about? Think of a possible story for each headline.

Lost weekend – Minister to resign

Red card for footballer who 'fell'

They asked me the time then hit me!

Star may not fight for kids

2 **9.1** Now listen to news reports related to three of the headlines. Which headline has no news report?

3 Discuss possible answers to these questions about the news stories.

Story 1
a What will happen if John Steele sues his ex-wife?
b What will happen if he doesn't try to get his children back?

Story 2
a What will happen if Jeremy Carlton denies the rumours?
b What will happen if he says and does nothing?

Story 3
a Why haven't the other passengers given the police a description of Paul Lewis' attackers?
b What will happen if the police do not find out who the attackers are?

Vocabulary

1 Match the crimes in the picture with words from the list below.

arson   assault   blackmail   burglary   fraud
hijacking   kidnapping   mugging   murder
robbery   shoplifting   theft

2 Now use all the words above to make two lists: crimes against people and crimes against property.

Have your say

Work in pairs.

1 Each choose one of the crimes against people. What normally happens in your country to people who commit these crimes?

2 What **should** happen to them?

Grammar review: Conditional sentences (1)

1 There are two types of conditional sentences below. Which sentences refer to
a something that is possible in the future?
b something that normally happens?
1 *If you drive dangerously, you lose your driving licence.*
2 *Steele's children will have to appear in court if he sues his ex-wife.*
3 *If he doesn't try to get his children back, he'll never see them again.*
4 *You go to jail for life if you are found guilty of murdering someone.*
5 *Everyone will think Jeremy Carlton is guilty if he says nothing.*
6 *If he denies the rumours, people will call him a liar.*

2 a Which sentences 1–6 above refer to
1 the future (first conditional)?
2 any / all time (zero conditional)?
b How are these two conditionals formed?

3 In each of these pairs of sentences, which sentence is more certain?
a *You'll go to prison if they find you guilty of shoplifting.*
You may go to prison if they find you guilty of shoplifting.
b *If he doesn't try to get his children back, he may never see them again.*
If he doesn't try to get his children back, he'll never see them again.

▶ **Language commentary p.134**

Check

4 Complete these sentences with the correct form of one of the verbs from the list.

burn   buy   drink   freeze   get (x2)   fall   fall asleep   pass   play
smoke   watch

a If I .... my driving test tomorrow, I .... a car at the weekend.
b If I .... TV late at night, I usually .... in the armchair.
c If you .... that computer game much longer, you .... a headache.
d Water .... if the temperature .... below zero.
e That coffee's really hot. If you .... it now, you .... your mouth.
f Everyone knows that if you .... too much, you .... a cough.

5 Answer these questions for yourself, then compare answers with a partner.
a What do you do …
1 … if you have a headache?
2 … if you can't sleep at night?
3 … if you get hiccups?
b What will you do …
1 … if you have some free time this evening?
2 … if you get a pay rise soon?
3 … if the weather is bad at the weekend?

▶ Conditional sentences (2)   p.87
▶ Expressing purpose and reason   p.90

Listening

In your experience

1 a Have you ever felt irritated or angry because someone was making a lot of noise? If so, how did you react? If not, how would you react?

b Has anyone ever complained to you that you were making too much noise? What did you do?

2 a This is a list of the Top Ten noises British people complain most about. How do you react to these noises? Rank them from 1 (the most annoying) to 10.

Barking dogs	Building sites	Car alarms
Noisy neighbours	Noisy parties	Aeroplanes
Pubs and restaurants	Road works	Traffic noise
Radios or personal stereos in public places		

b A survey like this was done in Britain. Turn to p.159 to find the results.

Listen

1 **9.2** You are going to listen to part of a radio programme about noise and the law. Tick (✓) the noises in the list in **2a** which are mentioned in the recording.

2 What other noises are mentioned?

Understanding ideas

Listen again and answer these questions.

1 Why are all foreigners told the story of the flat-warming party as soon as they arrive in Switzerland? Who do you think tells them?

2 Why was Monica Greentree surprised when her neighbours called the police?

3 According to the Dutch man, how are the police and people in his country different from the Swiss?

4 How are police powers in Scotland different from those in England?

5 Why do you think complaints about noise have been rising steadily?

Vocabulary

1 Fill the gaps in these sentences with words related to the words in *italics*.

a *complaint*
The last time I .... was when …

b *neighbour*
The people in the .... house / flat are …

c *foreigner*
My favourite .... food is …

d *invite*
The last .... I received was to …

e *irritation*
What .... me most about my neighbours is …

f *violence*
I think more children are .... these days because …

2 Now finish sentences 1a–f with ideas of your own.

3 Compare and discuss your sentences with a partner.

Have your say

1 Do you agree that people should sometimes be free to make as much noise as they want?

2 If you could introduce one new law to control noise, what would it be? How would you enforce this law?

Conditional sentences (2)

Exploring concepts

1 Underline the verbs in these conditional sentences.

   a *The neighbours would complain if we didn't invite them.*

   b *The police would laugh if someone complained about a party.*

   c *The police could arrest you if you refused to stop making a noise.*

   d *If I were younger, I'd go and work in another country for a year or two.*

   e *If Joe told the police, they might help him look for his car.*

2 Answer these questions about sentences 1a–e.

   a In **1a** do you think the speaker will invite the neighbours?

   b In **1b** do you think many people call to complain about parties?

   c In **1c** do you think many people refuse to stop making a noise?

   d In **1d** how do we know that the speaker will not go and work abroad?

   e In **1e** do you think Joe will tell the police? If he tells them, will they help him to find his car?

3 a Look at the sentences again. Which refer to
   1 an improbable future event or situation?
   2 an impossible present situation?

   b Sentences 1a–e include the second conditional. How is it formed?

▶ **Language commentary p.135**

Exploitation

1 a Look at this cartoon and read the people's words and thoughts.

   b What would or might happen if Nick went to the party with Liz? Make up five sentences like this:
   If Nick went to the party, Sara would be very angry.
                         Sara might throw him out of their home.

   c Compare sentences with a partner, then together think about the results of your sentences.
   Example
   If Sara threw him out of their home, Nick would / might be homeless.

   d Now make up sentences with *would* and *might* about this cartoon.

2 a Finish these sentences in ways which are true for you personally.
   1 If I were younger …
   2 If I were a man … / a woman …
   3 If I had more money … / more time …
   4 If I didn't have to go to work …

   b Now ask your partner questions to find their answers.
   Example
   What would you do if you were younger?

   c Find other students in the class who have similar answers to yours.

Free speech

3 Work in pairs or groups. Imagine some of the problems you might have in these situations. Discuss the problems and some possible solutions.

   a You are driving along the motorway at night. You are alone.

   b You wake up one morning to find a large number of newspaper reporters and photographers camping in your garden.

   c You lose all your money in a foreign country.

Skills

Listen and speak

1 You are going to listen to four people describing everyday situations. Look at the illustrations. What do you think the situations are?

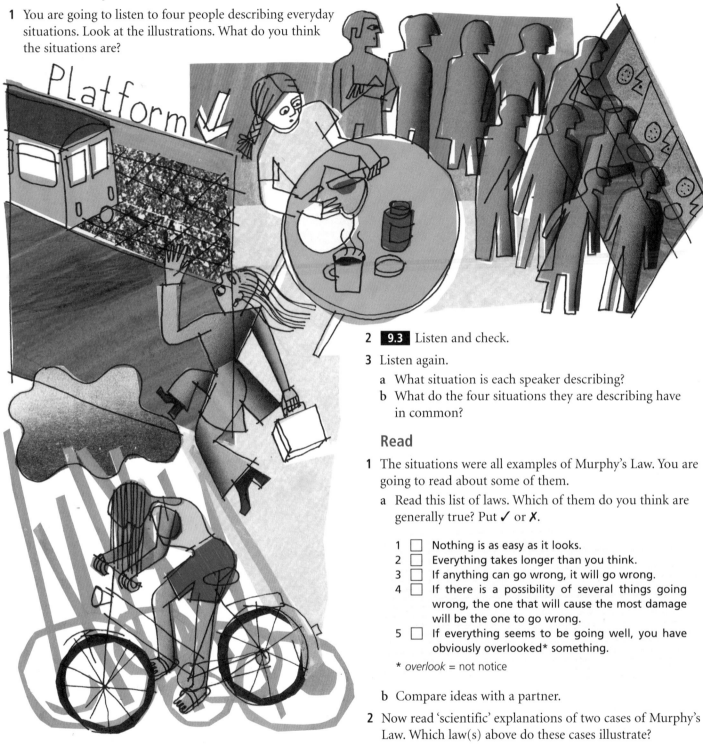

2 **9.3** Listen and check.

3 Listen again.
  a What situation is each speaker describing?
  b What do the four situations they are describing have in common?

Read

1 The situations were all examples of Murphy's Law. You are going to read about some of them.

  a Read this list of laws. Which of them do you think are generally true? Put ✓ or ✗.

  1 ☐ Nothing is as easy as it looks.
  2 ☐ Everything takes longer than you think.
  3 ☐ If anything can go wrong, it will go wrong.
  4 ☐ If there is a possibility of several things going wrong, the one that will cause the most damage will be the one to go wrong.
  5 ☐ If everything seems to be going well, you have obviously overlooked* something.

  * *overlook* = not notice

  b Compare ideas with a partner.

2 Now read 'scientific' explanations of two cases of Murphy's Law. Which law(s) above do these cases illustrate?

Explaining Murphy's Law

We all have bad days when we should simply stay in bed. At breakfast, our toast slides off our plate and lands on the floor – butter-side down. At the supermarket, we queue up at the checkout – we go nowhere, while the
5 queue next to us gets through in no time.

If you have always thought that such irritations are not just bad luck, I have news for you. I can confirm that your suspicions are right: Murphy's Third Law is at work. This says: 'If anything can go wrong, it will go wrong.'

10 For years, most scientists have rejected Murphy's Law. But recently, using mathematical techniques, I have found that the scientists are wrong.

Take the falling toast which lands butter-side down. When toast lands on the floor, it is usually after it has
15 fallen off a plate. Try this experiment: put a thin book face-up on the table. Now slowly push it over the edge like a piece of toast sliding off a plate. As it goes over the edge, the book starts to fall and spin. Unfortunately, the book simply doesn't spin fast
20 enough to come face-up again before it reaches the floor. This means that the book – or toast – will end up face-down almost every time.

I've found another example of Murphy's Law which can be explained. That is Murphy's Law of supermarket
25 queues: 'In supermarkets your queue is always slower than the next queue.' Of course supermarket queues actually all move at the same average speed. This means that when we queue up, our own queue and the two queues next to us have an equal chance of finishing
30 first. But in supermarkets nobody's interested in average speeds – we want our queue to finish first. The chance that ours will move faster than the next queue is actually 1 in 3. That means that 66% of the time, one of the queues next to us will finish before us.

Understanding ideas

1 Without looking at the text again, explain to a partner …
   • why toast often lands butter-side down   OR
   • why people often join a supermarket queue that is slower than the queues next to it.

2 a Why does the writer say *we should simply stay in bed*?
   b Why do you think *scientists have rejected Murphy's Law*?
   c How could the experiment be changed so that the book landed face-up, not face-down?
   d Why does toast end up face-down **almost** *every time*, not *every time*?

3 What do the words or phrases in **bold** from the texts mean? Choose the best alternative.
   a *Nothing is as easy as it **looks**.*   sees / seems
   b *… the queue next to us gets through **in no time**.*   quickly / slowly
   c ***Take** the falling toast …*   hold on to / think of as an example

Have your say

1 Have you been in any situations like the ones described?

2 Do you believe in good or bad luck? Are some people 'naturally' luckier than others?

3 What sort of people believe in Murphy's Law?

Speak and write

1 Here are some more modern 'laws'. How true do you think they are? Try to think of real-life examples.
   • Weiler's Law
     Nothing is impossible for the man who doesn't have to do it himself.
   • Forsyth's Law
     Just when you see light at the end of the tunnel, the roof falls in.
   • Parkinson's Law
     Work increases to fill the amount of time you have to do it in.
   • Gilb's Law
     Computers are unreliable, but humans are even more unreliable.

2 a Work with a partner. Write a law of your own. Give it a name and follow the style of some of the laws you have just read about.
   b Now exchange laws with another pair. If you have to explain your law, rewrite it to make it clearer.

Grammar extra

Expressing purpose and reason

Read

What does this article tell you about giraffes? Read it and choose the best summary.
- Giraffes are not good fighters because they have long legs.
- Giraffes follow rules when they fight each other.
- Giraffes are cruel, violent animals.

The law of the jungle

When giraffes are attacked by an enemy such as a lion, they kick out with their feet <u>in order to</u> injure the other animal seriously.

But when they fight amongst themselves, they do not kick, they neck. Two fighting males stand next to each other. They begin by stretching their necks as high as they can to frighten each other. As neither giraffe is frightened, one usually bends his neck and swings it back so that the short horns on his head hit his enemy. The other giraffe does the same. As the fight gets more violent, the two animals move their front legs outwards so as not to fall over. It would be quite easy for them to kick each other, but they never do this, because it is against the rules.

Exploring concepts

1 Read the text again and underline the six words or phrases which tell us **why** something happens. The first one is done as an example.

2 Which of the words and phrases you have underlined are followed by a clause and a main verb? What are the others followed by?

3 a Read these sentences. What are the two different ways of using *because*?
   1 *We stayed in at the weekend because of the rain.*
   2 *We stayed in at the weekend because it was raining.*

   b *As* can introduce a reason, but what does it mean in this sentence?
   As the fight gets more violent, the two animals move their front legs outwards …

▶ Language commentary p.135

Exploitation

1 a Answer these questions about human behaviour with a purpose / reason word or phrase, and ideas of your own. Think of unusual or original answers.
   1 Why do some people climb mountains?
   2 Why do some people smoke cigarettes?
   3 Why do some people get married?
   4 Why do people yawn?
   5 Why do people sneeze?
   6 Why do people shiver?

   b Compare answers in pairs or groups. Which is the most interesting answer to each question?

Free speech

2 Work in groups. Explain the actions of the people in these photographs.

Exploring words

Crime and the law

1 a How many correct sentences can you make using words from columns A, B and C?

Example
The police arrest criminals.

A	B	C
criminals	arrest	the accused
judges	break	cases / a case
police officers /	catch	(their) clients
the police	commit	compensation
solicitors (lawyers)	defend	crimes
victims of crime	give	criminals
witnesses	enforce	defendants
	prosecute	evidence
	question	laws / a law
	sentence	offences / an offence
	win	a suspect / suspects

b Complete these sentences with the appropriate form of a verb from column B.
1 A 33-year-old woman has .... damages of £1 million from her employers after an accident at work.
2 Last week police officers .... a ten-year-old boy for stealing from a supermarket.
3 In many countries over half the crimes are .... by young men between the ages of 16 and 25.
4 The number of motoring accidents has gone down because the police .... the speeding laws more strictly.
5 Police officers .... the suspect for eight hours before he finally confessed.
6 If you drive at more than 110 kilometres an hour on motorways, you .... the law.

c Discuss two or three of these questions for a few minutes. Talk about the situation in your country. Give real examples if you can.
1 Is it possible for ordinary people to arrest criminals? Would you do this if the situation arose?
2 What kinds of crimes are more often committed by young people?
3 Can an accused person defend themselves in court?
4 How easy is it for the victims of crime to win compensation?
5 Is it an offence to beg for money in public?

2 a Put these six illustrations into the correct order by reading the story.

After a member of the public had *tipped them off*, the police *picked up* Darren Bogart as he arrived home on Tuesday evening and *took him in* for questioning. A second man *gave himself up* the same evening. The two men were later charged with burglary. The court heard how Mr Bogart had been watching the post office for several weeks before *breaking in* and *making off* with £50,000 from the safe.

b Now match each phrasal verb in the text with the word or phrase from the list which has the same meaning.

accompany to the police station   arrest   inform
enter (a building) illegally and by force   leave quickly
allow yourself to be arrested

3 Work in pairs.
a Choose a minor crime, then decide on a suitable punishment for someone found guilty of this crime. Write the crime and the punishment on a piece of paper.

Example
Crime *parking illegally*
Punishment *five-year driving ban*

b Exchange pieces of paper with another pair. Do they agree or disagree?

Writing

A personal letter to a friend

Discuss

1 What would you do if you discovered that one of your colleagues was doing something dishonest or illegal at work – for example, stealing money, making fraudulent expenses claims, or blackmailing a younger employee?

2 Would you react in the same way if the colleague in question was
   • a friend?
   • someone you knew but didn't like?
   • someone you didn't know personally?
   • your manager?

Read

1 a Read this extract from a letter you have received from your friend, Raquel. How do you think she feels?

> Everything was going well in my new job until a couple of weeks ago when something terrible happened. I found out, quite by accident, that one of the computer experts in my department is regularly transferring small amounts of money from customers' accounts into his own personal bank account. The thing is, he seems like a really nice guy – we've even been out together a couple of times and I really fancy him. To make matters even worse, my boss's son is his best friend.
>
> I feel like simply confronting him and saying, 'Look, either you stop this right now and pay all the money back, or I'm going to the police.' On the other hand, I could tell the boss in confidence or simply go straight to the police.
>
> What do you think I should do? The problem is, I really like my job and I don't want to lose it.

b What is your instant reaction to this problem? Compare ideas with a partner.

Brainstorm and notes

Work in groups.

1 Talk in more detail about the situation described in the letter. Think about these points.
   • The relationship between the letter writer and her colleague
   • The friendship between the colleague and the boss's son
   • The fact that the letter writer is new to her job
   • The fact that only small amounts of money are involved

2 What would you say to your friend? Make a note of the main ideas that came up in the discussion.
   Example
   Phone the police immediately.
   Think carefully – don't do anything you might regret later.

Write

1 Write the first draft of your reply to your friend's letter, referring to the notes you made during the discussion. Write about 120 words.

   Follow this paragraph plan.
   1 Thank your friend for her letter. Say how you feel about her news.
   2 Say what you think your friend should do. Make one or two practical suggestions.
   3 Tell your friend to contact you again if she wants to talk more about her situation.

2 a Exchange letters with a partner from another group. Read your partner's letter and suggest improvements. Read the second paragraph particularly carefully.
   • Are the ideas clear and well expressed?
   • How would you feel if you received a letter like this from a friend?

   b Discuss your ideas for improvements with your partner.
   c Finally, rewrite your letter including any improvements you and your partner agreed about.

> **Reminder**
> • Write in a conversational style.
> • Express opinions.
> • Don't sound negative.

Language in action

Asking for and giving reasons

Introduction

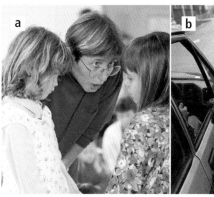

1 These photographs all show people talking to each other. In each case one person is asking for reasons and the other is giving reasons.

  a In pairs, imagine what each conversation is about.

  b Choose one of the situations and make up a four- or five-line conversation between the two people.

  c Make a note of any expressions you used to ask for or give reasons.

2 a **9.4** Now listen to extracts from the four conversations and match them with the photographs. Were any of your guesses correct?

  b Listen again. This time note down some of the language the speakers use.
  Student A Note expressions speakers use to ask for reasons.
  Student B Note expressions speakers use to give reasons.

  c Tell each other the expressions you heard. Make lists under these headings:
  • asking for reasons
  • giving reasons.
  Add the reason expressions you noted in 1 to your lists.

▶ **Pronunciation p.153**

Practice

Role play

1 Choose one of these situations. Turn to the back of the book and read your role card.
  Student A Turn to p.157.
  Student B Turn to p.158.

Car	A	motorist	B	police officer
Hospital	A	doctor	B	patient
Supermarket	A	shop detective	B	shoplifter

2 Make up the conversation for your situation.

Unit 9 Language check

In this unit you have worked on the following language points:
- Conditional sentences (1): zero, first
- Conditional sentences (2): second
- Expressing purpose and reason

- Vocabulary: crime and the law
- Writing: a personal letter to a friend
- Asking for and giving reasons
- Pronunciation: *wh-* questions; strong and weak forms

10 A roof over your head

Preview

Your thoughts

Work in pairs or groups.

1 What is your idea of a home? Could you imagine yourself living in any of the homes shown in the photographs?

2 Match these words with the appropriate photos.

| apartment | bungalow | boat | converted coach | cottage | hotel | hut | tent |

Read

The American columnist Mike Bellah makes three suggestions about *what makes home home*. Rank these three things in order of importance for you.

What makes home home? I have three suggestions.

A place

We need a place to call home. Ask any homeless person; everyone needs a physical location – if only a tent, mud hut or corner of a room to call his or her own.

People

Yet a place and even things still don't make a home, not without people. People you love make a home home.

Acceptance

'Home is the place where, when you have to go there, they have to take you in,' wrote Robert Frost. Home is where we belong, where everyone knows our name, where we can be ourselves, where we're wanted and valued and loved.

Listen

1 **10.1** Listen to five people talking about what the word *home* means to them. Do any of the speakers have similar ideas to yours?

2 Listen again and note down answers to these questions.

  a Which speakers talk about two different homes?

  b Which speaker describes a home they are not living in now?

  c Which speakers describe old buildings?

Vocabulary

1 Match the words and phrases **a–f** used by the speakers with their meanings **1–5**.

a … *a place where I'm **accepted*** …	**1** condition
b … *where I can just **be myself*** …	**2** trouble / disturb
c … *it was in a terrible **state*** …	**3** made to feel welcome
d … *nobody can **bother** me* …	**4** large / with a lot of room
e *It's nice because it's so **spacious*** …	**5** behave normally

2 Now answer these questions.

  a Have you ever been anywhere where you were not *accepted* for some reason?

  b Are there places you go where you find it difficult to *be yourself*?

  c What *state* is your house or your room in?

  d Is your home a place where people don't *bother* you? Do you like this?

  e Do you like buildings and rooms to be *spacious*? Or do you sometimes prefer them to be small and cosy?

Have your say

Describe your dream home or your nightmare home. Say where it would be as well as what it would be like.

Grammar review: Passive and active verb forms

1 Underline the passive verb forms and circle the other verbs in these sentences.

  a *It's a place where I can just be myself and a place where I'm accepted.*

  b *It's the place where I was born, where my parents live.*

  c *It's a lovely old house – it was built in 1780 …*

  d *My dad worked in the army, so we were often moved around.*

  e *My house was decorated five years ago.*

2 Look at the passive verb forms in sentences **1a–e**.

  a Which tenses are they?

  b How is the passive formed?

3 We choose the passive to show that we are more interested in the person or thing *affected* by an action (the *object* of an active sentence) than in who or what *did* the action (the *subject*). In sentences **1a–e** above:

  a What is the action?

  b Who or what is affected by the action?

  c Who or what does the action? (There may not be a clear answer to this.)

▶ **Language commentary p.136**

Check

4 Rewrite these sentences using the passive.

  a They built many multi-storey apartment blocks in the 1960s.

  b The postman delivers letters to our house twice a day.

  c They elect the American President every four years.

  d My parents brought me up in a lonely country area.

  e They sent me to a school in the city centre.

  f The police arrested the two men who broke into my house.

5 What do you know about these buildings? Answer as many of the questions as you can.

  a Where are they?

  b When were they built?

  c Why were they built? / Who by?

▶ Passive verb forms (2)   p.97
▶ Relative clauses (2)   p.100

Reading

In your experience

1 a What are the most important characteristics of a building for you? Rank these characteristics in order of importance and add two of your own ideas.
- light
- noise
- space
- temperature

b Compare your order with a partner's.

Read

1 What reasons do you think people have for living in a home underground? What would you ask them? Think of two or three questions.

2 Read the article quickly.

a Can you find the answers to any of your questions?

b Does the article focus on the positive or the negative aspects of living underground?

Close up

1.4 The plural of *roof* is *roofs*. What is the usual plural form of nouns ending in *-f*? Make a list of examples.

1.15 *northern* is the adjective related to the compass point *north*. What are the other compass points and what are the adjectives related to them?

1.29 Jason Dunbar says his house is *economical to run*. Can you think of an alternative to *run* here? What other meanings does *run* have?

Going Underground

Deep in the Devon countryside, you can find one of Britain's most unusual homes. From the outside, there isn't much to see: no walls, no visible windows or roof – just a heavy door in a hillside.

5   This house is not just invisible, it's underground. It may seem unlikely, but the owners, Jonathan Rodney-Jones and his partner, are turning an underground water tank into their dream home. 'People think we're mad,' says Rodney-Jones, 'but we
10 wanted something different. We liked the idea of a building which would be cheap to heat and which would not harm the countryside.'

    Underground living isn't so unusual. For example, more than 40 million people live in underground
15 homes in northern China. These shelters are easy and cheap to build and they protect people against the extremes of temperature. But not all underground homes have been built recently. Caves are still popular as homes in parts of Europe and the Middle East.
20 In France, caves were created in the 18th century by masons when they were cutting the stone to build the great chateaux of the Loire Valley. These caves are now being turned into holiday homes for Parisians.

    But who wants to live or work in a dark, miserable
25 hole in the ground? Jason Dunbar, who also lives in an underground house, laughs at the question. 'We have lots of roof windows, so it's always very light. It's also less draughty and much quieter than most ordinary houses, and it's economical to run because it
30 requires hardly any heating or repair work.'

    Town planners are increasingly realizing one major advantage of underground building: less space is needed for each home. Homes can be built much closer together. An average American suburb with
35 200 houses takes up about 14 hectares of land. An underground scheme with the same number of homes would cover an area of just 2.7 hectares.

Understanding ideas

1 Answer these questions.

a In what ways might ordinary houses *harm the countryside*?

b Why do you think underground homes are *easy and cheap to build*?

c What kind of *repair work* could an underground house require?

d Why do you think underground homes can be built closer together than ordinary homes?

2 a Can you think of alternatives for these adjectives from the text?

1 *People think we're **mad** …* (l.9)

2 *… who wants to live in a **dark**, **miserable** hole in the ground?* (l.24)

3 *It's … **quieter** than most **ordinary** houses …* (l.28)

4 *… one **major** advantage …* (l.31)

b What is the opposite of the adjectives in this context?

Have your say

Now that you have read the article, are you one of the people who think Jonathan Rodney-Jones and his partner are mad because they want to live underground?

Passive verb forms (2)

Exploring concepts

1 What are the tenses of the passive in these extracts from the article? How are they formed?

a … *not all underground homes* **have been built** *recently.*
b … *caves* **were created** *in the 18th century by masons …*
c *These caves* **are** *now* **being turned** *into holiday homes …*
d … *less space* **is needed** *for each home.*

2 What form of the passive is used in this sentence and how is it formed?
The houses can **be built** *much closer together.*

3 Discuss these questions about sentences **1a–d** in pairs.

a What is the writer's main interest in sentence:
   1a – the homes or the people who built the homes?
   1b – the masons or the caves?
   1c – the caves or the people who are turning the caves into holiday homes?

b What is the writer's main interest in sentence **1d**?

c In which sentence do we know who does or did the action?

d Why do you think the person who does the action is not mentioned in extracts **1a** and **1c**? Choose one or more of these reasons.
   • We don't know or we don't want to say who did the action.
   • The person who did the action is unimportant or no one in particular.
   • It is obvious who did the action and so we don't need to say.

4 The passive is often used to describe processes. Which of these descriptions sounds more personal and which more scientific?

a *First the tank was cleaned and repaired. Then the electrical system was put in and the internal walls were built. Finally the whole place was decorated.*

b *First we cleaned and repaired the tank. Then electricians put in the electrical system and builders built the internal walls. Finally we decorated the whole place.*

▶ **Language commentary p.136**

Exploitation

1 Passive verbs are often used in newspapers to make descriptions sound less personal. Sentences **a–g** describe the effects of a storm. Make them less personal by using passive verbs. Decide whether to mention who or what does or did the action.

UK hit by storm chaos

a A falling tree killed a man as he was driving home.
b Police are moving old people from their homes and taking them to public halls and schools.
c Lifeboats have rescued ten men from a boat in the North Sea.
d Strong winds have blown the roofs off many houses in the area.
e The police have closed roads in several seaside towns because of high seas.
f An overturned lorry blocked the M25 motorway for several hours.
g Lightning has hit a 20-storey office block in the centre of Leeds.

2 a Use the information in this diagram to describe how a group makes a CD. The words you need are given; the appropriate verbs are in brackets. Make sentences like this:
Recording equipment is set up in the studio.

1 recording equipment (set up) in studio
2 instruments and voices (record)
3 recorded sounds (mix)
4 effects (add)
5 final mix (transfer) to master CD
6 copies (make) from master CD

b Work in pairs. Choose one of these processes, write the first stage of the process, then pass your paper to another pair to continue.
   • Making wine
   • Cooking pasta
   • Making and cooking a pizza
   • Video-recording a TV programme
   • Recording a CD on to a cassette

Free speech

3 Work in pairs or groups.

a Choose a town or city you know. What could be done to improve it:
   • for the residents?
   • for tourists from other countries?

b Make a list of improvements you agree about.

Skills

Speak

1 Look at photographs **a–c** of buildings designed by the Austrian painter and architect Friedensreich Hundertwasser.
   a How are they different from 'normal' modern buildings?
   b What do you think the buildings are used for?

2 Would you like to live in or near to one of these buildings? Why? Why not?

Listen

You are going to hear some conversations in which people talk about Hundertwasser's architecture.

1 Here are some of the words and phrases which the speakers use to show their opinions. Do they have positive, negative or neutral meanings?

---
amazing   unusual   a real breath of fresh air   cool   brilliant
dull   grey and boring   colourful   dreadful   OK   gimmicky
fun to look at   they brighten the place up   artistic   cosy
they don't do anything for me

---

2 **a** **10.2** Listen to the conversations. In which conversation(s) do the two speakers agree?
   b In the conversation(s) where they disagree, who likes the buildings more, the man or the woman?

3 **a** Listen again. Make a note of any opinions you hear that you particularly agree with.
   b Compare ideas with a partner.

Read

Read this article. What do these people think of Hundertwasser's work?
   • Ordinary people
   • Tourists
   • Other architects

MAKING WAVES

As a young painter, Friedensreich Hundertwasser was fascinated by cities and these were the main subjects of his colourful paintings. Since then he has become famous as the architect who brought humanity and happiness
5 back into architecture. People queue up for the chance to live in his buildings and his fantastic housing projects are tourist attractions.

The spectacular Hundertwasserhaus stands out in Vienna's dull streets like a fairy-tale palace. This was
10 Hundertwasser's reply to the greyness of 20th-century architecture: 'I just wanted to show it was possible for a non-architect to make a humane building.'

Much of his work has been as an 'architecture doctor', invited to cure 'sick' buildings and make them beautiful.
15 A good example is his transformation of the waste incinerator at Spittelau near Vienna.

Hundertwasser has an intense dislike of straight lines. He says, 'When we are in cities exposed to straight lines we get headaches, we feel unwell, and we don't know why.
20 People get violent and they don't know why. All these straight lines are destroying our world. I find this architecture criminal. It is the destruction of our dreams.' Hundertwasser also believes that ground removed to build a building should be replaced on top of that building.
25 All his buildings have grass roofs or trees growing from balconies and on the roof. An example of this is the spa resort at Rogner-Bad Blumau, which he designed. The fronts of the coloured buildings grow out of the grassy hillsides which are their roofs. It has been called
30 'the world's largest habitable work of art', and has 247 double rooms and 24 apartments, with sports facilities and hot springs.

Although Hundertwasser's architecture is popular with ordinary people, many other architects dislike it. One critic
35 explains: 'Hundertwasser's architecture is very attractive for two minutes but it has no complexity. He should work for the Disney Corporation.'

Hundertwasser is still really a painter: 'I try to paint, but this involvement with architecture is very annoying.
40 Painters have sleepless nights because they can't get one colour right in a painting. Imagine what happens to me with a building I'm working on.'

a

b

c

Understanding ideas

1 Think of possible answers to these questions.

   a What does Hundertwasser mean by a *humane* building? (l.12)

   b What is a *sick* building and how can sick buildings be cured? (l.14)

   c Why does Hundertwasser dislike straight lines? (l.17)

   d What is a *habitable work of art*? (l.30)

   e What do critics have against Hundertwasser's architecture?

2 What do the words in **bold** in these extracts from the text refer to?

   Example

   … *these were the main subjects of his colourful paintings.* (l.2)

   these = cities

   a *Since* **then** *he has become famous as the architect who brought …* (l.3)

   b **This** *was Hundertwasser's reply to the greyness …* (l.9)

   c **It** *is the destruction of our dreams.* (l.22)

   d *An example of* **this** *is the spa resort at Rogner-Bad Blumau, …* (l.26)

   e *… many other architects dislike* **it**. (l.34)

Have your say

1 Do you think Hundertwasser is a genius or an eccentric dreamer?

2 Do you agree that he should work for the Disney Corporation?

Speak

Role play

Work in groups. You are a committee planning a large new public building in a town or city you know well. It could be a museum, a hospital, an art gallery, etc. Your task is to choose the architect for the new building. You have these three styles to choose from.

1 Decide which town or city and what type of public building you are going to discuss.

2 Discuss the advantages and disadvantages of each architectural style in relation to the type of building you have chosen. Express your own opinions about the different styles.

3 After about five minutes, stop the discussion and take a vote.

4 Present your ideas and the results of your vote to the rest of the class.

Grammar extra

Relative clauses (2)

Read

1 Why does Miss Barton have to move out of her home?

2 How does she feel about having to move?

> Miss Barton, (who) is 72 years old, lives alone. The cottage where she has lived happily for the last 20 years is in a small Scottish village. Now, at a time when Miss Barton simply wants to live a quiet life, the council says that she must leave her home because it is unfit to live in. The inspector whose report led to the council's decision said: 'There's no glass in the windows, no electricity and no running water. It's a very unhealthy place, especially for an elderly person.' It is unlikely that Miss Barton will be able to afford the necessary repairs, which could cost as much as £20,000. Miss Barton, who has three months to find a new home, blames the previous owners of the cottage. 'They promised to pay for any repairs which were needed before I moved in,' she says. 'This is the reason why I am so angry now.' The neighbours are sympathetic, but Miss Barton is not the kind of woman who accepts help easily.

Exploring concepts

1 Read the text again and circle the relative pronouns and underline the clauses that they introduce. The first one has been done as an example.

2 Which of the relative clauses add extra (non-essential) information and which give essential information?

3 Answer these questions about the nine relative pronouns in the text.

  a Which two pronouns refer to people and things? When can these pronouns be replaced by *that*?

  b Which pronoun refers to something which belongs to or is associated with someone?

  c Which pronoun refers to a place?

  d Which pronoun refers to an explanation?

  e Which pronoun refers to a time?

▶ **Language commentary p.136**

Exploitation

1 Complete these phrases and then talk in pairs about the subjects.

  a A place .... I'd like to live.

  b Someone .... opinions I respect.

  c Reasons .... I love my country.

2 Read this text about the Pompidou Centre in Paris, then rewrite it, adding the extra facts from the box in the places marked and a relative pronoun. Follow the example.

The Pompidou Centre

The Pompidou Centre, *which is also known as Beaubourg,*[1] is a famous art and culture museum in Paris[2]. The Centre[3] is located in an old part of the city. Georges Pompidou first thought of the idea in 1969[4]. The building was designed by Renzo Piano[5] and Richard Rogers[6]. The Centre is made up of a huge transparent box and a frame of steel tubes. The lifts[7], the escalators[8] and a series of brightly coloured giant tubes[9] are all clearly visible on the outside of the building. When the building first opened, many people disliked its ultra-modern style[10]. Despite this, the Centre[11] has been a great success.

Extra facts

- *The Pompidou Centre is also known as Beaubourg.* ✓
- *In this museum visitors can see permanent and temporary exhibitions of all kinds of art.*
- *The Pompidou Centre was finished in 1978.*
- *Georges Pompidou became the President of France in 1969.*
- *Renzo Piano is Italian.*
- *Rogers' other designs include the Lloyds Building in London.*
- *The lifts are painted red.*
- *The escalators are in clear plastic tunnels.*
- *Giant tubes carry water, electricity and air around the Centre.*
- *Many people thought the style of the building was too industrial.*
- *The Centre attracts 26,000 visitors every day.*

3 a Choose three of these places and write descriptions. Each description should be 25–30 words long and include at least one relative clause.

  • A place of natural beauty you like visiting

  • A street you like walking along

  • Your favourite room

  • A shop you enjoy visiting

  • Your favourite café, bar or restaurant

  • A place where you have felt bored, frightened or unhappy

  b Exchange descriptions with a partner. Decide as a pair which of the descriptions is the most interesting.

Exploring words

Buildings and materials

1 a Label the numbered parts of these buildings with words
from the list. There are four extra words.

aerial arch attic balcony basement chimney
doorway drainpipe gate gutter roof shutters steps
tiles wall window

b What do you think the different parts of the buildings
are made of? Here are some common building materials.

bricks concrete glass metal (e.g. steel) plastic
stone wood

Example
The doorways are probably made of wood.

c *Steel* is a kind of metal.
   1 What other kinds of metal do you know? Make lists
      of precious and non-precious metals.
   2 What common objects are made out of the metals
      on your lists? Think about your own belongings and
      about everyday household objects.

2 How many of these shape adjectives can you find in
the photographs?

curved flat oval pointed rectangular round sloping
square straight

3 Work in groups. One student thinks of an object.
The others try to find out what the object is, by asking
questions about
   • size
   • colour
   • shape
   • what it is made of.

The student thinking of the object can only answer *Yes*
or *No*.

Writing

A letter expressing opinions

Discuss

1 Are unemployment and homelessness among young people common problems in your country?

2 What can be done to solve these problems?

Read

As you read this newspaper report, imagine how each of these people would react to the story.
- A resident of Oak Street
- An unemployed, homeless young person in the town
- Someone living five kilometres from Oak Street

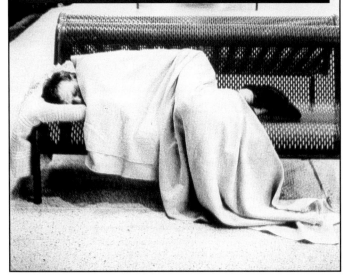

City to open refuge in Oak Street

The city council yesterday announced that it is planning to turn 17, Oak Street into a refuge for homeless young people. The four-storey building, which was once a fashionable hotel, had been empty for two years until it was bought by the council last month.

A council representative explained that the building needed repairs and complete redecoration before it could take in young people. It is expected to open some time in the new year and will provide temporary accommodation for between 30 and 40 young people.

As soon as the news of the refuge was announced, Terry Brown, a spokesman for the Oak Street residents, wrote to the council objecting to the use of the house as a refuge. Mr Brown, who lives with his family at 15, Oak Street, said, 'We are in favour of providing young people with somewhere to live, but Oak Street is not suitable. There are elderly people and families with young children living here.' Mr Brown added, 'This part of town is no good for the young people themselves as there is no work in the area.'

Brainstorm and notes

Work in groups.

1 Think of and note reasons you can think of for and against the refuge in Oak Street.

For	Against
• Homeless young people need somewhere to sleep – at the moment they only have the streets and parks.	• The refuge may disturb the other residents of Oak Street.
•	•
•	•

2 You are going to write a letter to the editor of the local newspaper supporting or attacking the use of 17, Oak Street as a refuge.
Write notes under these paragraph headings.
1 The subject of your letter: the refuge story
2 Opinion: your main reason for being for or against the refuge
3 Opinion: your second reason
4 What you want to happen next

Write

1 Write the first draft of your letter, referring to your notes. Write about 120 words.

2 Exchange letters with a partner whose opinions on the subject you do not know. As you read each other's stories, think about these questions.
- Are the writer's opinions clear?
- Does the writer use good arguments to support these opinions?
- Are the language and layout appropriate for a formal letter?

3 Discuss your ideas. Suggest one or two improvements your partner could make to their letter.

4 Write the final versions of your letter, incorporating any points you discussed with your partner.

> **Reminder**
> - Write formally.
> - Use the right layout.
> - Begin and end in the right way.

Language in action

Checking and correcting

Introduction

1 **10.3** Listen to this telephone conversation in which someone is checking that the information they have is correct.
   a Who are the two speakers?
   b Why is the woman telephoning the man?
   c How many mistakes does the caller make?

2 Now listen again and correct the wrong information.

Mr / Mrs / Ms	Mr
Name	Smythe
First names	Michael, Stuart, Humphrey
Address	33, Salisbury Avenue
Postcode	CO3 3FG

3 a What checking and correcting expressions can you remember from the conversation? Make two lists under these headings:
   • checking information
   • correcting information.
   b Now check your lists by looking at **Tapescript 10.3** on p.147. Add any expressions not on your lists. Add any other similar expressions you already know.

   ▶ **Pronunciation p.153**

Practice

1 Work with a partner.
   a Write down any facts you know about them, including first names, family name, address, telephone number, date of birth, etc.
   b Now take turns to check with your partner that the details you have written are right. Remember to check the spelling of names, etc. Make conversations similar to the telephone conversation you have just listened to.

Role play

2 Work in pairs. You are going to take turns to phone each other to check whether some information you have is correct. Sit back to back with your partner.

Situation 1
Student A Turn to p.157.
Student B
You want to book a holiday home, but your brochure is two years old, and so the details you have may be wrong. Phone the advertisers to check which of the information is still correct.

St Martin (Burgundy)
1 km from centre of village
for 2 adults + 2 children
Facilities include
TV • Fridge (no freezer)
Telephone • Washing machine
Pets welcome
Available, May–September only
Price €305 per week.

Situation 2
Student B Turn to p.158.
Student A
You want to order a pizza to be delivered to your house, but you only have an old leaflet, and so the details you have may be wrong. Phone the shop to check which of the information is still correct.

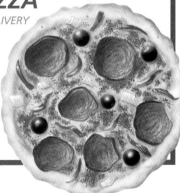

PRONTO PIZZA
TAKE AWAY AND FREE DELIVERY
Free delivery – in the city
Minimum order of £10
5% DISCOUNT FOR TAKE AWAY
OPENING TIMES
5.00 p.m. – 12 midnight
SUNDAY– THURSDAY
4.00 p.m.– 2.00 a.m.
FRIDAY & SATURDAY

Unit 10 Language check

In this unit you have worked on the following language points:

• Passive and active verb forms
• Passive verb forms (2): continuous, perfect and infinitive forms
• Relative clauses (2): *whose, where, why, when*

• Vocabulary: buildings and materials
• Writing: a letter expressing opinions
• Checking information and correcting what someone says
• Pronunciation: stress for emphasis

11 Fashions

Preview

LIFESTYLES

This week we look at attitudes towards food and eating in the United States.

American people eat a lot of fast food, which is hardly surprising. The USA may not have invented the hot-dog or the hamburger, but it was responsible for selling them back to the world. Now there is hardly a corner of the globe without a McDonald's, Burger King, Kentucky Fried Chicken or the like.

And it seems that fast food is getting even more popular. Why is this? Is it because the average American is getting lazier? Certainly it's much easier to get a take-away, have a pizza delivered, or pop a ready-cooked meal in the microwave than to slave for hours over a hot stove. And there is the added bonus that you don't have to do much washing up, if any, afterwards. Or is it because Americans don't have time to cook? It is true that Americans today work far harder than they did thirty years ago. And that fewer women are full-time housewives.

But it also seems that people's attitudes towards food and eating have changed. Eating is seen more and more as something you do while you are doing something else. People don't stop for meals any more. You see more and more people eating on the subway, in the street, or at their computer. And the evening meal is often eaten from a tray in front of the TV. It's sad really, but that's the way it is.

Your thoughts

Discuss these questions in pairs or groups.

1 Have your personal eating styles changed over the years? Think about what, when, where, how often, how much and how you eat.

2 Have eating styles in your country changed in the last 20 years? If so, how?

Read

1 You are going to read a magazine article about eating styles in the USA. Before you read it answer these questions.

  a What kinds of fast food do you know?

  b Why do you think people eat fast food?

2 Read the article. How many of your ideas were mentioned?

Vocabulary

Work out or guess the meaning of the words and phrases in **bold** from the article.

a … which is **hardly** surprising.

b … without a McDonald's, Burger King, Kentucky Fried Chicken or **the like**.

c … **pop** a ready-cooked meal in the microwave.

d It's much easier … than **to slave for hours over a hot stove**.

e And there is **the added bonus** that you don't have to do much washing-up.

Listen

1 **11.1** Listen to Marilyn Franks, from Canada, talking about the changes she has noticed in people's eating habits in Spain. Which of the reasons she mentions is the same as one in the article?

2 Listen again. Are these sentences True or False?

a Spanish women spend less time cooking than in the past.

b Ready-made meals are very popular in Spain.

c People have a long lunch break.

d Most people have a big family meal at the weekend.

e Young people's eating habits have changed a lot.

f Marilyn uses her microwave a lot.

Have your say

1 'Fast food will be the death of us.' What is your view?

2 What is a healthy way of eating? Think about what, when, how and how often you eat.

Review: *have* and *get*

1 Match the examples of *have* to meanings 1–5 below.

a *A lot of people just **have** a sandwich for lunch. **I'm having** a cheese sandwich for lunch today.*

b *Do people **have** microwaves?*

c *You **don't have to** do much washing up afterwards.*

d *'What's Tom doing?' 'I think **he's having** a shower. He usually **has** one before he goes out.'*

e *'**I'm having** problems understanding these instructions.' 'You always **have** problems.'*

1 take
2 eat or drink
3 possess or own
4 experience
5 need to

With which meanings of *have* can we use both the simple and continuous forms?

2 a In which two sentences in 1a–e can you use *have got (to)* instead of *have*?

   b What's the past tense of *have got*?

3 Match the examples of *get* to meanings 1–3 below.

a *More and more people **are getting** microwaves.*

b *Is it because the average American **is getting** lazier?*

c *I **got** it for Christmas.*

1 receive
2 buy / obtain
3 become

▶ **Language commentary p.137**

Check

4 Choose the correct alternative in these sentences. In which sentences are both alternatives possible?

a *I have / I'm having* a mobile phone.

b I'm sorry, but *I have to / I've got to* go. I'm already late.

c *Have you got / Do you have* the time, please?

d Ivan *had / had got* a beard when he was at university.

e Paula *has / has got* a new job in a multinational company.

f You *haven't to / don't have to* apologize. It wasn't your fault.

5 Work in pairs. Choose four of these questions and discuss them.

a Do you prefer to have a bath or a shower? Why?

b Do you have any of these qualities:
   • a sense of humour?   • a quick temper?   • a lot of patience?

c How many colds did you have last year? What other illnesses did you have?

d Do you have snacks during the day? What do you have and when?

e Do you ever have dreams or nightmares?

f What do you have to do in your job? In class?

g Do you ever get homesick?

h How many personal letters, faxes and e-mails did you get last week?

> ▶ *have something done*   p.107
> ▶ *so* and *such*   p.110

Listening

In your experience

1 Do most girls and women in your country have pierced ears? At what age do they have their ears pierced? What about men?

2 Is it fashionable to have a tattoo? What do you think of tattoos?

Listen

1 a **11.2** You are going to hear five people talking about these subjects. Complete this table with short answers to the questions.

Speaker	1	2	3	4	5
1 What have they had pierced, their ear(s) or their nose?					
2 When did they have it done?					

b Listen again. Who doesn't wear their earring or nose-stud any more? Why not?

2 a Speaker 2 says, '*I stopped wearing the earring when I got a proper job 'cos I was told it looked unprofessional.*' What do you think he means by *a proper job*? What kind of job do you think he did before?

b Speaker 5 says, '*My teenage daughters quite liked the idea of their father approaching middle age with still a little rebellion left in him.*' Why do you think wearing an earring shows *a little rebellion*? What other ways of showing rebellion are there?

3 **11.3** You are going to hear someone talking about his tattoos. Listen and answer these questions.

a On what parts of his body does he have tattoos?

b Why did he stop getting tattoos done?

c How does he feel about his tattoos now?

Have your say

1 Do you think people should be allowed to dress as they like when they like?

2 How do you feel about middle-aged people who follow teenage fashion?

Vocabulary

1 a What are the adjectives related to these nouns? They end in *-al, -ant, -ent, -able, -ive* or *-ful*.

attraction   care   comfort
confidence   effect   emotion
expense   fashion   importance
intelligence   patience   power
protection   reason   significance
success   use

b Most of the adjectives form a negative with *un-*. Which ones are different?

2 Discuss these questions.

a Do you think beards and moustaches are attractive?

b Would you wear something fashionable if it didn't suit you or if it was uncomfortable?

c Can the way you look make you feel self-confident?

d Do you have expensive tastes in clothes?

e What do you think is a reasonable amount of money to spend on a pair of shoes?

have something done

Exploring concepts

1 Read these sentences and answer the questions below.

a *I had my ears pierced when I was 16.*

b *I pierced my ears when I was 16.*

c *I had pierced my ears before I was 16.*

1 In which sentence(s) did the speaker do the action herself?

2 In which sentence(s) did another person do the action for her?

2 a How is the structure *have something done* formed?

b What is the difference in word order between this structure and the Past perfect (sentence 1c)?

3 Read these sentences and complete the rules below with *have* or *get*.

a '*I get my hair cut when it starts to annoy me. What about you?*' '*I have mine cut when the boss tells me it's too long.*'

b '*Get your hair cut!*' *the army sergeant shouted at the new recruit.*

c *Johann looks really different. He's had his hair cut really short.*

We often use *get* instead of *have* but sometimes only one form is possible:

• We can only use .... in imperatives.

• We can only use .... in the Present perfect.

▶ **Language commentary p.137**

Exploitation

1 Put the words in these sentences in the correct order. (The actions are all done by someone else.) The first word is in **bold**.

a decide / whether / her / pierced / get / **She** / ears / to / can't

b fixed / get / had / they / glasses / to / my / **I** / were / because / broken

c yet / window / **Have** / the / had / you / repaired?

d get / **She** / skirt / shortened / going / to / is / her

e house / **I** / to / had / the / delivered / her / flowers

2 a Work in pairs. Find out which of these things or actions your partner does, and which they have done by somebody else.

cut their hair   decorate their flat or house
clean their shoes   repair their car   wash their car
develop and print their films

b Find out the last time they did or had these things done.

3 Work in pairs. In three minutes, list as many things as you can think of that you can have done at these places.

• At the hairdresser's

• At the dentist's

• At a garage

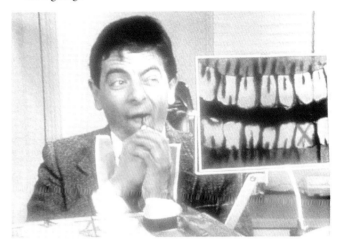

4 You've just won a fortune.

• How would you use the money to improve your house / flat?

• What changes (if any) would you make to your appearance?

Example

I'd have cosmetic surgery done on my eyes.

I'd have my house painted bright yellow.

Skills

Speak and write

1 Work in pairs. Add two questions of your own to this questionnaire about music.

Music survey

1 What kind of music do you like?
Rock ☐ Pop ☐ Classical ☐
Other ☐ – what? [   ]

2 What kind of music do your parents like?
Rock ☐ Pop ☐ Classical ☐
Other ☐ – what? [   ]

3 How many cassettes or CDs do you buy a month?
None ☐ 1 or 2 ☐ 3 or 4 ☐
More than 4 ☐ – how many?
[   ]

4 How much time do you spend listening to music a day?
An hour or less ☐ 1–3 hours ☐
More than 3 hours ☐ – how long? [   ]

5 [   ]
  [   ]

6 [   ]

2 Change pairs and interview each other.

3 Tell the class briefly about your partner's tastes in music.

Read

Read this article about tastes in popular music. Why are the Beatles still popular with teenagers in Britain today?

Still with the Beatles

Isn't there something wrong if today's teenagers rate their parents' favourite groups ahead of the groups of today?

The most comprehensive survey ever of popular music taste was published recently. In the survey the Beatles *Revolver* was voted the best album ever
5 with three other Beatles albums also in the top 5. And, says Colin Larkin, who compiled the list, the Beatles are favourites among all ages.

Being into what your mum and dad like is usually seen as very uncool. 'But,' says Colin Larkin, 'many 12-year-olds put *Revolver* above albums by other contemporary groups, and almost every list from a teenager had at least one
10 Beatles album on it.'

David Morgan, 14, says he grew up loving the Beatles. 'My mum and dad have all their albums. I like chart songs, but the Beatles are more solid and real, not so throwaway.'

Karen Bishop, 19, isn't surprised at their lasting appeal. 'You tend to absorb
15 Beatles songs when you're quite young, like nursery rhymes almost. You hear songs like *Yesterday* all the time.'

For many youngsters, however, the Beatles are not much more than a name. 'I've heard of the Beatles but I don't really know a lot about them,' says 11-year-old Natalie.

20 Stephen Timus, 13, prefers dance music. 'I don't like the Beatles or the Rolling Stones – it's not my scene.'

John Hindmarch, 25, who writes for *Smash Hits*, is disbelieving about the Beatles' supposed army of teen fans. 'When you're that age there is a strong belief that the music of the moment is good, and older music is for mum
25 and dad,' he says. 'It's a generation thing to think that your own music is best.'

He went on, 'Kids nowadays have their own CD players and spend a lot of money on music.' Reflecting this, pop culture is changing. 'These days artists get big very quickly. But they can be the biggest thing on the planet one minute and forgotten the next. Perhaps it's the disposable aspect of today's idols
30 that allows groups like the Beatles to last.' *The Independent on Sunday*

Guessing meanings

1 Guess the meanings of these words from the article.

a *rate* (l.1)
On a scale of 1–5, what would you *rate* a song that was OK?

b *comprehensive* (l.3)
If you have a *comprehensive* guide to New York, what information does it give you?

c *lasting appeal* (l.14)
What does the verb *last* mean? If something *appeals* to you, how do you feel about it?

d *absorb* (l.14)
What happens if you put a paper tissue on top of some liquid?

e *disposable* (l.29)
Many items nowadays are *disposable*; for example, babies' nappies, paper plates. What do you do with them when you have finished with them?

2 What do you think these slang expressions from the article mean?

a ***Being into** what your mum and dad like is usually seen as very **uncool**.* (l.7)

b ***… it's not my scene.*** (l.21)

Understanding ideas

Read the text again and answer these questions.

1 Who do you think took part in the survey?

2 Which two words tell us that John Hindmarsh doesn't accept the results of the survey?

3 *Reflecting **this**, pop culture is changing* (l.27). What does *this* refer to?

4 Why do you think today's artists are *disposable*?

Listen

1 You are going to hear a brief history of pop music. Before you listen, see how much you know. Complete these sentences with one of these periods of time.

| 1940s 1950s 1960s 1970s 1980s 1990s |

a Modern pop music dates from the ....

b Dozens of British groups were successful in the United States in the ....

c Singer-songwriter-poets like Bob Dylan and Joan Baez became popular in the ....

d Everyone was dancing to disco music with the Bee Gees in the ....

e Groups like the Spice Girls and The Back Street Boys were popular in the ....

2 **11.4** Listen and check your answers.

3 Listen again and answer these questions.

a Why did American parents dislike rock and roll?

b Why were singers like Bob Dylan popular with some young people?

c Which decade(s) had the most different styles of pop music?

d What three predictions does Rod Wallace make about pop music in the future?

Have your say

1 Work in groups. Discuss these quotations about music. Which do you agree with most? Which do you disagree with most?

a People who say that classical music and opera are better than pop music are just snobs.

b Pop music is bubblegum for the ears.

c Pop music reflects the world we live in.

d Good marketing is more important than musical talent.

2 Each write a controversial statement about music. Exchange statements with another group. Which one do you like best?

Grammar extra

so and *such*

Listen

11.5 You are going to hear an interview with Beatrice Noble, who used to be a fashion model. As you listen, answer these questions.

a Why did she want to be a model?
b What surprised her when she started modelling?
c What was her most embarrassing experience?
d What does she think is the main problem about a career in modelling?

Exploring concepts

1 How much do you know? Fill the gaps with *so* or *such*.

- Use ...... before *a / an* + adjective + singular countable noun (*difficult career*).
  before an adjective + uncountable noun (*hard work*).
  before an adjective + countable plural noun (*long hours*).
- Use ...... before an adjective without a noun (*glamorous*).
  before *much / many*.

2 *So* and *such* expressions can be followed by a *that* clause. Does this clause express a reason, or a result / consequence?

*At one show the heels I had to wear were **so** high **that I fell over**.*

▶ Language commentary p.138

Exploitation

1 a Match these sentence beginnings 1–6 with their endings a–f.

   1 She ate so little that …
   2 She is so well-known that …
   3 She put on so much weight that …
   4 She is such a good model that …
   5 She works so hard that …
   6 She has such an outgoing personality that …

   a she can demand very high fees.
   b she is recognized everywhere she goes.
   c she has no time for a social life.
   d she lost weight very quickly.
   e everyone enjoys working with her.
   f her clothes were too tight.

   b Now think of alternative ways of ending the sentences in 1a.

2 Fill the gaps in these sentences with *so*, *such* or *such a*, and then complete the sentences by adding an appropriate result or consequence.

   a Andy likes clothes .... much that …
   b Designer clothes are .... expensive that …
   c There were .... many people in the shop that …
   d The jacket was .... good bargain that …
   e Paul has .... big feet that …
   f We spend .... much time shopping that …

3 a Make brief notes about these topics.
   - An actor you like
   - A film you disliked
   - A place you don't like
   - Your favourite month
   - A colour you like

   b Now tell your partner what you like or dislike about the topic you have chosen.
   Example
   I like Brad Pitt because he's so good-looking. He's also such a …

Exploring words

The arts

1 Have you done any of these things recently?
   • been to the cinema, the theatre, a concert or an art exhibition?
   • bought a cassette or CD, or read a book?
   What did you see, buy or read? What was it like?

2 a Which do you prefer in each category and why?
   • classic films (like *Gone with the Wind*, Hitchcock's *Psycho*) or modern-day blockbusters?
   • classic novels (by authors like Tolstoy, Dickens, Cervantes) or modern best-sellers?
   • classical music or popular music?
   • classical plays (like Shakespeare or Molière) or modern plays?
   • the 'Old Masters' (like Rembrandt or Goya) or modern artists?

   b Read these quotations. What do you think the speakers are talking about?
   1 This was the first time I'd seen him playing live. He was brilliant.
   2 The set is minimal but effective – a bare stage with few props. The lighting is excellent.
   3 The works on display are on loan from galleries around the world.
   4 By chapter ten you knew what was going to happen.
   5 *The Killer Whale* will be on screens throughout the country from tomorrow.

3 Write the words below under the right heading. Some words can go under more than one.

acting   album   artist   author   autobiography   biography
cast   conductor   director   fiction   landscape   live   lyrics
non-fiction   novelist   orchestra   pen-name   performance
play   playwright   plot   portrait   recording   screen   script
story   title role   track

Cinema	Music	Theatre	Books	Art
director				artist

4 a Can you think of a film of each of these types?
   • thriller   • cartoon   • war film   • western
   • historical film   • horror film   • disaster movie
   • comedy   • romantic comedy   • science-fiction
   • musical

   b What kind of films do you like or dislike?
   c Which modern films do you think will become classics?

5 a Work in groups. You are going to plan a new blockbuster movie. Decide on the following: the type of film, actors, setting and time period, storyline.

   b Present the ideas for your movie to the class. Which movie do you think will be the most successful?

Writing

Reviews

Read

1 Read these reviews. How many stars do you think the reviewers gave the book, the album, the film and the TV programme?

Star ratings:	***** excellent **** very good
	*** good ** average * poor

The Voyage of the Narwhal by Andrea Barrett tells the story of Erasmus Wells, an American naturalist who goes on an expedition to the Arctic in 1855 in search of the lost crew of explorer Sir John Franklin. A word of mouth bestseller in the US, this beautifully written narrative is more than an adventure story – it is also about the quest for personal knowledge and self-realization.

Joni Mitchell's album *Taming the Tiger* is the first in four years from the American singer-songwriter. The lyrics are clever but a bit repetitive. The music is the usual blend of soft acoustic guitar and occasional jazzy saxophone. Quite relaxing.

Elizabeth Under the direction of the Indian director Shekhar Kapur, this story of the early years of the reign of Queen Elizabeth 1 unfolds like a political thriller. It begins with the death of Henry VIII and ends when, aged 29, Elizabeth declares herself to be the Virgin Queen. An international cast dominated by two Australians – Cate Blanchett in the title role and Geoffrey Rush as Walsingham, the Queen's main protector. Both actors give superb performances. Highly recommended.

Smile of the Shark – Wednesday, Cable and Satellite channels
There's something about sharks. It doesn't matter how many wildlife programmes they show about them, people always want ˙ more. This documentary takes a new angle, following the divers whose fascination for the world's most dangerous predators leads them to take extraordinary risks. Some good camera work. Worth watching.

2 a Would you be interested in the film or TV programme, the album or the book in the reviews in 1?

b How useful are reviews? Do you take any notice of them?

Brainstorm and notes

Work in pairs or groups. You are going to write a review. Think of a film, video, book, TV programme or album you all know. Make notes about the ideas in one of these checklists.

Book	Album	Film	TV programme
title	title	title	name
author	singer / band	director	when it's on
story	type of music	actors	channel
	good tracks	story	kind of programme
			what it's about
What's good / bad			
Opinion or recommendation			
*** rating			

Write

1 Write the first draft of your review using the notes you have made.

2 a Exchange reviews with someone who wrote about something different.

b Read the review. Does it give you enough information? Is the opinion or recommendation clear? Suggest one or two improvements.

c Discuss the improvement ideas, then write the final version of your review.

> **Reminder**
> - Give useful information.
> - Give your opinion or recommendation.

Language in action

Apologizing

Introduction

1 You are going to hear four conversations. Someone is apologizing in the four situations above.

   a In pairs, discuss what each person is apologizing for. What explanations might the people give?

   b Note down your ideas.

2 a **11.6** Listen to the conversations. How many of your ideas are the same?

   b Listen again.

   Student A Note expressions people use to apologize.

   Student B Note expressions people use to accept an apology.

   Tell each other the expressions you heard.

   c Listen again. This time note the language the speakers use to prepare someone for an apology.
   Example
   You know that tape you lent me?

   d Make lists under these headings:
   • preparing someone for an apology
   • apologizing
   • accepting an apology.

▶ **Pronunciation p.153**

Practice

Role play

Work in pairs.
Student A Read the instructions on this page. Spend a few minutes preparing what you will say in Situation 1 before you start the role play.
Student B Turn to p.157.

Student A
Situation 1
You have been staying in your friend's flat while they were on holiday. Start the conversation with Student B. Explain how the following things happened and apologize.
• There's a paint stain on the living room carpet.
• The parrot is dead.
• The kitchen window is broken.
• The washing machine isn't working.

Situation 2
You were out of town last night. Student B is a friend of yours and rents a room in your flat. You have just returned to your flat to find Student B looking rather ashamed. Student B will start the conversation.

Unit 11 Language check

In this unit you have worked on the following language points:

• *have* and *get*
• *have something done*
• *so* and *such*

• Vocabulary: the arts
• Writing: reviews
• Apologizing
• Pronunciation: giving bad news; sentence stress

12 Success

Preview

Your thoughts

1 Write down three personal ambitions. Say when you would like to achieve them by.

2 Exchange ideas with a partner. How similar are your ambitions?

3 Do you think it is important to have ambitions? Why?

Listen

1 You are going to hear part of a radio advice phone-in about problems connected with people's ambitions. Read these extracts from the programme and try to predict what the problems are.

Speaker 1
My daughter Zoe is nine years old and wants to be a successful skater … I don't think that's any kind of life for a nine-year-old but it's one against two in our house …

Speaker 2
I'm twenty-five years old and I work for a large international company. The job's OK, the money's quite good but …

Speaker 3
I'm fourteen years old and my parents want me to be …

2 **12.1** Listen to the callers. What is each speaker's problem? What advice would you give them?

3 **12.2** Listen to the reply to Speaker 2. What advice do the members of the panel give? Do you agree with their advice?

Vocabulary

Work out or guess the meanings of these words and phrases in **bold** from the programme.

a *She's travelling **the length and breadth** of the country …*
b *… not spending her time **chasing a dream**.*
c *I'm **in two minds** about **the whole thing**.*
d *My parents won't **take me seriously**.*
e *There is definitely **a gap in the market** for the product.*
f *If I were you, I would **put your plans on hold** for now.*

Read

1 Read these headings from the book *Yes, You Can!* Which ones do you think would be useful to Nicole?

- ◇ Increase your self-esteem
- ◇ Make your work fun
- ◇ Get organized
- ◇ Avoid negative self-talk
- ◇ Increase your energy
- ◇ Make better decisions
- ◇ Increase your job security
- ◇ Reduce your worry
- ◇ Win an argument
- ◇ Improve your memory
- ◇ Express family love more fully
- ◇ Feel more optimistic

2 Would you be interested in reading more about any of the topics? Which do you think would be a waste of time?

Have your say

1 Would you ever contact a radio programme for advice?

2 How useful do you think self-help manuals and videos are?

Review: Advice

1 These verbs and phrases are all used to give advice. What verb form follows them?

a *You **should** just do it, go for it.*

b *I think you **ought to** consider doing a self-improvement course.*

c ***Why don't you** read one of the books there are on the subject?*

d ***If I were you, I would** put your plans on hold for now. **I wouldn't** do anything until you yourself feel more confident that it's going to work.*

2 What are the negative forms of these three sentences?

a *He ought to tell his boss.*   **b** *She should apologize.*   **c** *I think you should go.*

3 Read these two sentences. Which sentence means it's a good idea, and which means it's essential?

a *You must speak to your father.*   **b** *You should speak to your father.*

▶ **Language commentary p.138**

Check

4 a A friend of yours is going for an interview for a new job. Complete these pieces of advice to them with an appropriate word or phrase.

1 You shouldn't …
2 You ought to …
3 If I were you, I would …

b A friend of yours is bored with their life. Complete these pieces of advice to them in an appropriate way.

1 Why don't you …
2 You oughtn't to …
3 You should …

c You think a third friend is working too hard. Give them advice using these words and phrases.

1 I don't think you ought to …   3 If I were you, I would …
2 You should …

5 a In pairs, write a letter in 50 words or fewer to the problem page of a magazine.

- Say what your problem is.   • Ask for advice.

> *Dear Problem Page,*
> *I have been going out with David for five years. When I asked him when we were going to get married, he said he didn't want to get married. He was quite happy as he was. What should I do?*
> *Desperate.*

b Give your letter to another pair. Discuss what advice to give and write a reply.

> *Dear Desperate,*
> *Is he still living at home? Maybe his mother is making life too comfortable for him! I think you ought to have a word with her about your problem.*

▶ Conditional sentences (3)   p.117
▶ *all, both, either, neither, none*   p.120

Reading

In your experience

1 Which are the three most popular spectator sports in your country? Why are they so popular? Are they equally popular with men and women? Do you like them?

2 Are there any sports in your country which women or men generally don't do? Why is this?

Read

1 You are going to read an article about a women's football team. First, read these questions.

   a Do any of the team play for England?

   b How many spectators went to women's football matches in 1920?

   c How many women's football clubs are there nowadays?

   d Who split up with her boyfriend because of football?

   e What does Sheila Edmunds do?

2 You now have two minutes to find the answers in the article.

Close up

1.13, 14 What other word has a similar meaning to *ban*? What things can be *banned*?

1.24 *Success* is a noun. What are the related verb, adjective and adverb?

1.29 A *mate* is a friend. A *team-mate* is someone who plays in the same team as you. What other 'mates' do you know?

Belles of the ball

Doncaster Belles are the cream of women's football. They have won a large number of trophies, and several of the team play for England.

But Doncaster Belles, like all women's football teams in England, are amateurs. None of the Belles is paid to play, and while 50,000 fans regularly watch a match

5 played by the top male professional clubs, a crowd of 200 is considered a good turnout for one of the Belle's matches.

When women's soccer first emerged during the First World War (1914–18), it attracted huge crowds. By

10 1920 games were watched by more than 50,000 spectators. Then everything changed. It was decided that football was 'quite unsuitable for females', and women were banned from playing at stadiums belonging to the professional clubs. The ban lasted 50 years and

15 although women still continued to play football, the women's game went into decline.

Recently, however, there has been a revival of interest. With 15,000 women now playing for 500 clubs, women's football is one of the fastest growing sports in

20 England. And Doncaster Belles is one of the most successful women's teams.

Karen 'Kaz' Walker, the team's star player, thinks that the fact that the players are close friends off the pitch accounts partly for their success. 'We're all mates so we

25 all want to do our best for each other,' she says.

Players have had to make sacrifices, however. Lou Ryde, an ex-Belle, split up with her boyfriend when he forced her to choose between football and him. Tracey Kilner's relationship wouldn't have ended if she hadn't spent all her free time with her team-mates.

30 But physiotherapist Sheila Edmunds, one of the Belles' founders, thinks sacrifices like these have usually been worth making. 'Some of the players would have had different lives,' she admits. 'They would have married early and had kids. Instead they have the chance to express themselves and, when they play for England, to travel abroad.'

Understanding ideas

Read the text more carefully, then answer these questions.

1 In what way do you think Doncaster Belles are *the **cream** of women's football*?

2 Why do you think women's soccer was so popular during and just after the First World War (1914–18)?

3 Why do you think women were banned from playing at professional stadiums in 1920? Why do you think the ban had such a negative effect on women's football?

4 *The players are close friends **off the pitch**.* What does this mean? What do you think they do?

— Grammar —

Conditional sentences (3)

Exploring concepts

1 We use the third conditional to describe imagined situations and consequences. Do these sentences refer to the present, the future or the past?
   a *Some of the players would have had different lives. They would have married early and had kids.*
   b *If Lou Ryde's boyfriend hadn't forced her to choose between football and him, she probably wouldn't have split up with him.*
   c *Tracey Kilner's relationship wouldn't have ended if she hadn't spent all her free time with her team-mates.*

2 How is the third conditional formed?

3 What is the position of the *if-* clause in the sentence? What do you notice about the punctuation?

   ▶ **Language commentary p.138**

Exploitation

1 a Read this short text.

   Last Sunday Luke went to Diana's party. The party didn't finish till 4.00 a.m. so he went to bed late. Unfortunately, because he was tired, he forgot to set his alarm clock and overslept. The phone woke him at 8.30 a.m. It was a colleague who wondered if he was ill. He got to the office as quickly as he could but still arrived an hour late. His boss was annoyed. In the afternoon Luke was so tired that he fell asleep in the middle of an important meeting with his boss.

   b Two of the following sentences about the text are correct. The others contain mistakes in one of the parts in *italics*. Correct the mistakes.
   1 If Luke *had gone* to Diana's party, he *would have gone* to bed earlier.
   2 He *wouldn't have gone* to bed so late if the party *had finished* earlier.
   3 If he *wasn't* so tired, he *would have remembered* to set his alarm clock.
   4 He *wouldn't oversleep* if he *hadn't forgotten* to set his alarm clock.
   5 He *wouldn't have woken up* if a colleague *phoned* him.
   6 If a colleague *hadn't wondered* if he was ill, he *didn't phone* him.
   7 If he *hadn't been* on time, his boss *wouldn't have been* annoyed.
   8 He *would have stayed* awake during the meeting if he *hadn't been* so tired.

Have your say

Professional sportsmen are generally better paid than professional sportswomen. Why does this happen? Is it fair?

2 Use the picture prompts to help you make third conditional sentences.

3 Read this situation. What would / wouldn't you have done?

Michael decided to go for a walk in the mountains. Although it was February, it was a beautiful sunny day. He didn't tell anyone at his hotel where he was going. He wore trainers, jeans and a light-coloured jacket and carried a packet of crisps, some chewing gum and a can of cola in his pockets. Halfway up it started to snow. He decided to go on.

Free speech

Think about three important events in your life. Tell your partner how these events affected you.

Skills

Speak

1 What kind of person do you have to be in order to be successful? Choose three ideas from the box and rank them in order of importance.

> You have to be
> aggressive ambitious* clever confident*
> creative dedicated* determined* energetic*
> enthusiastic* flexible focused good with people
> hard-working intelligent* lucky motivated*
> single-minded talented*
>
> You have to have
> self-belief a sense of humour

2 Compare ideas with a partner. Do you have any other ideas?

3 What are the nouns from the adjectives marked *?

Listen

You are going to hear nine people answering the question.

1 **12.3** Listen and tick (✓) the ideas you hear.

2 Do any speakers share your views?

Read

1 You are going to read an article about how to become a success. Do you think the following statements are generally True or False?

You are more likely to be successful in life:
a if you are brought up by two parents
b if you get good qualifications at school
c if your parents are rich
d if you are beautiful.

2 Now read the article to check your ideas. Were they correct?

So you want to be a success?

Lose a parent: only 5% of successful entrepreneurs had both parents present through childhood

You would think that you would need the loving support of two parents for the best start in life, but surprisingly
5 this is not always the case. For entrepreneurs the death or long-term absence of a parent appears to be what actually launches them on a successful career. Unstable family backgrounds have a similar effect on artists, but not, strangely enough, on those who make science their
10 career. Studies show that future scientists only do well if their home-life is stable and secure.

Do badly at school: almost two-thirds of our top earners left school early

You would expect a good academic record at school to
15 be a guarantee of future success. But the rules and regulations of the classroom tend to irritate future entrepreneurs, who often leave school as soon as they can, usually without any formal qualifications. However, those planning a more orthodox career – as employees in a large
20 organization, for example – should try to do as well at school as they can.

Start off rich: 25% of those who head large companies were born into wealthy families

There is a popular saying that the first million is the
25 hardest to make. But there is one sure short-cut: inherit it. Even today, wealth gives an advantage right at the start of their careers to those who possess it. Of course, those who are born rich have little incentive to fight their way towards a fortune. But the self-confidence that comes
30 from having money undoubtedly helps its owners to get top jobs.

Be born beautiful: good looks open up routes to the top that have nothing to do with merit

It is unfair, but beautiful people also often seem to have
35 a bigger than average share of intelligence and charm. However, it can be a disadvantage to be too beautiful, especially if you are a woman. You may be seen simply as a decorative ornament, and find that your less attractive contemporaries fight their way to the top ahead of you.

Focus

Guessing meanings

Guess the meanings of these words from the article.

a *launch* (l.7)
How are rockets sent into space?

b *short-cut* (l.25)
What is the most direct route from A to B?

c *incentive* (l.28)
What do most people need to encourage them to do something difficult, for example, work harder?

d *charm* (l.35)
What special quality do some people have which attracts people to them?

Understanding ideas

Read the text again, then answer these questions.

1 Why do you think an unstable, insecure family background has a positive effect on artists?

2 Give some examples of orthodox and unorthodox jobs.

3 *You may be seen simply as* **a decorative ornament**. (l.38) What does this mean? What kind of job might you be given in a big company?

4 What advantage might *less attractive contemporaries* have over you?

Listen

1 **12.4** You are going to hear three people talking about their personal achievements. As you listen, write down what each speaker is proud of and why.

2 What do you think these words and expressions in **bold** mean?

a *I decided* **to take the matter in hand** *and so I went to evening classes.* (Speaker 1)

b *And that was quite* **time-consuming** *but I think in the end it* **worked**. (Speaker 2)

c *I had to* **overcome** *a total loss of confidence.* (Speaker 3)

Have your say

What are your personal successes? What have you done that you are proud of?

Speak

1 What is your personal definition of success?

2 a Work in groups. Agree on a definition.
   b Design a five-point plan for being successful.
   c Present your plan to the rest of the class and take a vote on the best.

Grammar extra

all, both, either, neither, none

Read

1 Do you like exams? Do you usually do well in exams? Why or why not?

2 Read this short text. Has something similar ever happened to you or to someone you know?

To do well at school, college or university you usually need to do well in exams. 'All students hate exams' may be a generalization, but it is a fairly true one. Certainly, all of the students I've known disliked doing exams. None of them thought that the exam system was fair; to do well in an exam you simply had to be able to predict the questions which would be asked. This was the case as regards two students in my class at college. Both of them were exceptionally bright, but in the final year exam neither of them got an A grade. In fact, they both got Cs. The exam had tested us on questions which had come up the previous year. They had both assumed that the same questions wouldn't come up again, and hadn't prepared for them.

Exploring concepts

1 Underline the phrases in the text which refer to two or more people, as in the example.

2 Which of the underlined expressions is
  a a generalization?
  b something specific about more than two people?
  c something specific about two people (positive)?
  d something specific about two people (negative)?

3 Read these sentences and answer the questions about *both*, *none*, *neither*, *either* below.

  a ***Both*** students are clever.
  b ***Neither*** student has the necessary qualifications. ***Neither of them*** has the necessary qualifications.
  c ***None*** of the students has failed the exam.
  d Antonio sat two exams but he didn't pass ***either*** exam.

  • Which words can be followed by a singular noun?
  • Which word is followed by a plural noun?
  • Which words usually follow *none*?

▶ **Language commentary p.139**

Exploitation

1 Complete the sentences with an appropriate word: *all*, *none*, *both*, *neither*, *either*.

  a Giovanna and Tina are .... studying to be music teachers.
  b .... Luis nor Pedro can play a musical instrument, although they .... like music.
  c .... the people at the concert said how much they had enjoyed it. .... of them was disappointed.
  d I didn't like .... film. One was too long and the other was just boring.
  e They have sold .... the tickets for the opera.

2 a Work in threes. Take turns to say two things that you think the other two students have in common. Correct any wrong information. Use these ideas.

  | age   marital status   job   hobbies and interests   languages favourite colours   birthday   music |

  Example
  I think you are both married.
  I don't think either of you smokes.

  b Tell the class at least two things that two people in your group have in common.
  Example
  Pedro and Juan both like studying English.
  Neither of them is very good at sports.

  c Now find four or five things that everyone in your group has in common. Then tell the class.
  Example
  All of us are under 20.
  None of us has a car.

Exploring words

The language of money

1 a Choose the correct alternative in *italics*. What does the other word mean?

1 'What does Boris do when he isn't working?'
   'He *spends / wastes* all his free time on his computer.'
2 Do you think I could *lend / borrow* some money? I need to buy Alicia a birthday present.
3 We're going into business together. The bank has agreed to give us a *loan / mortgage*.
4 Have you got any *cash / change* for the drinks machine? It doesn't accept £1 coins.
5 When people reach the age of sixty or sixty-five, they get *a pension / an inheritance* from the state.
6 The bank has sent me a letter to tell me that my account is *in the red / bankrupt*.
7 The *cost / value* of our flat has gone up since we bought it.
8 I'd love to go out tonight but unfortunately I'm *poor / broke*.
9 Daniella's parents are rich and her husband's parents are *well off / well earned* too.

b Answer these questions.

1 What things can you *spend* and *waste*?
2 What does *rich* mean in these phrases?
   rich colours   *rich* in vitamins   a *rich* and varied life
   a *rich* chocolate cake   *rich* soil

3 What do these expressions with *red* mean?
   a I was *in the red*.
   b The woman was *in red*.
   c The traffic lights were *on red*.
4 Choose the correct verb in these sentences.
   a Radka *got out / took out* a loan and a mortgage.
   b When she was eighteen, Francesca *came into / took up* her inheritance.
   c David *got / went* bankrupt when his business failed.
   d They *set up / put up* in business together.

2 a Decide if the words in *italics* in these sentences are correct. Replace any wrong words with an appropriate word from this list.

value	values	valuable	valuables	invaluable	expense
expenses	expensive	price	priceless	worthless	

1 The notice said, 'Please leave your *values* in the safe'
2 When I go on a course, the company pays all my *expenses* – hotel, travel, etc.
3 I'd throw that old vase away. It's *priceless*.
4 My parents have very traditional *values*. They don't believe in divorce.
5 The museum contains *worthless* treasures from ancient Egypt.
6 Running a car is a big *price*.
7 I really couldn't have done it without you. Your help was *invaluable*.

b Ask and answer these questions in pairs.

1 What is the most valuable thing you own?
2 What is your greatest expense?
3 Do you have any traditional values? What are they?
4 Have you ever been given invaluable advice? What was it?

3 Work in groups.

a You have inherited a large old house. It is set in 25 acres of uncultivated land, ten kilometres from the nearest town. The house is in very poor condition and you would need to spend a lot of money (which you don't have) on it. Decide on the best way to make the most of your inheritance.

b Present your plan to the class. Which plan do you think would be the most effective?

Writing

Articles

Read

Read this magazine article on winning the lottery. Does the writer think there are more advantages or more disadvantages?

Congratulations!
You've just won £12,000,000!

Great, you think. All my worries are over.
- I'll be able to give up work. (Just think! No more getting up at 7.00 a.m.!)
- I'll be able to buy that red Ferrari I've always wanted. (Just imagine! Racing along the motorway with the wind in your hair!)
- I'll be able to go and live in Florida. Have a big house with a swimming pool. (Your dreams come true! Sunshine all year round, and Disneyworld on your doorstep!)

BUT ... Wouldn't there be some disadvantages too?
- What about friends? Would you be able to tell who was interested in you and who was just interested in your money?
- How would you spend your time? You can't spend the rest of your life doing nothing. You would soon get tired of the easy life! You'd get bored, start thinking too much, get depressed and ... wish you hadn't won the lottery?

Maybe it's better if our dreams don't come true after all?

Brainstorm and notes

Work in pairs or groups. You are going to write a short article about the advantages and disadvantages of one of these topics.

- Being President
- Being a famous actor or singer
- Being a world-class athlete
- Finding a wallet containing $50,000

1 Decide which topic you are going to write about.

2 Think of two or three advantages and two or three disadvantages and make notes.

3 Think of an interesting beginning. It could be a statement or a question.

4 Decide whether there are more advantages than disadvantages and write a final summarizing sentence.

Write

1 Write the first draft of the article, using the notes you have made. Write about 150 words.

2 a Exchange articles with someone from another group.

   b Read the article. Are the advantages and disadvantages clear? Does the summary tell you what the writer thinks? Suggest one or two improvements.

   c Discuss the improvement ideas in pairs, then write the final version of your article.

> **Reminder**
> - Catch the reader's attention.
> - Use a personal, informal tone.
> - Make the ending interesting.

Language in action

Review

Discuss

Work in groups of three or four. You have decided to go into business together.

1 First of all, decide what business it is going to be. Here are some ideas.
- a small company which makes and / or sells something
- a service (for example, dog-walking, house / flat-sitting, car-washing)
- a language school

2 a Depending on the business you have chosen, make decisions about the following.

Small company / service
1 Product or service
2 Location: area / type of building
3 Advertising
4 Furniture / equipment
5 Employees needed
6 Capital needed

Language school
1 Languages
2 Location: area / type of building
3 Number of students / nationalities
4 Class size / number of teachers
5 Furniture / equipment
6 Capital needed

b Note down the decisions you make – you will need to refer to them later.

Role play

1 Complete this application form. Make a few mistakes, for example in the spelling.

> **Loan application form**
> Name: ....
> Address: ....
> ....
> Telephone number: ....
> Loan required: ....

2 You are each going to ask the bank manager for a loan. Work with a student from another group. Read the notes below, then take turns to be the bank manager. Before you start, exchange loan application forms.

Bank manager
- Check the information on the loan application form. (A bank clerk took the details over the telephone.) Make any necessary corrections.
- Ask questions to find out the following information: type of business; plans for the business.
- Decide whether to give the loan or not and the conditions of repayment (?% interest over ? years).

Applicant for loan
- Answer the bank manager's questions. Be prepared to answer questions about your business plans.
- You may need to persuade the manager to give you the loan.

Follow up

1 Report back to the group. Decide on the best offer.

2 Write an advertisement for your school, company or service. Mention the main selling points that will give it an advantage over any other similar businesses.

Unit 12 Language check

In this unit you have worked on the following language points:

- Advice: *should, ought to, Why don't you, If I were you, I'd …*
- Conditional sentences (3): third
- *all, both, either, neither, none*

- Vocabulary: the language of money
- Writing: articles
- Review of functional language

Language commentary

► Frequency expressions with the Present simple

a Present simple

Check you remember these main uses of the Present simple.
1 Habitual actions.   *I **wake up** at 7.30 every morning.*
2 Permanent situations.   *My uncle **lives** in Australia.*
3 Facts that are always true.   *Cars **cause** pollution.*

b Frequency adverbs

1 These adverbs are used with the Present simple to say how often something happens. Here are some in order.

| always   usually   often   sometimes   occasionally |
| hardly ever   rarely   never |

2 These adverbs usually come before the main verb but after the verb *be*.
*You **always arrive** late! You **are never** on time!*

3 *Sometimes* goes before *don't* and *doesn't*; *usually* and *often* can go before or after *don't* and *doesn't*, depending on the meaning.
*He **sometimes doesn't** have breakfast.*
*I **don't usually** stay in at the weekend.*
*I **often don't** go out in the evening.*

4 *Usually*, *sometimes* and *occasionally* can also start or end a sentence.
***Usually** I arrive home late.*
*I miss the last train **sometimes**.*
*I walk home **occasionally**.*

c Other frequency expressions

1 Here are some more frequency expressions.

| every day   week   month   year   once a day |
| twice a week   three times a month   four times a year |
| on Fridays   at weekends |

2 These expressions usually come at the end of a sentence but can also come at the beginning.
*I exercise **every day**.*
*I go swimming **twice a week**.*
***On Fridays** I cycle to work.*

d Questions

To find out how often people do things we can ask the questions:
How often do you ..?   Do you ever ..?

► Present perfect simple and adverbs

(The contrast between the Present perfect and the Past simple is dealt with in Unit 2. The contrast between the Present perfect simple and the Present perfect continuous is dealt with in Unit 3.)

a Form

The Present perfect simple is formed with *have* or *has* + past participle.

*I **have swum** 1000 metres.*	*They **haven't run** very far.*
*He **has cycled** 20 kilometres.*	*She **hasn't been** to America.*
***Have** you **seen** my keys?*	*Yes, I **have**. / I **have seen** your keys.*
	*No, I **haven't**. / I **haven't** seen them.*

b Uses

1 We can use the Present perfect to point out a connection between a past event or activity and the present.
At last, I've found my keys.

Event	Present effect results
I found my keys.	*Now I can (un)lock the door.*
	Now I can get into my car and drive away.

2 We can emphasize this link between the past and the present by using different adverbs.

| already   just   yet   so far   still   never |

- *already* = at some time in the past before now.
*I'm not hungry, thanks. I've **already** eaten.*
*I don't want to go to the cinema. I've seen that film **already**.*

- *just* = very recently, a short time ago.
*He's **just** come in. Can he phone you back later?*

- *yet* = not in the past, but soon. It is used to talk about something which hasn't happened but which you expect will happen soon. It is used in questions and negative statements.
*Have you stopped smoking **yet**?*
*I haven't been to sleep **yet**.*

- *so far* = up to the present time. It suggests that this is a temporary fact – the situation will probably change in the future.
***So far** she's applied for ten jobs. (She'll apply for more next week.)*

- *still* is used to talk about actions that haven't happened yet. This is surprising or unexpected in some way. It is usually used in negative statements.
*Jo **still** hasn't phoned. I'm getting quite worried.*

- *never* = at no time before now.
*I've **never** been to Japan.*

3 Note the position of the adverbs.
already – after *have* or at the end of the clause.
just – after *have*.
So far – at the beginning or end of the clause.
still – before *have*.

4 In Present perfect simple questions, the word *ever* is used to emphasize the idea of the whole period of past time leading up to the present.
*Have you **ever** smoked a pipe?*
Ever here means at any time in your life.

5 *For* and *since* are both used with the Present Perfect to talk about something that started in the past and has continued until now.
For tells us how long the action has continued, and is followed by a period of time.
*They've had their car **for** four years.*
Since tells us when the action started, and is followed by a point in time.
*I've known him **since** last December.*
*She's been here **since** 1995.*

▶ Comparison of adjectives

a Form: regular adjectives

1 To make the comparative of one syllable adjectives ending in one vowel + one consonant (e.g. *hot*), double the last letter and add *-er*.

2 To make the comparative of two-syllable adjectives ending in *-y* (e.g. *healthy*) change the last letter to *i* and add *-er*.

3 To make the comparative of most adjectives of two or more syllables put *more* or *less* in front of the adjective.

4 To make the superlative of one-syllable adjectives ending in *-e*, add *-st*.

5 To make the superlative of three- or four-syllable adjectives (e.g. *uninteresting*) put *the most* or *the least* in front of the adjective.

Summary table 1: one-syllable adjectives

Adjective	Comparative	Superlative
tall	tall**er**	the tall**est**
light	light**er**	the light**est**
large	larg**er**	the larg**est**
big	big**ger**	the big**gest**

Summary table 2: adjectives of two or more syllables

Adjective	Comparative	Superlative
modern	**more** modern	**the most** modern
comfortable	**more** comfortable	**the most** comfortable
easy	eas**ier**	the eas**iest**

b Form: irregular adjectives

Some adjectives have irregular comparative and superlative forms.

Summary table 3: irregular adjectives

Adjective	Comparative	Superlative
good	**better**	the best
bad	**worse**	the worst
far	**farther** or **further**	the farthest or the furthest

c *than*

Than is used with comparative adjectives.
*Russia is bigger **than** Spain.*
*Cycling is more interesting **than** going by car.*

d *(just) as … as*

This is used to compare two things which are the same.
*My father is **as** tall **as** my mother.*
*This chair is **just as** uncomfortable **as** that one.*
Just here means exactly.

e *not as … as / not so … as*

These are used to compare two things which are different.
*I am **not as** tall **as** my brother.*
*She is**n't so** tall **as** you.*

f *less / the least*

Less and *the least* mean the opposite of *more* and *the most* and are also used with adjectives to compare.
*She is **less** intelligent than her sister.*
*That was **the least** interesting film I've ever seen.*

g Qualifying comparative adjectives

These expressions are used to say how much difference there is between two things.

1 To refer to big differences use: *a lot / far / much*.
*I'm **a lot** heavier than I was.*
*He's **far** friendlier than his parents.*
*This car's **much** more expensive than the one I've got now.*

2 To refer to small differences use: *a bit / a little / slightly*.
*I think it's **a bit** colder today than it was yesterday.*
*Do you? I think it's **slightly** warmer.*
*The second part was **a little** more interesting than the first.*

3 *Far* and *a little* are the most formal words in each list.
A lot and *a bit* are the most informal. *Much* and *slightly* are neutral.

Unit 2

▶ *used to*

a Uses

We use *used to* to talk about habitual or repeated actions or situations in the past.

1 We use *used to* to talk about actions or situations which happened in the past but don't happen now.
*Andy **used to** smoke.* = Andy smoked regularly in the past but he doesn't smoke now.
*Sandra **used to** be married.* = Sandra was married in the past but now she is either separated or divorced.

2 We use *didn't use to* or *never used to* to talk about actions or situations which didn't happen in the past but happen regularly now.
*Andy **didn't use to** smoke.* = Andy didn't smoke before but he smokes now.
*Mike **never used to** be so bad-tempered.* = Mike wasn't bad-tempered before but he is nowadays.

3 We only use *used to* to talk about habitual or repeated actions or situations. For something which happened once, we use the Past simple.
On one occasion he said *something extremely rude.*

4 We do not use *used to* when we talk about how long something lasted or how many times it happened. We use the Past simple.
I **lived** in Paris **for two years.**
I **visited** my friend **several times last year.**

5 We can use the Past simple tense to talk about a habitual repeated action in the past but the context must make this clear.
He **used to** drive all over the country while my mum, my sister and I **sat** in the car bored stiff.

6 If we use the Past simple form to describe a habitual past action, we often use adverbs of frequency or a frequency time expression to make it absolutely clear that the past action was repeated.
Every time he **was** in port, my mother **took** my brother and me to see him.
We **always had** lunch on the ship with the captain.

b Form

Used to is followed by the infinitive without *to.* Its form is like that of a regular past tense verb.
Question *How* **did** *you* **use to** *spend weekends as a family?*
Affirmative *We* **used to** *eat out a lot.*
Negative *It* **didn't use to** *bother me.*
We **never used to** visit our relations when we were young.
Short forms *Yes, (I, etc.)* **did**./ *No, (I, etc.)* **didn't.**

▶ Present perfect and Past simple

(See also Unit 1 and Unit 3 for Present perfect.)

a Present perfect

We use the Present perfect:
1 to talk about something which began in the past, is still true now and could continue into the future.
People **have celebrated** *the festival for hundreds of years.*
I've **lived** *here since 1998.*

2 to talk about something which happened in the past but in an unfinished time period like *today, this week, this year, this century.*
I've **sent out** thirty invitations this week.
We've **cleared** the house today.
Sometimes expressions with *this* can refer to finished time and we need to use the Past simple.
I've **written** two letters this morning. (said in the morning)
I **wrote** two letters this morning. (said in the afternoon or evening)

3 to refer to a completed past action, activity or experience without saying when it happened. We are more interested in the fact that something happened than when it happened.
He's thirty on Saturday so **I've organized** *a party for him.*

4 We use the question form *Have ... ever ..?* to ask a question about an experience in the past.
Have you **ever met** anyone famous?
When we continue the conversation, we use the Past simple because we are now talking about an event that happened at an exact time and place.
Who **did** you **meet?** I **met** the Pope.

b Past simple

We use the Past simple tense:
1 to talk about completed actions or events that happened at a particular time in the past when the exact time or place is mentioned.
My last birthday **was** *about two weeks ago and I* **celebrated** *it in France.*
The first guests **arrived** *at 8.00 p.m.*

2 to talk about past states and actions that were habitual or repeated over a period of time.
When I **was** *young I always* **played** *jokes on my parents and my teachers on April 1*
Every summer we **went** *to the seaside.*
Sometimes we use time expressions which refer to past time, for example *yesterday, last night.* Sometimes we use time clauses to refer to a period in the past, for example *when I was young.* Sometimes we do not use a time expression because the speaker and listener both know exactly when the action or event happened.

▶ Adjective order

1 When we use more than one adjective to describe a noun, the order of the adjectives is important. Here are some general rules of order.

1	**Opinion**	beautiful	smart	nice	horrible	cheap
		expensive	elegant			
2	**Size**	long	large	short	knee-length	tall
3	**Age**	old	modern	new		
4	**Shape**	tight-fitting	full	short-sleeved	rectangular	
5	**Colour**	yellow	white	red and blue		
6	**Where from**	Indian	Egyptian	Moroccan	Japanese	
7	**Material**	silk	cotton	metal	woollen	plastic
		linen	leather			
8	**NOUN**	sari	jacket	trousers	skirt	top	blouse
		boots	kimono			

It is not usual to use more than three adjectives in front of a noun.

2 Opinion adjectives always come before other adjectives.
A **comfortable** red leather chair.
When there is more than one opinion adjective, the more general adjective comes first.
Horrible cheap plastic sandals. NOT ~~Cheap horrible plastic sandals.~~
A **lovely well-furnished** modern flat. NOT ~~A well-furnished lovely modern flat.~~

3 When we want to find out about an object, we ask questions like this.

General   *What's it like?*
Size   *How big is it? How tall is it?* etc.
Age   *How old is it?*
Shape   *What shape is it?*
Colour   *What colour is it?*
Where from   *Where's it from?*
Material   *What's it made of?*

Unit 3

▶ Present continuous

(The Present continuous referring to a future arrangement is dealt with in Unit 5.)

We use the Present continuous to talk about:

1 An action which is in progress at the moment of speaking.
*I'll be there in a minute. **I'm talking** to someone on the phone at the moment.*

2 Something happening now or around now, which may change.
***I'm working** at home this week.* (But this is probably a temporary situation.)
Compare this with the use of the Present simple to talk about permanent facts or situations which are generally true.
*I **live in** London.* (This is my permanent home.)
***I'm living** in London.* (For a short time only.)

3 A trend, i.e. a changing or developing situation.
*More and more people **are working** at home these days.*
Compare this with the use of the Present simple to talk about traditions.
*Most people **drive** to work.* (A tradition.)
*Many people **are cycling** to work nowadays.* (A trend or new development).

4 A repeated action happening around now.
*Some British managers **are** regularly **working** until 10 or 11 o'clock at night.*

▶ Present perfect continuous

a Form

The Present perfect continuous is formed with *have* or *has* + *been* + verb *-ing* form.
*What **have** you **been doing** since we last met?*
***I've been repairing** my car.*
*She **hasn't been telling** the truth.*

b Uses

Like the Present perfect simple, the Present perfect continuous makes a connection between the past and the present. The Present perfect continuous refers to an action which started in the past and is still happening now.

1 It can refer to a single continuing activity or situation.
***We've been living** in Sydney for seven years now.*

2 It can refer to an activity which has been repeated over a period of time leading up to the present.
***He's been arriving** home late every night recently.*

3 It can be used with *for* and *since* to say how long.
*My **father's been working** for the same company for over forty years.*
***I've been studying** law since I was eighteen.*

c Present perfect simple or continuous?

1 The Present perfect simple describes completed actions.
*This week **I've written** three reports and **sent** over a hundred e-mails and faxes.*

2 The Present perfect continuous describes incomplete actions or actions which are still in progress.
***She's been writing** letters all morning.*
(And she has some more to write.)
***I've been waiting** to see him for over three hours.*
(And I still haven't seen him.)

Note Certain verbs are not usually used in the continuous form, or are not used in the continuous form when they have certain meanings.
I've known her for many years. (NOT *I've been knowing …*)
*How long **have** you **had** your computer?* (NOT *have you been having*)
Some others are:
believe hate (dis)like want look seem smell taste (dis)agree
be need own depend

▶ Word order: time and place words and phrases / adverbs of manner

a Time expressions

1 These are some commonly used time expressions.

for	*for* (over / more than / less than) *eight years*
since	*since 1996 / since this morning*
at	*at the moment / at night / at six o'clock*
in	*in the past / in the future / in September / in 1999*
during	*during the day / during the morning / during the afternoon / during the evening*
on	*on Monday / on 6th January*
after	*after dark / after work*
from	*from 9.00 a.m. to 5.00 p.m. / from June to December*
last / next	*week / month / year*

2 Expressions of time usually come at the end of a sentence, but can also come at the beginning.
*He starts works **at 10 o'clock in the evening**.*
***At the moment** he's an elephant keeper.*

b Place expressions

1 These are some examples of place expressions.

in	*in the park / in the garden / in the town centre*
at	*at the station / at the zoo / at the supermarket*
here / there	
opposite	*opposite the bank*
next to	*next to the cinema*
behind / in front of	*behind the theatre*
between	*between the shoe shop and the restaurant*

2 Expressions of place usually come towards the end of a sentence, but before time expressions.
*Andrew Hayton has worked **at Longleat** for over eight years.*
*Andrew works **in the park** from 8.30 a.m. to 4.00 p.m.*
*I've been working **in the garden** since lunchtime.*

3 Expressions of place can start a sentence when we want to emphasize location.
Behind the cinema *there's a car park.*
In the park *children were playing all kinds of games.*

c Adverbs of manner

We use an adverb of manner to say how an action is done.

1 Most adverbs of manner are formed by adding *-ly* to adjectives.

slowly	impatiently	carefully	neatly	smartly
politely	gratefully			

2 The adverb related to *good* is *well*.

3 The most usual position for adverbs of manner is after the verb or after the verb + object.
*He filled the application form in **neatly** … then waited **patiently** for the reply.*

Note Frequency adverbs (which tell us how often something happens) usually go before the main verb. *Brad **usually** wore jeans.* See Unit 1.

Unit 4

▶ Past continuous

We use the Past continuous:

1 to talk about a situation or event which was in progress at a specific time in the past.
***This time last year** my family and I **were travelling** around Australia.*

2 to refer to a past situation or event which was in progress when another shorter event happened.
*When the stewardess came down to check all the passengers were on board, everybody **was sitting** at the back.*
*When the train pulled into the station I **was crying** too.*
Sometimes the situation or event in progress is interrupted by another event.
*Carlos **was phoning** Antonio when I **arrived**.*
*I **was watching** TV when I **heard** a knock at the door.*

3 to talk about two continuous past actions which were happening at the same time.
*She **was hugging** me and she **was crying** at the same time.*

Note When one finished action follows another, we use the Past simple tense for both actions.
*When the bus **arrived** at his stop, Gianni **got off**.*
*Carlos **phoned** Antonio when I **arrived**.*

▶ Past perfect

a Form

The Past perfect is formed with *had* + Past participle.
*I **had decided**. (**I'd decided**.)*
*She **hadn't heard**.*

b Uses

1 To show which of two or more past events or situations happened first[1].
*When I **was**[2] eight I **had** already **decided**[1] on my future.*
*I **had not been**[1] abroad before I **went**[2] on the ski-trip to Austria.*
*They **had heard**[1] a lot about each other before they **met**[2].*

2 To explain the reason for an event or actions.
*The car stopped because **I'd forgotten** to fill up the petrol tank.*

3 With many adverbs, for example *already, just, never … before.*
*I wasn't hungry because I **had already eaten**.*
*When we arrived the plane **had just left**.*
*The boys **had never been** to the seaside **before**.*
The adverbs *already, just* and *never* usually go between *had* and the Past participle. The adverb *before* goes at the end of the sentence.

4 After many conjunctions, for example *when, after, as soon as, until.*
*I felt much better **after** I **had drunk** the water.*
As soon as she'd written *the letter she went out to post it.*

Note
1 When the sequence of past events is clear we often use the Past simple for both events.
*As soon as I **sat** down (had sat down), the phone **rang**.*
*I **threw** the letter away after I **read** (had read) it.*
2 Sometimes the meaning depends on the tense we use.
*When I was eight, I **decided** on my future.*
(At the age of eight I decided on my future.)
*When I was eight, I **had decided** on my future.*
(I decided on my future before the age of eight.)
*I **called** Tim when I **heard** the news.*
(I heard the news and then I called Tim.)
*I **had called** Tim when I **heard** the news.*
(I called Tim before I heard the news.)

▶ Time clauses and sequencers

a Time clauses

1 We use the conjunctions *as soon as, after, before, when, while* to show the relation between events in the subsidiary clause and events in the main clause.

subsidiary clause	main clause

As soon as *the balloon was inflated, everyone climbed in.*

*The balloon started to rise **when** the pilot turned on the gas burners.*

***While / when** the pilot was flying the balloon, he was talking to the lorry driver, who was following below.*

***Just before** we landed, he told us to crouch down and hold tight onto the ropes.*

***After** everyone had helped to deflate the balloon, it was rolled up.*

Notes
1   *As soon as* can be used instead of *when* to emphasize that one event happens immediately after another.
    *They stopped the tennis match **as soon as** it started to rain.*
2   Both *when* and *while* can be used when we want to show that two events happen at the same time.

2   Time clauses can come at the beginning or at the end of a sentence. When they come at the beginning, they are separated from the main clause by a comma.
    ***Before she went on the balloon trip**, Sara had to book.*
    *Sara had to book **before she went on the balloon trip**.*

3   We can use time clauses to talk about events in the present, future and past.
    ***When the pilot turns on the burners**, the balloon starts to rise.* (Present)
    ***When you go on a balloon trip**, you will probably get a certificate too.* (Future)
    ***When the pilot decided (had decided) we were high enough up**, he turned down the burners.* (Past)

Notes
1   We use the Present simple tense of the verb in the time clause to refer to both present and future events.
2   We use the Past simple or Past perfect tense in the time clause to refer to a past event.

b   Sequencers

1   We use sequence words and phrases to show the order in which a series of events happens.
2   Sequence words and phrases usually come at the beginning of a sentence but most of them can also come at the end. When they come at the beginning, they are separated from the rest of the sentence by a comma.
    ***First of all**, we took the balloon off the lorry.*
    *We took the balloon off the lorry **first of all**.*

Note   *Then* is not usually followed by a comma and often comes at the beginning of a clause or sentence.
*I got up and **then** I went downstairs.   I got up. **Then** I went downstairs.*

3   These groups of words are similar in meaning.
    First   Firstly   First of all   To start with
    Then   After that   Next   Later   Afterwards
    Finally   In the end

Note
Compare these.
After + noun   ***After my walk**, I wrote some letters.*
After + clause   ***After I'd been for a walk**, I wrote some letters.*
After that   *I went for a walk. **After that**, I wrote some letters.*
Afterwards   *I went for a walk. **Afterwards**, I wrote some letters.*

Unit 5

▶ The future – predictions, expectations, arrangements, intentions

a   *will* + infinitive without *to*

We use *will* to talk about predictions or expectations.
The negative form of *will* is *won't*.
*I expect things **will be** quieter at the end of the tourist season.*
*Do you think life **will be** less stressful in the future?*
*The world **won't be** very different in 20 years' time.*

Notes
1   We say: *I don't think life will be less stressful.*
    NOT ~~I think life won't be less stressful.~~
2   *Probably* and *definitely* come after *will* and before *won't*.
    *I'll **probably** stay in a hotel.*
    *They **definitely** won't be here before 6.00.*

b   *going to* + infinitive without *to*

We use *going to* to talk about intentions or plans.
***We're going to run** a bar in Puharras or Epilmilma.*
***I'm going to fly out** next month.*
***Are** you **going to see** Jane tomorrow?*
***I'm not going to tell** you. It's a secret.*

Note   We do not usually use *going to* with the verb *go*. We usually use the Present continuous.
I'm going to China next week. NOT ~~I'm going to go to China next week.~~

c   Present continuous

We use the Present continuous tense to talk about future actions or events which have already been arranged.
***We're going** back to Playa de Las Americas, where we were last year.*
***We're** even **staying** in the same apartment.*
***I'm meeting** my sister at 6.00 tomorrow.*

▶ *will* and *going to*: other uses

a   *will*

We also use *will* to talk about future facts and to make instant decisions, offers and promises.
1   Future facts
    *This **will be** the first hotel built on the island.*
2   Instant decisions
    *'Are you ready to order? The fish is very good.' 'OK, **I'll have** the fish.'*
3   Offers
    *'I don't have time to do this.' '**I'll do** it if you want.'*
4   Promises
    *'Let me know when you arrive.' 'Sure. **I'll phone** as soon as I get there.'*
    *'It's very important that you are at the meeting.' '**I'll be** there.'*

b *going to*

We use *going to* to make predictions which are based on present evidence or knowledge; something we already know or can see.

*It's clear that Eigg **is going to have** a bright future.*
*Look at those black clouds. **It's going to rain.***

▶ Articles

a The indefinite article, *a* / *an*

We use *a* / *an*:

1 to refer to something or someone for the first time.
   *Ana and Jake live in **a** block of flats in Ursynów.*
   *I've got **a** new car.*

2 to refer to a person or thing (but not a specific person or thing). The speaker or writer cannot or does not want to say which person they are referring to, or it does not matter.
   *They live in **a** small village.*
   *The woman next door brought round **a** cake.*

3 to classify; to say what someone or something is, or what someone does.
   *It's **an** apple.*
   *Jake, **an** American from Oregon, is **a** university lecturer.*

4 with some numbers.
   ***a** hundred   **a** thousand   **a** million   **a** billion*

   We use *a* before a noun which begins with a consonant sound, and *an* before a noun which begins with a vowel sound.
   ***a** city   **a** university*
   ***an** hour   **an** umbrella*

b The definite article, *the*

We use *the*:

1 to refer to something which has been mentioned before.
   *They bought a small house. **The** house has a big garden.*

2 when there is only one of something in a particular context.
   ***The** centre of London   **The** President of the United States*

3 in a superlative expression.
   ***The** biggest disadvantage of living here is …*

4 with names of oceans, seas, rivers, mountain ranges.
   ***the** Atlantic ocean   **the** Dead Sea   **the** River Vistula*
   ***the** Bieszczady mountains*

5 with the names of some countries and groups of islands.
   ***the** USA   **the** United Kingdom   **the** Dominican Republic*
   ***the** West Indies   **the** Seychelles*

6 with certain public buildings.
   *We go to **the** cinema or **the** theatre.*

7 to refer to something both the speaker and listener know about.
   ***The** party was good, wasn't it?*

c No article (Ø)

We do not use an article:

1 with plural countable nouns (when we are speaking generally).
   ***Temperatures** often fall below zero.*

2 with uncountable nouns (when we are speaking generally).
   *It's so nice to be close to **nature**.*
   ***Chocolate** is fattening.*

3 with names of towns, cities and most countries.
   *They live in **Warsaw**.*

4 with nouns for certain types of place.
   *Our children can walk to **school**.*
   *He can drive to **work**.*

5 with *by* and means of transport.
   *He can go by **underground**.*

Unit 6

▶ Permission, obligation, prohibition

a Permission: *can* / *can't*

1 We use *can* (+ infinitive without *to*) to express permission.
   *In Japan women **can get married** when they are sixteen.*
   *You **can leave** at any time you like.*

2 We use *can't* to talk about absence of permission.
   *Amish couples **can't get married** any time they like.*
   *You **can't go** in during the concert.*

b Obligation: *must, have to* / *don't have to*

1 We use *must* (+ infinitive without *to*) to talk about rules, laws and obligations.
   *They **must keep** them secret until July or August.*
   *All visitors **must have** a valid passport.*

2 We also use *have to* to refer to rules, laws and obligations. Sometimes there is no real difference between *must* and *have to*.
   *16-year-olds **have to have** their parents' permission to get married.*
   *16-year-olds **must have** their parents' permission to get married.*
   *You **have to be** here by 8.00 a.m.*
   *You **must be** here by 8.00 a.m.*
   Sometimes we use *have to* to show that the rules, laws and obligations were not made by us, but by somebody else.
   *I can't leave early. I **have to work** late. (The boss says so.)*
   *I **have to work** till 5.30 every day. (It's in my contract.)*
   We use the negative form of *have to* to talk about absence of obligation.
   *You **don't have to get married** in a church. (You can if you want to but it isn't a legal obligation.)*

c Prohibition: *mustn't*

We use *mustn't* to talk about prohibition.
*The couple **mustn't tell** anyone their plans.*
*You **mustn't take** photographs during the performance.*

Note Sometimes *can't* and *mustn't* express the same idea.
*In most countries you **can't marry** a blood relative.*
*In most countries you **mustn't marry** a blood relative.*

▶ Permission and obligation (2)

a *had to / didn't have to*

1 We use *had to* to talk about obligation in the past.
   They **had to** accept things.
   We **had to wear** a uniform at school.
2 We use *didn't have to* to talk about absence of obligation in the past.
   Nimu **didn't have to get** her parents' permission to marry.
   We **didn't have to do** sport if we felt ill.
3 The question is formed like a regular past tense verb.
   Did you **have to do** any housework when you lived at home?
   Did you **have to repeat** a year at school?

b *could / couldn't*

1 We use *could* to talk about permission in the past.
   They **could** only **marry** men that their parents had chosen for them.
   We **could go** home at lunchtimes.
2 We use *couldn't* to talk about absence of permission in the past.
   In Asha's day, women **couldn't choose** who they married.
   We **couldn't wear** jewellery at school.
3 The question is formed with *could* + subject + infinitive without *to*.
   Could you **come** home as late as you liked?
   Could you **wear** make-up at school?

c *must / mustn't, can / can't, have to / don't have to*

Future and past
As with all verbs, the present form can sometimes be used to talk about the future. Look at this table.

Present	Past	Future
must	had to	must / will have to
mustn't	—	mustn't
can / can't	could/ couldn't	can / can't; will / won't be able to
have to / don't have to	had to / didn't have to	have to / don't have to; will / won't have to

I really must go now.
I had to leave before I finished.
I must see him tomorrow, if I can.
I'll have to leave work early on Friday, but I can stay late tomorrow if you like.
You mustn't make a noise if you come back late.
If you go to Scotland next January, you'll be able to ski but you won't be able to go swimming.
There is no past form of *mustn't*.

▶ Indefinite pronouns

a Form

Some-, any-, no-, every- can combine with *-one, -body* and *-thing*, and with *-where*.

People	Things and actions	Places
someone / somebody	something	somewhere
anyone / anybody	anything	anywhere
everyone / everybody	everything	everywhere
no one (no-one) / nobody	nothing	nowhere

b Use

This follows the same rules as for *some, any* and *no*.
1 We use *some-*:
   • in affirmative sentences.
     If **someone** made fun of him, he just smiled.
   • in questions when we expect to get the answer *yes*.
     Why are you wearing your coat? Are you going **somewhere**?
   • in requests.
     Could you do **something** for me?
   • in offers.
     Would you like **something** to eat?
2 We use *any-*:
   • in negative sentences.
     We didn't really have **anything** in common any more.
   • in questions when we don't know whether the answer will be *yes* or *no*.
     Is there **anybody** else we should invite?
3 We use *no-*:
   • as an alternative to *not + any-*. *No-* is used with an affirmative verb.
     There's **nothing** for young people to do. (There isn't anything for young people to do.)
     There's **nowhere** to sit. (There isn't anywhere to sit.)
4 They are used with singular verbs.
   Everybody **needs** friends.
   Has anybody **got** any change?

Note You can use singular pronouns with these words.
*Everyone has a best friend when **he or she** is young.*
However, it is also common to use the plural form to avoid repetition of both masculine and feminine pronouns.
*Everyone has a best friend when **they** are young.*

5 We use *anybody* and *anyone* to talk about one (unknown) person, or no person in particular. We use *everybody* and *everyone* to talk about all the people in a particular situation.
   *Do you know **anybody** who can speak Polish?*
   (= do you know one person.)
   ***Everybody** in my family can speak Polish.* (= all the people.)
   ***Anyone** can buy food if they have enough money.*
   (= a person who has enough money can buy food.)
   ***Everyone** needs food and clean water to live.*
   (= all the people.)
6 When we use adjectives with these words they come afterwards.
   *Are you going **anywhere nice**?*
   *I know **something interesting**.*

Unit 7

► can / could

a Past, present and future

1 We use *can* to talk about the present or the future.
*I **can swim** 50 metres underwater.*
*We **can come** to your party tomorrow.*

2 *Could* can refer to the past, the present or the future.
*She **could read** when she was only three.*
*There's someone at the door. It **could be** my sister.*
*We **could go** to the cinema at the weekend.*

b Uses

1 Ability
*'**Can you ride** a horse?' 'No, I **can't**.'* (Present)
*I **could beat** my father at chess when I was 7.* (Past)

2 Possibility
*Smoking cigarettes **can cause** heart disease.*
(Definite possibility)
*There **could be** a lot of traffic on the roads this evening.*
(Speculation – present or future)

3 Permission
*'**Can / could* I borrow** your car for the evening?'*
(Present or future)
*'Yes, you **can**.' 'No, I'm sorry, you **can't**.'* (*could* is not possible)

4 Requests and offers
Can / could you **tell** me the time, please?* (Present or future)
Can / could I **help** you with that?* (Present or future)

Note* Some people consider *could* to be more formal and so more polite than *can*.

► can, could, may, might

a *can*

We use *can* to talk about something that is possible in general or in some cases.
*It **can rain** in England in August.*
*Laughing **can be** highly infectious.*

b *could, may, might*

1 We use *could, may* and *might* to express uncertainty about a particular situation in the present or future. There is no real difference in meaning between the three words; they all suggest the same degree of uncertainty.
*I'm not sure where Mark is – he **could / may / might be** in the library.* (Present situation)
*Take an umbrella with you because it **could / may / might rain**.* (Future situation)

2 In general *could, may* and *might* are used to express possibility, uncertainty or doubt. There is little difference in meaning between the three verbs, but *might* is a little less certain than *may* or *could*.
*'Have you seen Joe?' 'No, but he **may / might / could be** at work.'* (Present possibility)
*I haven't decided where to go next year. I **may / might go** to Canada.* (Future possibility)

► Relative clauses (1)

(Relative clauses (2) on p.136 looks at the relative pronouns *when, where, whose*, etc.)

a Relative clauses

1 Relative clauses are often used to link two or more pieces of information in one sentence and so avoid short repetitive sentences.
*Humphrey Bogart, **who** played the detective Philip Marlowe, was married to Lauren Bacall.*
Instead of:
Humphrey Bogart played the detective Philip Marlowe.
Humphrey Bogart was married to Lauren Bacall.

Note Relative clauses are used more often in writing than in speech.

2 There are two kinds of relative clauses: defining and non-defining.
Defining relative clauses give essential information which defines exactly which person or thing we are referring to.
*The actor **who first played the part of James Bond** was Sean Connery.*
Without the information in this relative clause the sentence has no meaning.
Non-defining relative clauses add extra non-essential information.
*Sean Connery, **who played the part of James Bond**, has a strong Scottish accent.*
The main sentence has a meaning without the relative clause.

Note Commas separate non-defining relative clauses from the rest of the sentence they are in.

3 Relative clauses start with a relative pronoun and contain a verb.
*Billy Connolly, **who comes from Scotland**, is a famous comedian.*

4 A relative clause can be in the middle or at the end of a sentence.
*The film **which made Leonardo diCaprio world-famous** was Titanic.*
*Titanic was the film **which made Leonardo diCaprio world famous**.*

5 Relative pronouns refer back to people or things which have already been mentioned.
In *Billy Connolly, who comes …*, the pronoun *who* refers to *Billy Connolly*.
In *The film which made Leonardo …* the pronoun *which* refers to *The film*.

b Relative pronouns

1 *Who* refers to people.
***Humphrey Bogart, who** played …*

2 *Which* refers to things.
***The film which** made Leonardo diCaprio …*

3 *That* can refer to people or things.
*I like being with **people that** make me laugh.*
*There's **the car that** nearly knocked me down.*

Unit 8

► Reported speech (1): statements

a Direct speech and reported speech

1 Direct speech = the actual words someone uses when they speak.
 '*My name's Jean. I work in a bank.*'

2 Reported speech = the words we use to tell someone what another person has said. We don't use exactly the same words.
 She said **her** *name* **was** *Jean and she* **worked** *in a bank.*

b Differences between direct and reported speech

- Verbs

1 We often move the tense of the verb back in time, for example from present to past. This happens when we report someone's words some time after they have spoken.

Direct	Reported
Present simple	**Past Simple**
'I **live** in a flat in the town centre.'	He said he **lived** in a flat in the town centre.
Present continuous	**Past continuous**
'**I'm learning** to drive.'	She said she **was learning** to drive.
Present perfect	**Past perfect**
We've finished work early.	They said they **had finished** work early.
Past Simple	**Past perfect**
'I **arrived** at 10.00 a.m.'	She said she **had arrived** at 10.00 a.m.
will / won't future	**would**
'**I'll / I won't see** you on Friday.'	You said **you'd / you wouldn't see** me on Friday.
can / can't	**could / couldn't**
'I **can't wait** to get home.'	He said he **couldn't wait** to get home.

2 The verb tense does not have to change when the information we are reporting is still true.
 '**I'm learning** to drive.'
 → She said **she's learning** to drive.
 '*I* **saw** *him yesterday.*'
 → She said she **saw** him yesterday.
 The verb tense also does not change when the reporting verb is in the present tense.
 '*I'm learning to drive.*'
 → She **says** she's learning to drive.

- Pronouns

1 *I* changes to *he* or *she*.
 '*I feel tired.*'
 → He said **he** felt tired.

2 *We* changes to *they*.
 '**We're** *going soon.*'
 → They said **they** were going soon.

3 *You* changes to *I*.
 '**You** *don't look very well.*'
 → He said **I** didn't look very well.

4 Object pronouns also change.
 '*I'll give* **you** *a ring.*'
 → She said she'd give **me / us** a ring.
 '*They're coming to see* **me** *soon.*'
 → He / She said they were coming to see **him / her** soon.

- Time references
 References to time change when we report words at a different time.

Direct	Reported
next week / year, etc.	**the following** week / year the week / year **after**
last month / year	**the previous** month / year the month / year **before**
tomorrow	the next / following day
yesterday	the day before / the previous day
now	then / at that time
a week **ago**	a week **earlier / before**

- Place references
 References to place change when you are reporting words from a different place.

here	there
to come	to go

► Reported speech (2): questions

a Differences between direct and reported questions

1 We make the same changes to verb tenses, pronouns and time and place references as we do when we report statements.
 '**Can you come** to **my** party **next** weekend?' he asked.
 → He asked if **I could go** to **his** party **the following** weekend.

2 The word order in reported questions is the same as the word order in statements. The subject is after the verb.
 '*What* **have you done***?*' she asked.
 → She asked what **I had done**.

3 The auxiliary verbs *do / does / did* are not used in reported questions.
 '*Where* **do you live***?*' he asked.
 → He asked me where **I lived**.
 '*What time* **did you get up***?*' she asked.
 → She asked what time **I got up**.

b Different types of question

1 When we report *Wh-* questions we use the same question word(s).
 '**Why** *are you here?*' she asked.
 → She asked **why** I was there.
 '**How much** *do you earn?*' they asked.
 → They wanted to know **how much** I earned.

2 When we report *Yes / No* questions we need to add *if* or *whether*.
'Would you like a coffee?' she asked.
→ She asked **if / whether** I'd like a coffee.
'Are you going abroad for your holiday?' he asked.
→ He asked **whether / if** we were going abroad for our holiday.

▶ Expressing quantities

a Small quantities

- *few / a few*
1 *Few* and *a few* are followed by plural nouns.
Few people came to the match but millions watched on TV.
I'm going out with **a few friends** this evening.
2 *Few*, *a few* and *many* can also be followed by *of* + determiner + plural noun.
A few of my friends like classical music, but most of them prefer jazz.
3 *Few* means not many or hardly any. This sound negative.
A few means some or a small number. This sounds neutral or positive.

Note The expression *quite a few* means a surprising number, the same as *quite a lot*.

- *little / a little*
1 *Little* and *a little* are followed by uncountable* nouns.
We'd better hurry. There is **little time** left.
I've still got **a little** more **work** to do.
2 *A little* can also be followed by *of* + article + uncountable* noun.
I spent **a little of the money** on books.
A little means some or a small quantity. This sounds neutral or positive.
3 *Little* means not much or hardly any. This sounds negative.
You've got **little chance** of getting that job. Lots of people have applied for it.

*A countable noun is a noun which has a plural form. *Student(s) / computer(s)*
*An uncountable noun has no plural form, because it refers to something which we see as a 'mass', not as individual things. *Time / money / water*

b Large quantities

- *many / much*
1 *Many* is followed by a plural noun.
I don't get **many headaches**.
2 *Much* is followed by an uncountable noun.
We haven't got **much time**.
How **much money** have you got?
3 *Many* and *much* can also be followed by *of*.
Many of the people who were at university with me now work abroad.
How **much of your time** do you spend working?
4 *Many* means a large number.
Much means a large quantity.

5 *Many* and *much* are more often used in negative sentences and in questions than in affirmative statements.
How many birthday presents did you get?
I **didn't get much** sleep last night.

- *a lot of / lots of*
1 *A lot of* and *lots of* can be followed by a plural countable noun or an uncountable noun.
I've got **lots of time**.
A lot of my friends play tennis.
2 In affirmative statements, *a lot of* is usually used instead of *much* or *many*.
He had **a lot of** money.
She always meets **a lot of** people when she travels.
3 *Lots of* is more informal than *a lot of*.

- *plenty of*
1 *Plenty of* can be followed by a plural countable noun or an uncountable noun.
I'll pay for the drinks. I've got **plenty of money** with me
It's a great place for a holiday. There are **plenty of things** to do.
2 *Plenty of* means as much or as many as you need for a particular purpose.

- *some*
1 *Some* can be followed by a plural countable noun or an uncountable noun.
Some people have never used an answerphone.
Can you lend me **some money**?
2 *Some* means an unspecified quantity, not all.

Unit 9

▶ Conditional sentences (1)

(There are four common types of conditional sentences: zero, first, second and third.
- Zero and first conditional sentences: notes in this section.
- Second conditional sentences: notes on p.135.
- Third conditional sentences: notes on p.138.)

a Zero conditional

1 Zero conditional sentences are formed like this.
If + present, → present OR Present → *if* + present
If I **wake up** early, I **have** a cup of tea and **read** the newspaper.
I **walk** to work **if** it **isn't raining**.
2 Zero conditional sentences say what is usually true or always happens under certain conditions.
If it rains, I drive to work. (I always do this when it rains. This happens quite regularly.)
If you eat too much, you get fat. (This is generally true.)
3 In some zero conditional sentences we could say *when* or *whenever* instead of *if*.
When / whenever it rains, I drive to work.

b First conditional

1 First conditional sentences are formed like this.
If + present ➔ future with *will / may* OR
Future with *will / may* ➔ *if* + present
He **won't go** to work **if** he **feels** ill.
If I **don't feel** well, I **may go** and see the doctor.
If I **miss** the bus, **I'll take** a taxi.
You **may be** late **if** you **don't go** now.

2 First conditional sentences say what will or may happen in the future under certain conditions. *May* is less certain than *will*.
He **won't go** to work if he feels ill. (It is possible in the future that he will feel ill. Under these conditions he will not go to work – this is certain.)
If I don't feel well, I **may go** and see the doctor. (It is possible in the future that I will not feel well. Under these conditions I may or I may not go and see a doctor. I am not sure.)

▶ Conditional sentences (2)

Second conditional

a Form

Second conditional sentences are formed like this.
If + past ➔ *would / might* OR
would / might ➔ *if* + past
If I **felt** ill, I **would / might stop** smoking.
He **might lend** you some money **if** you **asked** him.

b Uses

1 Future
One use of the second conditional is to say what would or might happen in the future under certain conditions. We use the second conditional, not the first conditional, when we think that these conditions are improbable or unlikely. *Might* is less certain than *would*.
I **would** stop smoking if I felt ill. (It is possible that I will feel ill in the future, but I think it is improbable. Under these conditions, I would stop smoking. I am sure about this.)
If you asked him, he **might** lend you some money. (I know it is unlikely that you will ask him for money, but if you asked him, it is possible that he might lend you some money. I am not sure.)

2 Present
Another use of the second conditional is to say how things would or might be different under certain unreal or impossible conditions in the present.
If I were younger, I'd play squash. (I can never be younger than I am now, so this is an impossible condition. I am imagining this situation. Because of this I probably won't play squash.)
I'd buy a Rolls Royce car if I had a lot of money. (I do not have a lot of money and I will probably never have a lot of money, so I will never be able to buy a Rolls Royce.)

3 We can use *could* instead of *would be able to*.
If you were 18 you **could vote** in the election.

4 If I were
In formal and informal speech, we can use *were* instead of *was* in second conditional *if* clauses.
If I **were** you, I'd look for a new job.
If my brother **were** a teacher, he'd be very popular with the students.
Were is more common than *was* in formal writing.

▶ Expressing purpose and reason

Purpose and reason expressions both answer the question *Why?* Purpose expressions look forward and express an intention; reason expressions look backward and give an explanation.

a Purpose

1 *to* + infinitive
I came here **to see** you.
He emptied his pockets **to show** that he wasn't carrying a gun.

Note There is no negative form of this. We cannot say
~~I stopped smoking not to damage my baby's health.~~

2 *in order (not) to* + infinitive
He drove fast **in order to get** to the airport on time.
In order not to wake me he closed the door quietly.

3 *so as (not) to* + infinitive
I listen to the news **so as to find out** what's going on.
I stopped smoking **so as not to damage** my baby's health.

4 *so (that)* + clause
People wear gloves **so their hands don't get cold**.
I am leaving early **so that I don't get caught in the traffic**.

b Reason

1 *because* + clause
He had an accident **because he fell asleep in the car**.

2 *because of* + noun
The match was cancelled **because of the rain**.

3 *as* + clause
As I was feeling exhausted, I went to bed early.
I got up early, **as I couldn't sleep**.

Notes
1 *As* is often used to start a sentence. We use *as* when the reason is not as important as the rest of the sentence. Where the reason is important or surprising, we use *because*.
2 *As* also means while.
As I was walking home, I met someone I was at school with.

Unit 10

▶ Passive and active verb forms

a Introduction

1 In active sentences the person or thing who does the action is the subject.
Thousands of people play football on Sunday mornings.
The action is *play*. The subject is *Thousands of people*.

2 In passive sentences the person or thing that is affected by the action is the subject.
Football is played on Sunday mornings.
The action is *play*. The person or thing affected by the action is *Football*.

3 When we use the passive we can choose to include the agent or not. The agent is the person or thing who does the action.
Football is played by thousands of people on Sunday mornings.

b Form

The passive is formed with a tense of the verb *be* + the past participle of the main verb.
Present simple
*Our cat **is fed** twice a day.*
Past simple
*Our house **was built** in 1980.*

c Use

We choose the passive rather than the active when we are more interested in the person or thing that is affected by an action (the object of an active sentence) than in the person or thing that did the action (the subject of an active sentence).
My car was made in Germany. (In this sentence my car is more important than the company or the factory workers who made the car.)
My house was built in 1950. (It is not important who built the house.)

▶ Passive verb forms (2)

a Form

The passive is formed with the appropriate part of the verb *be* and the past participle.
Present continuous
*Many large houses **are being turned** into flats.*
Past continuous
*When I turned on the TV, a taxi driver **was being interviewed**.*
Present perfect
*Six people **have been injured** in a road accident.*
will future
*The new city hall **will be opened** by the President.*

Modal verbs
The passive of modal verbs is formed with the modal verb + *be* + the past participle.
*This recipe **can be made** in 10–15 minutes.*
*Drunk drivers **should be fined** and **banned** from driving.*

b Use

The main reason for choosing the passive is always that we are more interested in the person or thing affected by the action than the person or thing that did the action. (See c Use opposite.)

c Agent

The agent follows the passive verb and is introduced by *by*.
*Our cat is fed **by my brother** twice a day.*
*Our house was built in 1980 **by a large building company**.*

We do not use the agent in a passive sentence when:

1 we do not know or do not want to say who did the action.
Our house was built in 1980. (The house was built by unknown builders.)
The police were told where the thief lived. (The identity of the person who told the police is secret or unknown.)

2 the agent is unimportant or no one in particular.
This recipe can be made in 10–15 minutes. (Anyone or everyone can do this.)

3 the person or thing that did the action is obvious.
Drunk drivers should be fined and banned from driving. (Everyone knows that law-courts or judges punish people who do wrong.)

Notes
1 We often use the passive to describe processes because it shows we are more interested in the process itself than in the person doing it.
2 In a text, we use the passive to make a connection between sentences, to keep the same subject at the end of one sentence and the beginning of the next one.
I am reading an interesting book. It was written by Jane Austen.
(NOT *Jane Austen wrote the book.*)
One of the greatest medical developments this century is penicillin. It was discovered by Alexander Fleming.

▶ Relative clauses (2)

(Relative clauses (1) in Unit 7 introduced these aspects of relative clauses.
• The position of relative clauses: in the middle or at the end of a sentence.
• Relative pronouns: *who, which, that*
• The differences between defining and non-defining relative clauses.)

where, whose, why, when

1 *Where* refers to a place and means *in which* or *at which*.
*The town **where** I live is not far from the motorway.* (defining)
*Chester, **where** I was born, is in the north of England.* (non-defining)

2 *Whose* has a possessive meaning. It links a person with something that is theirs.
*The people **whose** house I am renting are on holiday in France.* (The house belongs to the people.)
Whose can also relate to animals and things.
*I am looking after a cat **whose** owners are away.*
*The company, **whose** workers are very well paid, has factories all over the world.*

3 *Why* refers to a reason and often follows the word 'reason'.
The reason **why** *I got up so early is that I couldn't sleep.*
(*I couldn't sleep* is the reason and *I got up so early* is the situation that needs an explanation.)
The word 'reason' is often left out.
I couldn't sleep. That's **why** *I got up so early.*

4 *When* refers to a time.
I remember the day **when** *we first met.*
The shops are usually very quiet between 12 and 2 o'clock, **when** *people are having their lunch.*

Unit 11

▶ have and get

a *have*

Have can have different meanings.

1 possess or own and other related meanings
Do *people* **have** *microwaves?*
She **has** *beautiful hair.*
He **has** *a great sense of humour.*
I **have** *one sister.*
I **have** *a terrible headache.*

2 experience
'**I'm having** *problems understanding these instructions.*'
'*You always* **have** *problems.*'
We **had** *a great time at the party.*

3 eat or drink
A lot of people just **have** *a sandwich for lunch.* **I'm having** *a cheese sandwich for lunch today.*
I usually **have** *a glass of milk for breakfast.*

4 take
I think **Jack's having** *a shower. He usually* **has** *one before he goes out.*
When I'm short of time, I **have** *a quick wash.*

5 need to
You don't **have to** *do much washing up afterwards.*
Alan is **having to** *work late all this week.*
With this meaning, *have* is followed by *to* + infinitive.

Note When *have* means to possess or own we do not use it in the continuous form. The other meanings of *have* can be used in both simple and continuous forms.

b *get*

Get also has different meanings.

1 receive
I **got** *it for Christmas.*
I **got** *two letters last week.*

2 obtain / buy
More and more people **are getting** *microwaves.*
What grade **did** *you* **get** *in the exam?*

3 become
It's getting *dark.*
Is it because the average American **is getting** *lazier?*

c *have got*

1 *Have got* can be used instead of *have* in the present tense when *have* means:
   a possess or own and other related meanings
   I've got *a new camera.*
   She's got *two younger brothers.*
   He's got *a terrible cold.*
   In informal English, *have got* is more usual than *have*.
   b need to
   I can't stay. **I've got to** *go.*
   She's got to *leave early tomorrow.*

2 The question form is *Have (you) got (to) ..?*
   Have *you* **got to** *leave now?*
   Has she got *any brothers and sisters?*

3 The past tense of *have got* is *had*.
   The last time I saw you, you **had** *long hair.*

Note Do not confuse this with the perfect forms of *get* (*have / had got*).

▶ have something done

a Use

1 We use the structure *have something done* when we want to show that another person did the action for the subject.
Anthony **had a tattoo done** *on his left arm.*
I **have my hair cut** *every six weeks.*
You can **have your photographs developed** *here.*

b Form

1 The structure is formed with *have* (in all tenses)+ object + past participle.
She's had her ears pierced.
The word order is very important.

	have	object	past participle
Julia	has	her hair	cut every six weeks.
I	had	my car	repaired yesterday.
They	have never had	their flat	painted.
She	is going to have	a dress	made.

2 Compare these sentences.
Past simple form of *have something done*
I **had my ears pierced** *when I was 16.*
Past perfect
I **had pierced** *my ears before I was 16.*
In the second sentence *I* did the action; in the first sentence someone else did it for me.

c *have* or *get*?

We sometimes use *get* instead of *have*.

1 We often use *get* in informal English, although we can also use *have*.
I **get my hair cut** *when it starts to annoy me.*

2 We usually use *have* in formal English.
Most hairdressers recommend that people should **have their hair trimmed** *every 6–8 weeks.*

3 We often use *get* when we want to show that the action is urgent.
I really must **get my hair cut**. *It looks awful!*

4 We must use *get* in the imperative.
   Get your hair cut!

5 In the Present perfect we can only use *have*.
   Have you had your hair cut? NOT ~~Have you got your hair cut?~~

▶ so and *such*

So and *such* are used to add emphasis to adjectives and adverbs.

a *so*

1 *so* + adjective or adverb (without a noun)
   Modelling had always looked **so glamorous** *on TV.*
   Don't speak **so quickly!** *I can't understand you.*

2 *so* + *much* (+ adjective) + uncountable noun
   Top models earn **so much money** *nowadays that they can choose who they work for.*
   I can't eat **so much food.**

3 *so* + *many* (+ adjective) + plural countable noun
   So many *young* **girls** *don't make it to the top.*
   I don't know why you have **so many clothes**

b *such*

1 *such* + adjective + uncountable noun
   I had no idea that modelling was **such hard work.**
   This is **such good coffee!**

2 *such* + adjective + countable plural noun
   I had no idea that I'd have to work **such long hours.**
   You have **such lovely eyes!**

3 *such* + *a / an* + adjective + singular countable noun
   It really is **such a difficult career** *to break into.*
   We had **such a good holiday.**

c *so / such* + *that* clause

We can express the result or consequence of one action or situation in a *so / such* + *that* clause.
(Situation) *Top models earn a lot of money nowadays.*
(Consequence) *They can choose who they work for.*
Top models earn **so much money nowadays that they can choose who they work for.**
(Situation) *She was very tired.*
(Consequence) *She went straight to bed.*
She was **so tired that she went straight to bed.**

▌Unit 12

▶ Advice

We often give advice using the following verbs and phrases.

a *should* (+ infinitive without *to*)

   You **should** *just* **do** *it, go for it.*
   She **shouldn't apologize.**
   Should *she* **tell** *him?*

Note the difference in meaning between *should* and *must*.
You **should speak** *to your father.* = it's a good idea (advice)
You **must speak** *to your father.* = it's essential (obligation)
Should is quite a direct way of giving advice.

b *ought to* (+ infinitive without *to*)

   I think you **ought to consider** *doing a self-improvement course.*
   He **ought not to tell** *his boss.*
   Ought I to send *in a written application?*

Note The question and negative forms of *ought to* are not usually used in British English. We prefer *should*.

c *If I were you* (*him*, etc.), + *would* (+ infinitive without *to*)

   If I were you, I would put *your plans on hold for now.*
   If I were you, I wouldn't do *anything.*
   If you were me, would you apply *for the job?*

Note We often miss out *If I were you*. 'What would you do?' 'I'd stay at home.'

d *Why don't you ...* (+ infinitive without *to*)

   Why don't you read *one of the books there are on the subject?*
   Why don't you look *for another job?*
   Why don't you ... is a less direct way of giving advice.

e Opinion words

1 We sometimes put phrases like *I think* before an advice verb.
   I think *you should think carefully before you do anything.*

2 The negative form of *I think you should* is *I don't think you should.*
   I don't think you should *go.*

▶ Conditional sentences (3)

(For zero and first conditional, see p.134 and p.135. For the second conditional, see p.135.)

a Use

We use the third conditional to describe imagined past situations and the consequences of these imagined situations. These consequences and situations are the opposites of what happened.
If I hadn't been ill, I would have gone. (I wanted to go but I was ill so I couldn't go.)
If I had gone to bed late, I would have been tired. (I didn't go to bed late so I'm not tired.)

b Form

1 The third conditional is formed with
   If + Past perfect, ➜ *would* + *have* + past participle OR *would* + *have* + past participle ➜ *if* + Past perfect
   If I had (I'd) seen *John, I* **would have told** *him.*
   If Dave had not (hadn't) invited *me, I* **would not (wouldn't) have come.**
   What **would** *you* **have done if you had (you'd) overslept?**

2 The *if-* clause can come before or after the main clause. If the *if-* clause comes first, it is separated from the main clause by a comma.
Tracey's relationship wouldn't have ended if she hadn't spent all her free time with her team-mates.
If Lou Ryde's boyfriend hadn't forced her to choose between football and him, she probably wouldn't have spilt up with him.

▶ all, both, either, neither, none

a *all*

1 *All* refers to a whole group of more than two people or things. It is used with plural nouns and uncountable nouns.
All students *hate exams.*
All homework *should be handed in on time.*

2 There is a difference in meaning between *all* + noun and *all* + *the* + noun.
All students *hate exams.* (Students in general hate exams.)
All the students *hate exams.* (A specific group of students hates exams.)

3 We can express the same idea in different ways.
All the students *studied hard for the exam.*
All of them *studied hard for the exam.*
The students all *studied hard for the exam.*

b *both*

1 *Both* refers to two people or things. It is used with plural nouns and means A and B.
Both students *were exceptionally bright.* (Robert was bright and Philip was bright.)

2 We can express the same idea in different ways.
Both (the) students *did badly in the exam.*
Both of them *did badly in the exam.*
The students both *did badly in the exam.*

3 *Both* cannot be used in a negative sentence. To express a negative idea, we must use *neither* with a positive verb.
Neither of those exams was / were *difficult.*
NOT ~~*Both those exams weren't difficult.*~~

c *none*

1 *None* also refers to a group of more than two people or things. It is the opposite of *all*. If it is followed by a noun, we use *none of* + *the*; if it is followed by a pronoun, we use *none of*.
None of the people *I studied with enjoyed doing exams.*
None of them *thought that the exam system was fair.*

2 In formal English, *none* is followed by a singular verb. In informal English, we often use a plural verb.
None of us **was listening** *to the music.* (Formal)
None of us **were listening** *to the music.* (Informal)

d *neither*

1 *Neither* refers to two people or things and means not A and not B.
Neither *of them got an A grade.* (Robert didn't get an A grade and Philip didn't get an A grade.)

2 *Neither* is used with a singular noun.
Neither **exam** *was difficult.*

3 *Neither* is also used with *of the* + plural noun, or *of* + pronoun. In this form you can use a singular or plural verb.
Neither of the exams was / were *difficult.*
Neither of us knows / know *the answer.*

4 We use *neither … nor* to name the two people or things we are talking about.
Neither *Luke* **nor** *Jake is coming to the party.*

e *either*

1 *Either* refers to two people or two things and means A or B.
We can **either** *go home* **or** *go out somewhere.*
Kate didn't pass **either exam**. (She didn't pass her History exam or her Chemistry exam.)

2 *not … either* can sometimes be used as an alternative to *neither … nor*. *Either* is the last word in the sentence.
Neither Robert nor Philip had bothered to study these areas.
Robert **had**n't *bothered to study these areas and Philip* **had**n't **either**.

Tapescripts

Speaker 1
Yeah – smoking. The thing is I gave up nearly a year ago, but I sometimes take cigarettes from other people instead of simply saying 'No thanks, I don't smoke any more.'

Speaker 2
Showers. I usually spend at least half an hour in the shower, just enjoying it. But I know it's a terrible waste of water – that's why I feel guilty.

Speaker 3
I occasionally go to sleep in front of the TV instead of doing more important things like helping the kids with their homework or tidying the house. The worst time is when you fall asleep and wake up at about three in the morning and you've completely wasted the whole evening.

Speaker 4
Yes – it's something I enjoy doing 'cos it makes my life easier – I always drive to work and I feel guilty about it, for obvious reasons, you know, because using a car in the city is generally a bad thing – it causes pollution. These days I never walk, not even on warm sunny days. I mean I feel guilty about driving, but I still do it.

Speaker 5
Buying expensive shoes – I've got funny feet and the only comfortable shoes I can find are really expensive. Well, you see, they last for ages – so I hardly ever buy new shoes. Well, that's my excuse, anyway.

Speaker 6
Surfing the Internet on my Dad's computer. I don't often do it and it's usually pretty cheap – but I feel guilty because Dad doesn't know I found out his password.

Speaker 7
Spending ages on the phone. The thing is, I ring my boyfriend two or three times a week when my parents are out, even though they're pretty hard up and can't afford high phone bills.

Speaker 8
That's easy – secretly buying chocolate. I buy a bar every day when I'm on my way home from college. I just feel so tired – I really need the sugar – then, when it's all gone, I feel terrible.

1.2

Speaker 1
My ideal holiday erm, my ideal holiday would be one where I forget completely about work, I think, er and one where I had as much money to spend as I wanted – that would be really good. Erm, every time I've been on holiday so far erm I've always been restricted in what I can do, erm, because I haven't got enough, enough money, so yeah, I think I could go anywhere and be happy if I had enough money to spend when I was there.

What kind of things would you do?

Erm, I dunno – I love the countryside so I think I'd do quite a lot of touring – erm, I'd like to eat in some nice restaurants and er I've never swum er in the sea because the sea in England, er the sea around England is so cold, so I'd love to go somewhere where I could swim in the sea – that would be great.

Speaker 2
A perfect holiday for me is is going to places of erm natural beauty – erm, I quite like the idea of – I would love to go to places like the Grand Canyon so, that would be my perfect holiday but not as a package tour – I would, I would sort of go ideally with friends and you know we would do things in our own time and sort of stay in in hotels just as they sort of come along but and the important thing is not to spend a massive amount of money either.

Speaker 3
My ideal holiday would be, erm, some kind of mixture of relaxing on a beach, doing some kind of strenuous activity like er, walking in the mountains or something a little bit adventurous, er I'd also, probably I'd also want some sort of culture, like er, galleries or ancient monuments or something similar and food – it would have to have good food, erm so I'd want to go somewhere where I could do something relaxing, er something cultural, something a bit strenuous and a bit challenging, and somewhere where I could experience erm the local food and drink and a little bit of the local culture.

Speaker 4
A perfect holiday, erm I think something where everything was organized for me, all my food was cooked, everything was planned and I didn't have to think about anything at all.

Somewhere warm but not too hot, somewhere near the sea, near water of some kind – I don't want to bake in the sun, but I don't want to spend all the time lying on a beach either.

I would like to look at wildlife somewhere – go to somewhere different and look at the wildlife – Africa – that would be quite a good thing because it's all very different but somewhere near the coast as well – East Africa I think that would be rather nice.

1.3

1 I When were you born?
   A On the 23rd of December 1976 – it was a Friday.
2 I How long have you worked here?
   A For nearly two years, now. Before that I worked for a Japanese computer company.
3 I Do you like your job?
   A Yes, I do. The pay is good and the people I work with are really friendly. It's like one big happy family here.
4 I How much do you earn?
   A I'm sorry, but that's my business, but it's certainly better than my last job, so I'm not complaining.
5 I Are you married?
   A No, not yet, but I will be this time next year. The wedding is fixed for June 21st.
6 I What does your girlfriend do?
   A She's an assistant editor on the local newspaper.
7 I What does she look like?
   A She's short and slim with dark hair and she sometimes wears glasses.
8 I Are you planning to have any children?
   A Sorry, I'd rather not answer that if you don't mind. It's too far in the future. Let's just say neither of us is quite ready yet.
9 I What do you do in your spare time?
   A I play the bass guitar in a rock band, I go to concerts, the cinema. I do all kinds of things, erm – I'm quite keen on sport.
10 I Do you do any sports yourself?
   A Yes, I do. Tennis in the summer and basketball all the year round.

2.1

Interview 1
I What do you remember about family outings when you were young?

M Well, my father was a keen photographer and because of that he used to drive all over the country looking for pretty views to photograph while my mum, my sister and I sat in the car, bored stiff.
I I can imagine.
M The worst thing was that he only wanted to take photographs when the sun was out, which wasn't, unfortunately, most of the time. So the three of us used to sit there praying for the sun to come out from behind a cloud so that we could get on our way.
I Right.
M The only problem was that we were on our way to the next photograph, the next cloud and the next wait in the car.
I Oh dear!

Interview 2
I When you were younger, how did you use to spend the summer holiday?
F We always spent our summer holiday as a family and every year we went to the same place – a small seaside town on the north coast of Spain called Laredo. Do you know it?
I No, I don't.
F Well, everyone there could speak English so there wasn't really any need for us to speak Spanish, but my father insisted on speaking it at every opportunity. The awful thing was that no one could understand him because he used to invent words – add an 'a' or an 'o' to an English word and think that that made it Spanish. Anyway, when we were first there, it didn't use to bother me because I didn't speak Spanish myself at that time. But then I started learning it at school and I realized just how bad his Spanish was.
I A bit embarrassing, yeah?
F Yeah, it was. We used to eat out a lot and I hated that because I was sure that all the waiters and other people in the restaurant were laughing at him. And I remember on one occasion he said something extremely rude and he didn't even realize. It was so embarrassing.
I I can imagine.

2.2

Speaker 1
On my last birthday I decided that I wasn't going to go out with loads of friends erm as I normally do. Erm, I think it was on a Friday and erm I went out with my boyfriend and I think we went for a quiet meal somewhere, and then probably just went home and watched television like we normally do.

Speaker 2
My last birthday was about two weeks ago and I celebrated it in France. It was very special because we were on holiday and my children brought me a cake and they brought me some presents ... and well they all sat on the bed ... and they sat around whilst I opened my presents.

Speaker 3
My last birthday? Erm, I've just had my last birthday. It was yesterday. My twenty-fifth. Oh, what did I do? Can't remember! No. I went out with some mates for a few drinks. We went on to a club. I got to bed late. I've got a bit of a hangover today so it must have been good.

Speaker 4
It's my boyfriend's birthday next week, actually. He's 30 on Saturday, which is a bit special, so I've organized a party for him. It's supposed to be a surprise party but I'm not sure if I'll be able to keep it a secret for much longer. I've hired a room above a

pub and there's going to be a live band playing. Er, I'm not sure how many people will come. I sent out 30 or so invitations last week and er, I've sent out the same number this week. I'm not sure if everyone'll be able to come, but it should be good anyway.

Speaker 5
My last birthday was my favourite birthday because I had five of my friends round and we went bowling and then we had a birthday tea afterwards and we played twister and and ate lots of popcorn.

2.3

I As you all know tomorrow is April 1st – April Fool's Day. So we thought it would be a nice idea to invite someone along to tell us a bit more about this festival. And to do just that we have Professor Stephen Pennington from the University of Hull. Good afternoon, Professor Pennington, and thank you for coming.

P Not at all. Good afternoon.

I Can I start by asking you a personal question, professor?

P By all means.

I Will you yourself be playing a joke on anyone tomorrow?

P But of course. That's the whole point of April Fool's Day.

I But isn't April Fool's Day more for children? I remember when I was young I always played jokes on my parents and my teachers on April 1st. The plastic fried egg on the breakfast plate – that sort of thing. But isn't it something people grow out of?

P Yes and no. Some adults get just as involved as children, believe me. You see, it's the one day in the year when you're allowed and even expected to be silly. And in the workplace it gives people the ideal opportunity to play a trick on their boss which they'd probably get the sack for any other day of the year.

I I see. So tell me, is April Fool's Day only celebrated in Britain?

P No, not at all. It's celebrated in many other European countries apart from Britain, though not always on April 1st. People have celebrated the festival for hundreds of years. It's actually believed to be linked to the ancient Roman festival of Hilaria.

I I didn't know that.

P Oh yes, although some people think it might have some connection with the spring Holi festival in India.

I I see. Tell us some April Fool jokes.

P Well, one of the best in my opinion was in the early sixties in England. In 1962, I think it was, a television company showed a short documentary film about spaghetti farming in Italy.

I Spaghetti farming?

P Yes. They showed villagers climbing up ladders and picking strings of spaghetti off the trees.

I They didn't.

P Yes, and the best thing was that they received hundreds of letters from viewers the next day asking how to grow spaghetti. That still makes me laugh.

I Amazing.

P Another good one was in the 70s in Holland when a Dutch newspaper announced on its front page that they had printed the paper with perfumed ink. Apparently loads of people were seen secretly sniffing their newspapers that day.

I What will they think of next? Well, I'm afraid we'll have to stop there Professor Pennington. Thank you. That's been both amusing and interesting.

P My pleasure.

2.4

A Have you finished answering the questions yet?

J Er, just a minute.

N Just finishing. OK.

A Right 'How to score'. OK. The scores are different for men. Right Nick? You'd better make a note of it.

N Yep.

A 'Men score: a: ten points; b: five points; c: minus five points.'

N Minus five points?

A Yeah. Ten points for a; five points for b and minus five points for c. Got that?

N Yeah.

J What about mine?

A Right. 'Women score: a: fifteen points; b: five points; c: minus five points.'

J a: fifteen; b: five and c: minus five.

A Uh huh.

J Why are the men's and women's scores different?

A Don't know. It doesn't say. OK. Are you ready to find out what your score means?

N/J Just a minute.
Hang on a minute.

2.5

A Right. What did you get Nick?

N I'm not saying till you tell me what it means.

A OK. It says 'Most men will score between 0 and 60. Most women will score between 50 and 100.'

N What happens if you don't?

A It says that 'men who score above 60 may show a female bias and women scoring below 50 may show a male bias.'

J What does that mean?

A Well, according to the article, men's and women's brains work in different ways. What did you get anyway, Nick?

N 65.

A Well, it just means that for some things your brain works like a woman's brain. I got 45 so that means that for some things my brain works like a man's brain. What did you get, Jan?

J 50.

A So you're fairly typical.

N I'm not sure I really agree.

J Just because you got 65! I'm not sure I really understand.

A OK. Well, according to scientific research, men and women use their brains differently. Before, scientists thought that everyone's brain worked in the same sort of way; the right side of the brain controlled some things and the left side of the brain controlled other things. But apparently, that's not the case. It depends on whether the brain is totally male or totally female, or whether it has some male characteristics, like mine does, or some female characteristics like yours does, Nick.

N I'm still not clear.

A OK. Well, generally speaking men's and women's brains work differently. For example, men use the right side of their brain for working on an abstract problem like a mathematical equation, while women use both sides of their brain. For language, although both use the left side of the brain for speaking and grammar, in women it's the front part of the brain that handles these skills and in men it's the back and the front part of the brain. It seems that when one skill is concentrated in one area of the brain we are better at it, or at least we find it easier. When a skill is spread over two areas of the brain we find it more difficult.

J I suppose that would help to explain why men are better than women at mathematics and women are better than men at languages.

A Yep. But each person's different. Don't forget that not all men have a typical male brain, and not all women have a typical female brain.

N OK. I understand now. I'm not sure if I agree, but it's interesting.

J What about the answers then?

A OK. Question 1 …

2.7

1 People come to the village from all over the world to watch this annual event, and although most of the competitors are Finns, there are also entrants from Norway, Germany and Switzerland. The race itself is run over 235 metres. The runner – a man – runs over the obstacle course with a woman, who must be at least 17, on his back. They have to run over sand, grass, asphalt, up hills, over fences, and through water. If the man drops the woman they are given a 15-second penalty.

2 See 2.8, paragraph 2.

2.8

The Annual Sweetwater Rattlesnake Round-up takes place, as its name suggests, in the town of Sweetwater in the state of Texas, USA. The event started in 1958 when a group of cattle ranchers and farmers paid people from out of town to round up the snakes and take them away from the area. The venomous snakes, which are found in particularly large numbers in this part of Texas, were proving a danger to humans and animals alike.

The Sweetwater Rattlesnake Round-up, which attracts more than 30,000 visitors to the town each year, is held on the second weekend of March. The festivities begin on the Thursday with a parade through the town. This is followed by a dance. While this is going on, the hunters, working in groups of 25, go out in search of snakes. Each group is accompanied by an official, who carries anti-venom antidote just in case anyone is bitten. For obvious safety reasons, tourists are not allowed to join in.

On the Friday, when the hunting groups return, and after a prize has been awarded to the group which has caught the most snakes, there are snake-handling exhibitions at which you can find out what to do if you come across a snake. Basically, don't play with it and don't run away from it either. Remember, it's more afraid of you than you are of it!

The big event on the Saturday is a cooking competition for the best chilli. A prize is given to the best chilli in several different categories, and you can try the end results for yourself. For the more adventurous there is rattlesnake chilli and for the less adventurous there is hamburger chilli, which you can wash down with a glass or two of beer if you like. The festivities don't end until the last bowl of chilli has been eaten.

2.9

1 B Hi, Sally. How are you doing?

S I'm fine. You?

B Oh, great! Actually, I'm glad I've bumped into you. You know it's Neil's birthday next Saturday?

S Oh, right.

B Well, it's his thirtieth, so we've decided to throw a surprise party for him. You will come, won't you?

S Yeah, great. What time?

B Nine-ish? Oh, and bring a bottle.

2 O Phil?

P Mm?

O Janice and I are going to stay at a friend's house for the weekend while they're away.

P   That sounds nice.
O   Yeah, well, actually it's in a really nice place, right by the sea. Would you and Martha like to come along?
P   Oh, we'd love to, but we're busy this weekend. Thanks for asking, though.

3   S   What's that you're reading?
    M   It's an invitation. Someone I was at university with is having an exhibition of her paintings. There's a party afterwards. It says 'Bring a partner'. Do you want to come?
    S   When is it?
    M   Saturday.
    S   This Saturday?
    M   Yes. From 8.00 p.m. on.
    S   Mm, Saturday night's a bit difficult.
    M   It doesn't matter. I'll ask Pete if he wants to come.

4   O   Karen?
    K   Yeah?
    O   Sam and I are going to the cinema tonight. Do you fancy coming?
    K   Thanks, I'd like that.

5   L   Hello, Sandra. It's Linda here. How are you?
    S   I'm fine thanks, Linda. And you?
    L   Not too bad. Look, the reason I'm ringing is that we're having a small dinner party a week on Friday and we'd like to invite you and David.
    S   Just a minute, Linda. I'll have to check my diary. Is that the 29th?
    L   Yeah.
    S   Oh, oh I'm really sorry, but we've arranged to go to the theatre that night.
    L   Ah, well, never mind … Some other time …

3.1

I   You've been working from home for nearly a year now. What's it like?
T   Brilliant! Absolutely brilliant!
I   No regrets at all?
T   None! I certainly wouldn't go back to spending three hours a day in my car just to work in an overheated office in the middle of a polluted city. In fact, I actually sold my car last month and since then I've been putting the money I save on travelling into a separate bank account.
I   OK, so what else do you like about teleworking apart from not having to travel every day?
T   So many things. I mean, on the personal front, I see more of my family. I didn't use to get home until seven in the evening, by which time I was so tired I just staggered in, had a meal, watched TV for a couple of hours and went to bed.
I   And now?
T   Well, for a start, I'm much less tired. Since I started working from home, I've been getting more sleep. And I've been seeing my friends more often.
I   What about work?
T   You'll have to ask my boss about that, but I'd say I was better at my job than I used to be. I can certainly concentrate more easily, and I probably have fewer breaks than my colleagues at head office.
I   How do you explain that?
T   I'm not really sure, but I've heard several people say this. One thing, I suppose, is that there aren't as many distractions at home, so I usually finish a job before I have a break. I'm sure the company has been getting more work out of me. So far this week, for example, I've written three reports, and sent over a hundred e-mails and faxes, I've made fifty or sixty phone calls and I've been preparing for a business trip to the Far East next week. I haven't stopped!
I   What about contact with other people? Doesn't it get lonely being at home all the time?

T   That's something that used to worry me, but I can honestly say that I don't feel cut off at all. I mean most days I speak to my colleagues in the office. And of course, I'm in regular contact with our branches in other countries. Today, for example, I've been talking on the phone to colleagues in Australia and Japan – that was a three-way conversation that lasted nearly an hour.
I   But what about face-to-face contact with other people?
T   No problem. Two or three of my friends who live locally also work from home – so from time to time we have lunch together. And I certainly don't miss the boss breathing down my neck – I work office hours, you know, so he can contact me whenever he needs to. No, strangely enough, I think I'm a more sociable person than I was, I mean, I've got to know several of my neighbours really well.
I   So is there nothing you miss about your old life?
T   Not really, no. I mean the food in the restaurant was very good, there was always coffee around – and, of course there was office gossip – but that's all really.
I   So, finally, what would you say to someone who's thinking about teleworking?
T   I'd say 'Go for it'.

3.3

Speaker 1
I spend all my time waiting for the phone to ring, which it does almost non-stop. You'd be amazed by the kind of questions people ask. It's quite difficult to stop yourself laughing sometimes. Someone rang me yesterday and said his mouse wasn't working. He moved it around but nothing happened. It turned out he had forgotten to connect it. Most of the problems are easy to put right. Most people ring because they're too lazy to read the manual. The hardest thing is being polite from nine in the morning till six in the evening.

Speaker 2
It's hard physical work, but I enjoy it 'cos it's out in the open and at that time of the year it's usually quite warm. The buses pick us up at seven in the morning and take us out of town to the fields. We start picking as soon as we get there – you've got to pick the fruit before it's too ripe. We put it into wooden boxes which are collected by tractor and taken to the sorting area where they're weighed and packed ready for the supermarkets.

Speaker 3
There are loads of people doing it now. It's so easy – all you need is a bucket of water and a cloth. The most important thing you've got to do is find yourself a really good place where cars have got to stop for at least half a minute. Traffic lights are best – especially in the rush hour when everyone's stopped or going very slowly. The money's not bad as long as you put the hours in.

3.4

A   Have you heard about PZM? I was absolutely amazed …
M   Oh, so was I.
C   I wasn't – they've been losing money for nearly a year now.
M   Everyone knew they were losing money, but I didn't think they'd close down completely.
A   Neither did I.
C   Oh, I did.
M   I thought they might make a hundred or so people redundant but this is going to have a terrible effect on the town.
C   That's true. I agree.
A   Yeah – you're right there.

C   Will it affect your family?
A   Yeah, my dad's worked there all his life.
M   I don't know what my dad'll do. He's too old to get another job.
A   I think my dad's quite pleased really, though he wouldn't actually admit it. He's never really liked working there.
M   My dad won't know what to do with himself. His work is his whole life.
C   I wonder what'll happen to the buildings.
M   Maybe another company'll move into the town and buy it.
C   I think that's a bit optimistic, Matt.
A   I agree. It'll probably just stay empty until the council decide to knock it down and build houses on the site.
M   I think it's so sad.
C   Mm, so do I.
A   I disagree – it's progress – nothing lasts for ever. If you ask me, PZM weren't very good employers – I mean lots of people work there but they pay really low wages and the working conditions are dreadful.
C   Oh, I don't agree. I worked there for a while a few years back and I've got very good memories.

4.1

Speaker 1
This time last year my family and I were travelling around Australia. One of the places we visited was the desert. We took a car from Alice Springs to Uluru. It was boiling hot outside and I can remember that the air-conditioning in the car wasn't working. I remember the first time I saw the rock in the distance it was glowing bright orange. It was absolutely spectacular!

Speaker 2
It was a really small plane. It was one of those planes where you go up about three steps and you're in the cabin. And erm I think there were about twenty of us and anyway the smoking section was at the back of the plane and when the stewardess came down to check all the passengers were on board everybody was erm sitting in the at the back in the smoking section. Erm, so she said 'Would some of you move to the front please? Would you like to move to the front?' and we said well nobody wanted to go because we thought well we all wanted to smoke. And since nobody put their hands up then she said, 'Well, I'm afraid I'll have to ask some of you to move to the front. You can smoke there if you like but we need to you know distribute evenly the weight of the plane.' And after she said that one er, one guy said 'She'll be asking us to put our hands out of the windows and wave our arms up and down next!' Everybody burst out laughing.

Speaker 3
I can remember the scene at the station very clearly. I was 22 I think, I'd never been away from home for any length of time and I was just about to go to Montreal to work there for a couple of years. My parents came to the station to see me off. I hadn't wanted them to, because I don't like long goodbyes. I remember my dad put his arm round me and told me to take care of myself. My mom was so upset she couldn't speak. She was hugging me and she was crying at the same time. When the train pulled into the station I was crying too. I felt really awful, really homesick. I got on the train and I cried all the way to Montreal.

4.2

Good afternoon. In today's programme we are going to look back at some of the great achievements of the twentieth century. Let's start by mentioning important breakthroughs in flight and space travel.

The most important of these was the first powered aircraft flight in 1903. The flight, though it lasted just twelve seconds, marked an important technological advance, and made Orville and Wilbur Wright household names overnight. Just thirty years later, in 1933, the first solo round-the-world flight was accomplished by another American, Wiley Post, with the first non-stop round-the-world flight being achieved in 1949.

Such advances in aviation technology paved the way for the space revolution and on 12th April 1961 Yuri Gagarin made history by being the first person to orbit the earth, doing so in a time of one hour and 48 minutes. Another important first in space travel was the first moon landing on 20th July 1969, with the American astronaut Neil Armstrong becoming the first person to walk on the moon.

But not all of the great achievements of the 20th century were technological. Some marked important triumphs of man over nature. For instance, the expeditions to the North Pole in 1909 and the South Pole in 1911. However, the race to the South Pole, which was won by the Norwegian Roald Amundsen, had unfortunate consequences for the British expedition team led by Captain Robert Scott, who died on the return journey from the Pole.

Another achievement we shouldn't forget was the first ascent of Everest. On 29th May 1953 the New Zealander Edmund Hillary, and the Sherpa, Tenzing Norgay, became the first two people to stand at the top of the highest mountain on earth.

In the field of sport there were major achievements too …

4.3

Everybody who was going on the balloon trip met in the car park. Then we were taken to a field. The balloon was actually on the back of a lorry and we all had to help to get it ready. First of all, we took the balloon off the lorry. Then four of the women had to get into the wicker basket – one in each corner – to balance it. The men then helped to inflate the balloon with a wind-machine. As soon as it was inflated, everyone climbed in. It started to rise when the pilot turned on the gas burners. It lifted off the ground very gently but went up extremely quickly – much faster than I'd expected – about 100 metres a minute – and then when the pilot decided we were high enough he turned down the burners a bit so we stayed at more or less the same height. While the pilot was flying the balloon, he was talking to the lorry driver, who was following below. He also gave us some information – told us how fast we were flying, pointed out some landmarks and so on, and people chatted and took photographs. I was waiting for the champagne, but there was no sign of any – much to my disappointment. One thing that surprised me was the fact that there wasn't any wind at all, and it was also extremely hot, I suppose because we were standing right under the burners. Anyway, when the hour was up the pilot started looking for somewhere to land. I was a bit worried about the landing but it was OK. It was quite straightforward really. Once the pilot spotted an appropriate site, he turned off the burners and the balloon started to descend. I was scared we were going to fall like a stone but it was quite gradual. Just before we landed he told us to crouch down and hold tight on to the ropes. We had to have our backs facing the direction the balloon was travelling in so that if it fell over we'd fall backwards rather than forwards. Anyway, it was a very gentle landing. After we landed, we got out and helped to deflate the balloon. Then we had to roll it up and after that, we put it on the back of the lorry again. And finally, we celebrated our safe return with a glass of champagne, and we were given a certificate to prove that we'd been on a balloon flight. It was great. I really enjoyed it.

4.4

W Excuse me. Is this seat free?
M Yes.
W Would you mind helping me with my suitcase?
M Not at all. Where would you like it?
W Could you put it up there?
M No problem.
W Thank you very much. The train's very busy today, isn't it?
M Yes, it is.
W Don't you think it's a bit stuffy in here? (*To woman*) Excuse me. I wonder if you could open the window a bit? Thank you. That's much better. (*To teenage boy*) Excuse me! EXCUSE ME. CAN YOU TURN THAT DOWN A BIT PLEASE? Thank you.
I Tickets please? I'm sorry madam but this ticket's out of date. It's for yesterday.
W Oh. I am sorry. Can you change the date on it?
I I'm afraid not. Thank you, 'kyou, 'kyou …
W Well, can't you just turn a blind eye? I am getting off at the next station.
I I'm sorry but that's not possible, madam.
W Oh, all right. How much is it?
…
W Excuse me. I'm sorry to bother you again but could you possibly get my case down for me?
M Certainly.
W That's very kind of you. Thank you.

5.1

Speaker 1
This year I'm doing the same as I did last year 'cos I enjoyed it so much. I'm going to Tenerife with three friends. We're going back to Playa de las Americas, where we were last year. We're even staying in the same apartment 'cos it's really handy for everywhere; it's near the beach and it's not far from the town centre. There's loads to do there. We go clubbing every night. There are some really great clubs. And there are hundreds of bars too. The nightlife is brilliant. You never get bored. You meet loads of people.

Speaker 2
It's quite hard being so far away from home, actually. The people I work with have been extremely nice, very hospitable, inviting me to their homes for meals and so on. But it's not the same as having your own family around you. I miss my kids a lot. Another thing is the language. Although most people in the company can speak some English, it's a different thing once you're outside the office. I'm afraid my Italian isn't very good yet. I can understand more than I can speak, but I feel a bit left out in conversations. I'm sure I'll feel more at home soon – once my Italian improves.

Speaker 3
We've always wanted to live in another country and my husband's always wanted to run his own business so we're going to combine the two. We're going to run a bar in Fiskardo on Cephalonia. We first went there for a holiday five years ago and we fell in love with the place. It's so quiet, so peaceful! My husband's already over there – there are one or two problems to sort out – and I'm going to fly out next month. I think our lives will change for the better once we've made the move. We'll get more job satisfaction 'cos it's our own business. And life will be much less stressful.

5.2

I decided to take a year off after finishing High School before I went to university and considering I was going to be studying French at university I thought the best way to improve my the way I spoke French was to go to France. Erm, I went for five months in all and I went with a programme which meant I was going to be staying with another with a French family for that time. At the beginning of my stay of course I felt homesick because France to Australia is a very long way. Erm, I wasn't with my family of course, and I missed my family and my friends. Erm, I was I couldn't I wasn't able to telephone them very often because of course it's very expensive and being surrounded by French all the time and me not being that wonderful at speaking French I had a few difficulties but once I got over that and started making friends and fitting in it was it just improved significantly.

I'm really glad I went because it gave me a lot more independence because I had to stand on my own two feet on my own without my family in a foreign country where I didn't necessarily speak the language very well. Er the distance from Australia meant that I had to be fully independent because I couldn't ring my parents all the time and say 'What do I do now? I don't understand' because Australia is a long long way from France and of course the telephone bills would have been enormous. Erm of course my French improved. Erm before I went I couldn't speak very well at all and when I left I can I can hold a conversation now in French er so of course that's good. It's definitely improved my confidence as well. Er, now I go into life with the attitude that if I managed to do something in a country where I didn't speak the language as my mother tongue then I can do it here. It's, it's not that hard. And I definitely think I'm a more mature person now. I can handle what life throws at me.

5.3

1 A Do you think it's a good idea for parents to send young children to nursery school?
   B How young?
   A Two or three years old.
   B It's difficult to say.
2 A What's your opinion of children living at home with their parents until they get married?
   B I don't think they should. I think it's a good idea to live on your own for a bit – it helps to make you independent, think for yourself, learn to manage your money, learn to cook, even.
3 A Do you have an opinion on young people having to do military service?
   B It's not something I've really thought about.
   A But don't you think it's unfair that boys have to do military service but girls don't?
   B I'm not sure. Maybe. Anyway, girls do have to do military service in some countries.
4 A What do you think about this idea of taking a year out between school and university?
   B I'd say it's a brilliant idea. I think the best time to travel is when you're young and have no ties.

6.2

Speaker 1
In the United States you can get married without your parents' permission when you're 16 or 18. It depends on the state. Every state has its own laws. I guess that the average age that people get married is about 25. That's the first marriage of course. As you probably know, we have a very high divorce rate in the States and an awful lot of people get married more than once. The actual wedding can be well

anywhere – church, City Hall, in your own home. I had a friend who got married in a bowling alley – 'cos that's where she met her husband.

Speaker 2
Britain apparently has the highest divorce rate in Europe but marriage is still very popular here. You can get married when you're 18 without your parents' permission, but I'd say most people wait until they're in their mid-twenties. You can actually get married in lots of places nowadays – at a football ground if you want – or even sky-diving – if you can find a vicar who's a sky-diver of course! But most people still get married in church or in a registry office.

Speaker 3
In Japan women can get married when they are 16, but they have to have their parents' permission. I don't know about men. When you are 18 you are free to choose who you marry. I suppose the average age that people get married is around 24 for women and 30 for men, but I'm not really sure. You don't have to get married in a church. You can get married in a registry office if you prefer.

6.3

Speaker 1
My car is a wonderful blue Fiat Panda, which is about 12 years old and it's been all over Europe. It's lived in Italy, Hungary and travelled many miles. It's a dear friend. It never lets me down and it always starts.

Speaker 2
My favourite car was a black mini. It was my first car and it had a lovely wooden dashboard and I think that's why I liked it so much. It was very special. I was quite fond of of this car because the registration number was TFN so we called it Tiffany and it had a name and a little personality so yes I was quite fond of that car. It was special.

Speaker 3
Er, my favourite car was a red Vauxhall Astra which I had for several years until it stopped working. I liked it best because it was reliable, it was comfortable and it had a good stereo.

Speaker 4
Erm when I was a student, I inherited my grandfather's Volkswagen Beetle and it was an orange one and it was very old. In fact it was older than than I am and em he'd looked after it really really well though and so it was, it was a really nice car to drive – not for going on long journeys …

Speaker 5
My favourite car is actually the the car I've got at the moment. It's a Peugeot 306 – petrol not diesel – and I suppose I like it mainly for two reasons. It's a lot faster than the car I had before and it's very good going round corners and also it's bigger so it's it's quite comfortable. A friend of mine was quite surprised when she saw it for the first time. She said, 'I didn't think of you as em a red car driver. I thought of you more as a blue car driver,' which rather upset me at the time although I got over it later.

6.5

1 J Sue? Hi, it's Jack.
  S Hi, Jack. How are you?
  J Fine. Erm, Sue?
  S Yeah?
  J Could I borrow your 'Best Rock Music Ever' CD? I'll let you have it back tomorrow.
  S I suppose so. But make sure you remember.
  J I will, don't worry. Can I come round to get it now?

2 A Is it OK if I join you?
  B Of course. I think you know Alan, don't you?
  A Hi.
  C Hi.

3 A Do you think I could borrow your car tonight for a couple of hours?
  B What for?
  A I promised Jenny I'd give her some extra driving lessons.
  B Jenny? No way! Anyway I'm using it myself tonight. Why don't you ask David?
  A (Shouts) David?
  D (From another room) Yeah?
  A Any chance of borrowing your car tonight?
  D My car?
  A Yes. I said I'd pick Jenny up from college.
  D Sure. Go ahead. I think the keys are on the table.

4 I Do you think I could possibly leave early tonight, Sara? It's my girlfriend's birthday.
  S I'm afraid not, Ian. We need to get this finished today.

5 A Do you mind if I take this chair?
  B No, not at all.
  A Hi, Sue! Come and join us!
  S Is it all right if I take this chair?
  B No problem. I'm just leaving anyway.

7.1

Speaker 1
Well I suppose I've got rather an individual sense of humour. All sorts of things can make me laugh – not always the things that are meant to be funny. For instance, I often laugh at things people say or do in real situations. I can't stand prepared jokes, you know the sort of corny jokes people tell in bars – jokes that you feel you ought to laugh at.

Speaker 2
Mmm, that's a really difficult question. I can tell you what I don't like – that's easy enough. I can't stand slapstick humour, you know like clowns, people slipping on banana skins, that kind of thing. There are a few comedians on TV I find funny – but it's difficult to say why they're funny – perhaps you could call it ironic humour.

Speaker 3
There are a few people I know, you know, friends of mine, who are just naturally funny. They can make me laugh at almost anything – but I'm not sure that's a particular kind of humour, is it? It's just an ability some people have got to make you laugh – a sort of natural wit. On the other hand, I'm not very keen on professional comedians – I just don't find them funny.

Speaker 4
Actually, I think humour's to do with age, I mean there's almost nothing on television that I find funny – it's all so middle-aged – especially sit-coms – they can be really dreadful, but my parents watch them and think they're absolutely hilarious. I sometimes go to the theatre – when there's a stand-up comedian on – some of the young ones are quite funny – pretty mad humour, but it makes me laugh.

Speaker 5
Mm, good question. I er, I don't like humour that's too obvious. I suppose what I really like is black humour – you know when you can see the funny side of something that is normally quite serious or er, even sad. Some people might call it sick humour, I suppose.

Speaker 6
My favourite kind of humour is something to do with words – definitely – I think people who can make jokes with words are really clever – you know – words with double meanings. I'm afraid I don't really like a lot of modern humour – to me it's just not funny.

7.3 and 7.4

1 Q How many Americans does it take to change a light bulb?
  A I don't know. How many Americans does it take to change a light bulb?
  Q Three – one to change the bulb and two to tell the rest of the world (on a chat show).

2 Jock, from Glasgow, went into the newspaper office. His wife had just died and he wanted to put a notice in the paper.
  'What would you like to say?' asked the clerk.
  'Jane's dead,' replied Jock.
  'You can have five more words for the same money,' said the clerk.
  'OK,' said Jock. 'I'll have: (Jane's dead. Red Toyota car for sale').

3 An Englishman, an Irishman, a Scotsman and an American who were complete strangers were shipwrecked on a desert island. The inhabitants of the island welcomed the four men and soon the American was building a small railway, the Scotsman had opened a shop, the Irishman was making whiskey, while the Englishman (was still waiting to be introduced)

7.5

R So, you're all in favour of the basic idea, then?
All Yeah!
  Absolutely!
R And have you thought of any other ideas you'd like us to consider in the future? We're planning now for next year.
TB I think everyone should get a free CD player and two CDs to listen to during the flight.
R If we did that, we'd have to put up air fares, I'm afraid.
M What about putting on a magic show – the kids would love that.
TB I wouldn't.
TG Nor would I.
M Then why not have general knowledge quizzes – one of the cabin crew could read out the questions and the passengers could all write down the answers and hand them in before the end of the flight.
W Mmm – that's not a bad idea.
TB You could give the winner a prize?
TG Yeah, like a free flight to New York.
R I'm not so sure about that. I don't think the company is quite that generous.
W How about fashion shows? The attendants could model the latest designer clothes.
Y No, I'm not keen on that idea – they've got enough to do without having to change their clothes every five minutes. No, I've been thinking, what about Karaoke competitions?
R Brilliant!

8.1

Speaker 1
I don't have a mobile phone, but I would like one so that I could call home when I was on the train, late home on the train.

Speaker 2
No, I don't have a mobile phone.
Would you like one?
I sometimes think it would be useful to have one on a motorway on a journey on my own just in case the car broke down and I was on my own with the children.

Speaker 3

I have got a mobile phone because when I was pregnant we were worried that I might get stuck in a car somewhere and not be able to contact someone so it was for safety reasons really. I don't use it very often erm just when I'm out and about.

Speaker 4

I've got a mobile phone but I mainly use it for phoning other people, er in my job I need to be available to er my staff.

Speaker 5

Erm, I can't think of any really really good reason why I should have a mobile phone. Erm – It means that you're accessible 24 hours a day if you've got a mobile phone …

Speaker 6

Yes, very recently. I've never used it however. I don't know how to use it yet.
But why have you got one?
Essentially for the for the car again it's that – as this car although it's a wonderful car of course it has broken down on a number of occasions and a mobile is very very useful for for for getting emergency help in the middle of nowhere and that's the main reason.

Speaker 7

I don't have a mobile phone. I considered buying one erm because I was doing a lot of motorway travelling and I thought it would be very useful, erm just in case I broke down because you never know when you you know where a motorway phone might be …

8.2

Speaker 1

I think they're a real pain in the neck – I find it really annoying when I'm on a train or I'm out for a walk and somebody's got a mobile phone in a shop or – I just think it's silly and it's unnecessary – erm I think people can be contacted at home and there should be some time and space where they don't have mobile phones.

Speaker 2

I get annoyed when mobile phones go off in church and erm when people are having a quiet time …

Speaker 3

It annoys me on public transport when people are talking on their mobile phones and in public places when the phones ring especially when they've got silly tunes – I find it very annoying.

Speaker 4

The most annoying thing about mobile phones is when they ring on trains and when people talk really loudly on their phones to let everybody else know they've got one.

Speaker 5

What really most annoys me about mobile phones is, as I've just said, that people have to answer them when they go off. You can't … You're talking to someone, their mobile phone goes off and they have no option but to answer it.

Speaker 6

I also find them very annoying especially when people are sitting in restaurants or on buses and their phones are going constantly and you have to overhear people's private conversations – they don't seem to have any er respect of either your privacy or their privacy funnily enough.

Speaker 7

I'm fairly resistant to the idea of mobile phones as fashion accessories which they obviously are for a lot of people because there's absolutely no reason to walk around with one clipped to your belt and the fact that some people do is, is purely to advertise the fact they've got a mobile phone …

8.3

It used to be terrible. Now I'm usually OK. I suppose it's worst in new situations especially if there are lots of people I don't know. Like at parties – I start feeling tense even before I get there – a sort of nervousness – I suppose you'd call it butterflies in the stomach. By the time I arrive my hands are sweaty and my throat's dry. I normally make straight for a friend, but if I can't see anyone I know, I just stand around feeling uncomfortable. If someone I don't know talks to me, I blush and sometimes I stammer when I talk. If I see someone I know a bit, I might try to start a conversation – sometimes it's OK, but not always. I went to an office party a couple of weeks ago and I started talking to a young woman I thought I knew. Anyway, I went up to her and asked her very politely if we'd met somewhere before. She said she didn't think we had. So I asked her where she worked. She said she didn't work. When I asked her if she knew anyone else in the room, she said, 'Yes'. So I asked her if she could introduce me to someone. But just then she saw a friend and she walked off. I found out later she was my boss's wife.

8.4

Of course it's hard being shy, especially if you're single. But I should say right at the start that almost everyone has certain situations when they feel tense or shy. In the end most people learn to cope with these feelings – keep them under control and not let them ruin their lives. If you're naturally a very shy person, this can be quite a long process – it may take years – in fact you may never get over it completely – but I hope that following some of my suggestions will help you, especially if you want to form positive relationships with other people.

OK, rule number one – stop yourself worrying what other people are thinking about you – especially in social situations. Do anything you can to take your mind off yourself.

Number two – focus on other people. If you're at a party and there's someone you'd like to talk to, focus on that person. As you walk towards them, say their name or look for something you like about them – it could be the colour of their eyes or what they're wearing.

Number three – think about successful past experiences. Remember times when you were not shy and enjoyed meeting other people.

Number four – improve your small talk. Have something interesting to talk about apart from your dog, your job or your past relationships.

Five – use well-practised lines if you suddenly feel shy, 'Hello, my name's whatever' or ask the person you're talking to whether they know anyone in the room, that kind of thing.

Number six – imagine the worst thing that could happen. If the very worst thing that you can possibly imagine happens, how will you handle it? You think, 'Well, I might feel so shy that I'd run out of the room.' So, what if you do run out of the room! That's not so bad, is it?

Seven – try talking about something that embarrasses you, such as blushing. Bringing a fear out in the open takes away its power to worry you.

Eight – relax your muscles and breathe deeply both before and during the situation.

Number nine – smile, smile, and smile some more. Everyone loves a smile.

And finally number ten – think of yourself climbing a ladder – overcoming shyness can be like that. You go up two steps, slide back down one, you go up two or three more steps, then just hold on and persuade yourself you can climb higher.

Well, that's it. It's up to you now. Good luck and whatever you do, don't give up hope.

8.5

A What's your name, please?
TA Anderson. Thomas Anderson.
A And where do you live please, Mr Anderson?
TA Yeah, it's 2678 Fairview Crescent, Vancouver, BC.
A And what's your postcode?
TA V6T 2BP.
A How do you want to pay for your order?
TA By credit card, if that's OK.
A That's fine. Can you give me your number, please?
TA 5543 5654 7869 4239.
A Thank you. And when is the expiry date?
TA September this year.
A Thank you. And do you want our Fastpost service?
TA Yes, please.
A OK, Mr Anderson. That should be with you some time tomorrow.
TA Thanks. Goodbye.

8.6

Speaker 1

P When did you start learning your second language?
A My first second language, as it were, I started learning when I was four and a half and that was Portuguese and I was very fluent in it and then after a couple of years we moved to Argentina from Brazil and I had to learn Spanish and I became very fluent in that. Subsequently more or less forgot it but then started learning French in a a French-speaking environment when I was about eleven, twelve, and I was in that environment, it was in Geneva, for many years, for ten, twelve years and I basically erm thought and wrote and spoke in French as if I was French and everybody still thinks I'm French when I speak French.
P Did you realize that you had … that this was a special thing?
A I suppose I did because erm I noticed that other people couldn't do it and at the same time I didn't necessarily think of it as very special because my father spoke so many languages, I mean he could speak about seventeen languages, so erm it didn't seem unusual to me – it seemed very obvious.
P Do you feel more comfortable in English?
A No, funnily enough I don't actually. In some ways and for … in some subjects … if I'm talking about erm feelings and philosophy and things like that I'm more comfortable in French than I am in English. I also have noticed that I gesticulate more when I'm speaking French and I also use a wider range of expressions – facial expressions and bodily expressions and so on.
P Were you ever confused about the languages?
A Not at all – not the least little bit, no.
P And have you found any disadvantages?
A Not that I can think of. I think it's always been a plus actually and part of the plus is knowing that I can erm communicate in lots of different languages and that other people don't necessarily know it, so I very often walk behind somebody talking Chinese on the street, for example, and I know what they're talking about and they don't know that I know what they're talking about.

Speaker 2

P When did you learn your second language?

L When I was … I started learning it when I was three – in Argentina.

P And when did you first realize that you could speak more than one language?

L Erm I think when I was four and a half, because I learnt to say the time in English before I learnt it in Spanish and suddenly I realized that some people couldn't understand it.

P And how did you … why did you become bilingual?

L Well that's a family story, it's because my parents didn't want me to go to the state system so I had to go to a private school and as I was going to a private school, they thought it was better if I learnt another language, so my father wanted me to learn English because it was a useful language and my mother wanted to learn, me to learn French because it was a nicer language, so I had to learn both.

P And do you feel, or did you ever or have … do you feel now more comfortable in one language than another?

L Yes, I always feel much more comfortable in Spanish, because you can … there is a certain nuance in your language and feelings feelings you can always say certain things in your own language, you know.

P So you feel very strongly that Spanish is your first language?

L Absolutely, yes, yeah.

P And were you ever confused?

L I don't remember being confused – I don't know, but I don't think I ever was, no.

P And have you ever found any disadvantages to being bilingual?

L Not really, no. I think it's quite a great advantage, I … My son is also bilingual and I think it's a great advantage.

P And how … in what way have you brought him up?

L Well, because he, he was born here in England so he … his first language is English, but at home we speak Spanish and when we lived in Holland he also had to speak Dutch so there was a routine by which he knew which language to speak when, so he knew that when we were the three of us alone he would speak Spanish, when he was alone with me, because we were living in Holland, to keep his English we would speak in English and when he was at school or with friends or whatever he would speak Dutch.

8.7

Message 1

Hi, I'm not here right now but my answerphone is, so you can talk to it instead. Wait for the bleep.

Message 2

Hi! Jenny's answering machine is broken. This is her fridge. Please speak slowly after the tone and I'll keep your message fresh for Jenny.

Message 3

There's nobody here at the moment to take your call, but if you leave your name and phone number after the long tone, I'll get back to you as soon as I can.

Message 4

Hi. I am here, but I'm just avoiding someone I don't like. Leave a message, and if I don't call back, it's you.

Message 5

If you are a burglar, then we're probably here cleaning our guns and can't get to the phone. So please hang up. If you aren't a burglar, we probably aren't here, so it's safe to leave us a message.

8.8

1 A Hello, Mediterranean Holidays. Can I help you?

B Yes, hello. Could I speak to someone about self-catering holidays, please?

A Yes, certainly. Who's calling, please?

B My name's Kirkby.

A Just one moment, Mr Kirkby, I'll put you through to one of our assistants.

C Hello, I'm sorry to keep you waiting. I understand you're interested in self-catering holidays.

B That's right. I've just seen your ad in the paper. Could you send me a brochure, please?

C I'm afraid next year's brochure isn't out yet, but if you give me your name and address, we'll put one in the post to you as soon as they're available.

B Thanks very much. My address is 72, West Street …

2 A Hello, Olden Days News, Jeremy speaking. How can I help?

B Hello. Erm. Yes, I'd like to order one of your original newspapers.

A Yes, of course. Just hold on a minute. OK, first of all, which newspaper and what date are you interested in?

B Sorry, could you speak up, please? It's a terrible line.

A Yes, which newspaper and what date are you interested in?

B Sorry, it's no good. I can't hear what you're saying. I'll ring back in a couple of minutes.

3 A Hello.

B Oh, hello. Is that Olden Days News?

A No, sorry. You've got the wrong number.

B Oh, I'm sorry.

4 A Hello, Olden Days News, newspaper department.

B Hello, I'd like one of your newspapers, please.

A Certainly, can I ask the newspaper and the date you're interested in?

B Well, I really need to know how much they cost.

A Between £10 and £200, depending on the newspaper and the date.

B I see. Could you send me a sample newspaper?

A No, I'm afraid not, but we could send you a photocopy of the front page.

B That'd be fine.

A OK. I'll put one in the post to you today.

B Thanks very much.

A Not at all. Thank you for calling.

5 A Hello, Mediterranean Holidays. Can I help you?

B Yes, this is Mrs Forest here. Could you put me through to your self-catering holidays department?

A I'm afraid all the lines are busy at the moment. Would you like to hold?

B Yes, thank you.

A The lines are still engaged. Do you still want to hold?

B No, thanks. I'll try again later.

A Can I take a message or get someone to phone you back?

B Yes, please. I'd like some information about holidays in May. The name's Forest and my number's 453879.

A Thanks for your call, Mrs Forest, I'll pass on your message.

9.1

1 Last night, John Steele, who is appearing in the latest Spielberg film, appealed to his ex-wife Matilda to return his three children. Mrs Steele took the children as they came out of school last Monday. Steele is considering suing his wife, but is not happy at the thought of his children appearing in court.

2 Friends of Jeremy Carlton claim that they do not know where he was last weekend. They say they do not believe he has done anything wrong and see no reason why he should resign. It is thought that the Prime Minister is trying to persuade Mr Carlton to explain where he was on the two days in question and to deny rumours that he was with Hollywood actress, Marlene Shaw.

3 The London train was full of passengers. The injured man, Paul Lewis, was standing near a door when the attack occurred. 'I was reading the paper when two men approached me. One asked me the time, and as I looked at my watch, the other one hit me in the stomach and stole my wallet. They both had knives. There were people all around me. I can't believe no one has given the police a full description of the men.'

9.2

PO Are you the owner of this house, sir?

M Yes, I am.

PO Then I have to tell you, sir, that you are breaking the new Night Noise Law and I am now officially asking you to end this party.

M But it's only eleven o'clock. Would it be OK if we turned the music down?

PO I'm sorry, sir, but under new laws we have to uphold complaints from members of the public who complain about late night noise.

M Look, officer, we've got all our friends here now. We can't just send them home.

PO I'm sorry, sir, but you have no choice.

P Yes, you're right – that wasn't a real life scene, but there are countries with strict anti-noise laws. In Switzerland, for example, neighbours can complain about any type of noise after ten o'clock at night. This law can cover everything from flushing toilets to crying babies and televisions. Here's Monica Greentree who lives in Switzerland.

MG When we arrived, we heard a story about a foreign couple who decided to have a party.

P Did you hear this from the couple themselves?

MG No, but apparently all foreigners are told this story as soon as they arrive in Switzerland. Anyway, this couple were warned about the Swiss attitude to noise so they invited their neighbours to their party, thinking, you know, 'If we invite the neighbours, they won't complain.' How wrong can you be? The neighbours accepted the invitation, drank lots of wine and left promptly at midnight. As soon as they got home they phoned the police to complain about the noise. The police arrived within minutes and put an end to the celebrations.

P That's incredible!

MG It is, isn't it?

P A Dutch person living in Geneva says that it is not the law, but the people who enforce the law who are to blame.

D In Holland we have similar laws, but people are tolerant and the police would laugh if someone complained about a party.

P Noise, it seems, is a cause of intense irritation for many people. Here in Britain, noise and badly-behaved children are the most common causes of arguments between neighbours. Complaints about neighbourhood noise in general have been rising steadily since the early 1980s. There is actually a very serious side to the subject. Here's a Chief Inspector of Police.

CI We are seeing more and more cases of violence associated with noise – sort of 'noise rage' if you like. People have actually died as a result of attacks by irate neighbours. There was a particularly strange case recently when a man was jailed for life for killing a neighbour who had complained about the volume of his music.

P   What powers do the British police have in this area?

CI Well, it depends where you are. In Scotland, for instance, the police could actually arrest you if you refused to stop making a disturbing noise. In England this job is left to environmental health officers. They cannot arrest people but they can remove the cause of noise.

P   In fact there was a famous case only last year, wasn't there?

CI That's right, a 16-year-old girl had her stereo taken away because she refused to turn down her music when her mother asked her to. Alarms are another area of growing concern for us – burglar alarms on houses and shops have been with us for a long time, but more and more people now have car alarms and it can be very disturbing if these go off at night, particularly if the car is parked some distance from where the driver lives.

P   Thank you, Chief Inspector. Well, that's about it for today. I'll say goodbye now and hope to have the pleasure of your company next week.

9.3

Speaker 1
Well again, connected to trains, erm I always find that the train never leaves on time – it's always four, five minutes late, maybe more, but the very day you arrive four or five minutes late, the train has just pulled out.

Speaker 2
… when I was very small and I was putting jam on my toast in the morning and I was standing up to have my breakfast and I dropped the piece of bread and it landed with the jam side down to the floor so of course picking up all the horrible bits off the floor …

Speaker 3
… you're in a supermarket or a bank or at the post office and you're standing in a queue waiting to pay and you notice that the queue next to you is moving faster, so you move into that queue and immediately it slows down and the queue you were in before starts moving faster …

Speaker 4
When I'm cycling in to work in the morning I try to …, not to carry too much on my bike because I have loads of bags to take because of the children's things, and er so if I think it's not going to rain, I won't bother to take my waterproofs but you can guarantee that if I don't take my waterproof in the morning, it'll be raining by the time I have to cycle home in the evening and then you know vice versa – if I, if I do take it, it's beautiful weather and by the time I cycle home, I'm just carrying four times too many coats and bags and things that I didn't need.

9.4

1 T   What's the matter? You were OK five minutes ago. Why are you crying?

   P   Because Ben took my sandwiches and ate them, and now I'm hungry.

   T   Come on, don't cry. I'll have a word with Ben. Have you any idea why Ben took your sandwiches?

   P   Dunno – maybe it was because I took his cake.

2 O   Perhaps you could tell me why your uniform is in such a mess? You've had three days to get it clean and tidy.

   S   Because I've been ill in bed since the weekend, that's why.

   O   That's why what?

   S   That's why my uniform is in a mess.

   O   That's why your uniform is in a mess, what?

   S   That's why my uniform is in a mess, sir.

3 T   Why on earth are you out of bed at this time of night?

   M   For the simple reason that it's three o'clock in the morning and we were worried about you.

   T   Why were you worried? I'm quite old enough to look after myself.

4 P   So, is there a reason why you didn't stop at the traffic lights at the corner of the High Street?

   D   The main reason was that they were green, not red.

   P   Don't get funny with me, sir. The last set of traffic lights were definitely red.

   D   Were they? Oh! Sorry.

   P   Could you blow into this for me, please, sir?

   D   Why should I?

   P   Because I think you've probably had too much to drink.

10.1

Speaker 1
Home to me is a place that I feel safe and comfortable – it's a place where I can just be myself and a place where I'm accepted and until I moved here home was always in New York State but over the past few months there are at least two different places here in Oxford that I consider home – friends' places and where I'm living now and it just feels like home because, as I said it's safe and comfortable and it's a place where I just be myself.

Speaker 2
Home means my house erm which I bought two years ago and which I love dearly because I did all the work on it – it was in a terrible state when I moved in and it needed complete redecoration and, because I did it myself, I feel more at home there than anywhere else, I think.

Speaker 3
To me it means the place I go home, shut the door, nobody can bother me, I can do what I like, erm – it also means the place where I was born where my parents live, so when I say I'm going home that's often what I mean is going to their their country house and relaxing. It's a lovely old house – it was built in 1780 – erm it's got four bedrooms erm it's very comfortable huge sofas and fireplace – the kind of place you can completely relax.

Speaker 4
Home … oh well … is two things. Home is, is next door where I live, I'm happy enough to, lucky enough to be living next, next to my workplace and of course it's where my Mum lives – that's in Paris and where my family and friends (live) – so erm yeah that's where I go back.

Speaker 5
Home, I always think of my parents' home – I think a lot of it is because I've moved around so much so I've never lived in one house for a very long time and I've always rented so, because of me moving around, so again I don't think you really, really think of it as your home until you actually buy all the furniture and do a bit of work on it maybe and stay there for quite a while.
Where is your parents' house?
Erm that's outside Manchester erm, and they still live in the old family house – they're talking about selling it now which will be quite sad and it's a, a large house and it's from the end of the last century, so it's, it's old.

It's got a very big garden with a summer house in it. It's, it's nice 'cos it's so spacious and so you can have lots of people to stay. I'm always taking people back there and my Mum and Dad enjoy it, so, so to me that's home really.

10.2

Conversation 1

A   Have you seen these buildings? They're amazing!

K   Let's have a look. Wow! They're really unusual. But what exactly are they?

A   Well, that's a block of flats in the middle of Vienna, that's an incinerator and this one's a health resort, apparently.

K   An incinerator?

A   Yeah, you know, where they burn the city's rubbish. So, what do you think of them?

K   They're fantastic! I mean, I think they're a real breath of fresh air – I'd love to live somewhere like that.

Conversation 2

T   I think they're absolutely dreadful – I could design better buildings than that myself. I think they should knock them down and start again.

J   They're OK, but they're not as wonderful as some people say – I mean they're fun to look at and they brighten the place up a bit, but they don't do anything for me.

Conversation 3

M   Cool! They're brilliant – I'm fed up with modern buildings, they're all grey and dull – I mean, why do they always have to use such boring colours? Why can't we have more bright, colourful buildings like this?

W   Oh that's not fair. Not all modern buildings are grey and boring. You're thinking of those typical 1960s office blocks – things have moved on you know – it's not just concrete these days – they can do amazing things with glass and steel. I must admit these places look like kids' playgrounds to me. I certainly wouldn't like to live in one – or even near one for that matter.

Conversation 4

R   If you ask me, the bloke who designed them is a genius. I'd love a few colourful buildings like those where I live. I think they're really artistic.

E   Me too, all those round shapes are sort of cosy – not hard and sharp like most things you get in modern cities, you know, all built by macho middle-aged architects trying to be different.

Conversation 5

E   I really like them, but they're not as different as all that. I mean, they're the same as all the others inside – they're only different on the outside.

G   Yeah, I expect people will get fed up with the colours in a year or two. They'll get dirty and messy and – and eventually nobody will want to live in them. I wouldn't be surprised if they end up knocking them down and replacing them with something less gimmicky.

10.3

B   Oh, hello, is that Mr Smith?

S   It's pronounced Smythe actually.

B   I'm sorry, Mr Smythe. This is the Sports Club here. We're just ringing to check that the information we have on our members' files is still correct. We've had a few problems recently with our new computer system – that's why we're contacting all our members. Have you got a few minutes to spare?

S   Yes, that's fine.

B Thank you – it shouldn't take too long. OK, I'd just like to check your name again. It's Smythe – and that's S-M-Y-T-H-E. Is that right?
S No, it isn't actually. In fact, there's no E on the end.
B OK, thank you. And your first names, Mr Smyth. We have Michael, Stuart, Humphrey. Is that correct?
S No, I'm afraid that's completely wrong. It should be Glen, Edward – I've only got two names.
B Oh dear, we're not doing very well, are we?
S No, are you sure you've got the right person?
B I certainly hope so, let me just check your address. Is it 33, Salisbury Avenue? Have we got that right?
S Yes, that's correct.
R And the postcode is CO3 3FG.
S No, I'm afraid that's not right. In fact, it isn't CO anything. It's CM5 6RD.
B Oh no. That's a different town. I'm so sorry. Let me just check again on the computer. I won't keep you a moment.
   Hello, Mr Smyth, I can't find your details anywhere on the computer.
S That's strange, I've been a member of the tennis club for more than 15 years now.
B This is not the tennis club, Mr Smyth, it's the squash club. I'm so sorry to have troubled you.

11.1

I You've lived in Spain for some time now.
M Yes, about twelve years.
I And have you noticed any changes in people's eating habits in that time?
M Oh yes.
I What kind of changes have you seen?
M Well, I suppose the biggest change is that women are spending less time in the kitchen than before. A lot of women, particularly in the cities, go out to work nowadays and, of course, have very busy lives. And it seems that they're less prepared to spend the free time they do have preparing elaborate meals.
I So they don't spend as much time cooking?
M That's right. They still cook but it tends to be fairly quick things.
I What about ready-cooked meals?
M Yes, they're getting more popular but they're still not nearly as popular as they are in Canada and the States.
I Do people have microwaves?
M Yes, they do. More and more people are getting microwaves.
I Hmm. Any other changes?
M Yes, lunch is changing. People used to spend a long time over lunch. Some still do, of course, but now a lot of people just have a sandwich for lunch. I'm talking about during the week, of course, not weekends.
I That's still the big family meal?
M On the whole, yes.
I What about young people? Have their eating habits changed?
M That's where I notice most of the changes. Fast food is very popular – McDonald's, Burger King, that sort of thing. Young people nowadays tend to prefer to eat hamburgers than the traditional Spanish 'tapas'.
I The snacks they serve in the bars?
M Yes. But of course, it's a fashion and like all fashions it could change tomorrow.
I Can I just ask you one last question?
M Sure.
I Have you got a microwave?
M I'm afraid I have to admit that I do. I got it for Christmas. It was a present from my mom – but it's still in its box.

11.2

Speaker 1
I had my ears pierced first when I was 16. Erm, I think it was a birthday present from my parents, that's the reason that I originally had it done, and then I had a second earring put in probably about three years later just because it was fashionable.

Speaker 2
I had my left ear pierced oh back at the end of the 1970s erm and I had a gold small gold ring in my ear for a long time and I occasionally would vary that but I stopped wearing it when I got a proper job 'cos I was told it looked unprofessional but I still put it in from time to time.

Speaker 3
I've taken them out recently erm because I don't know I've got too old, I've got too old for wearing them. They looked OK on me when I was young but now they look a bit daft so I've got rid of them.
When did you have it done?
When I was about 16.

Speaker 4
About two months ago I had my nose pierced with a silver stud. I'd been wanting to get it done for a long time but my mum told me that my nose was too big but I decided that I wanted to get it done anyway and I think it suits me but my mum didn't like it.

Speaker 5
I had my left ear lobe pierced about two or three years ago and I was goaded into it by my teenage daughters – and they quite liked the idea of their father approaching middle age with still a little rebellion left in him.

11.3

My first tattoos were the ones were ones on my hands done at school with a few mates – Indian ink – and they're probably the ones I hate the most now and they kind of grew. A friend of mine became a tattooist and I had an old tattoo on my right arm, which I didn't like. It was a skull and a snake and he covered it up quite nicely with a pattern and er then he showed me some more, so I had another on the inside of my arm then I moved over to my left arm and had a few on there to balance things up a little, erm, all of which I regret today. I wish I'd listened to dad who said, 'You'll regret those.' I didn't finish there. I had one on my leg as well but fortunately then I moved away from my friend who was quite good at giving me free tattoos – they didn't cost any money. I suppose these ones would cost quite a lot of money but no, I'd like to be free of tattoos and listen to dad. I wish I had …

11.5

I Beatrice, you run your own modelling agency now?
B Yes. I have done for quite a few years now.
I And you were, of course, a successful model in the 70s.
B Thank you.
I How would you say the modelling business has changed since you were a model?
B I can probably sum that up in one word – money. Top models earn so much money nowadays that they can choose who they work for, when they work. Really, there's no comparison.
I How did you get into modelling? Had you always wanted to be a model?
B I was lucky. Someone approached me at a fashion show and asked me if I'd like to be a model. I'd had no experience at all, but modelling had always looked so glamorous on TV and I thought it would

be exciting so I said 'Yes, please.'
I And was it exciting and glamorous?
B Yes, but I suppose I was a bit naive really. I had no idea that modelling was such hard work and that I'd have to work such long hours.
I What were the most memorable moments of your career?
B The most exciting was my first Paris Fashion Show. The most embarrassing was when I fell.
I On the catwalk?
B Yes. You remember the shoes that were fashionable in the 70s? At one show the heels I had to wear were so high that I fell over. It was rather embarrassing.
I I bet it was. Would you recommend modelling as a career to young girls?
B Yes, I would. The only problem is that not everyone is successful. So many young girls don't make it to the top. It really is such a difficult career to break into, but certainly it's a very exciting career if you're one of the lucky ones.

11.6

1 A Debbie?
   D Yeah?
   A You know that tape you lent me?
   D Mm? What about it?
   A Er, well, I'm afraid there's been a bit of an accident.
   D What have you done?
   A Well, actually, it wasn't me. It was my kid brother. He started playing with it and it got a bit tangled.
   D Tangled?
   A Yeah. It's more or less OK but I'm afraid it jumps a bit on one of the tracks.
   D Which track?
   A The title track.
   D Oh, no, that's my favourite.
   A I'm really sorry. I'll buy you another one.
   D No, I don't want you to buy me another one, honest. It doesn't matter. It's not the end of the world.
   A Well, thanks for being so nice about it.

2 A Ed, there's something I've got to tell you.
   E What?
   A You know your blue jacket?
   E The one I lent you?
   A Yes. I'm ever so sorry but I got tomato sauce all over it.
   E What? How on earth did that happen?
   A Sally and I had a bit of an argument and, well, she threw a plateful of spaghetti bolognese all over me.
   E In the restaurant?
   A Yes.
   E In front of everyone?
   A Yes! I tried to wash it out but, well, you can still see the stain quite clearly.
   E Oh well, it can't be helped.
   A I'm really sorry.
   E Oh, don't worry about it. It really doesn't matter.

3 M I really don't know how to tell you this.
   B Tell me what?
   M Your car. I can't tell you how sorry I am.
   B What's happened?
   M There's been a bit of an accident.
   B An accident? Are you all right?
   M Yes, I'm fine, but the front headlamp's smashed and the wing mirror on the same side. It's all my fault. This car stopped suddenly in front of me and I crashed into him.
   B Look, you're all right, aren't you?

M Yes, but …
B Well, that's all that matters. The insurance will cover the damage.
M But I feel really bad about it. You've only had it a few months.
B Matthew. Forget it! It's only a car!
4 B Christopher? It's Brian here. Look, I'm afraid I won't be able to come on Saturday. I've got to attend a conference in Prague.
C Oh well, never mind. It can't be helped.

12.1

Speaker 1
My daughter Zoe is nine years old and wants to be a successful skater. She's at the ice-rink at six o'clock in the morning and again after school for a couple of hours. She comes home exhausted, has something to eat, spends half an hour on her homework and goes straight to bed. Weekends she's either doing more training or travelling the length and breadth of the country going in for competitions. I don't think that's any kind of life for a nine-year-old but it's one against two in our house. It seems I'm the only one who thinks there's something wrong with it. I think Zoe should be out with her friends and should be concentrating on her schoolwork, not spending her time chasing a dream. I'd like to know what you think.

Speaker 2
I'm phoning in for some advice. I'm twenty-five years old and I work for a large international company. The job's OK, the money's quite good – but it's not very exciting and quite honestly I can't really see myself here for the rest of my working life. What I'd really like to do is set up my own company. I've got one or two ideas and I think I'd be able to get a bank loan but it's a big decision and I don't know whether I could make a success of it or not. I'm in two minds about the whole thing.

Speaker 3
Hallo. I'm fourteen years old and my parents want me to be a professional musician. They're both musicians themselves. I've been having piano and violin lessons since I was five and I'm quite good, but not really good enough to make a career out of it. I've tried telling my parents that I'd rather have music as a hobby and do something else as a career but they won't take me seriously. I really don't know how to convince them.

12.2

P You don't sound very confident, Nicole.
N No, I'm not really. I'm confident about the business – well, there is definitely a gap in the market for the product – but I've always worked for someone else before and the idea of being responsible for everything is quite scary.
P What do you think Nicole should do, James?
J Nicole?
N Yes?
J Is this what you really really want to do?
N Yes.
J Well, if you're absolutely positive that's what you want to do, you should just do it, go for it, because if you don't, you might regret it later on.
P Professor Webb?
W It seems to me from what I've heard that Nicole is lacking in self-confidence but, don't take this as a criticism, Nicole, but are you?
N I am, yes.
W Well, I think you ought to consider doing a self-improvement course. Do you know the kind of thing I mean?
N Yes, I know what you're talking about, but I'm not sure that's really for me.

W Well, if you don't like the idea of doing a course, why don't you read one of the books there are on the subject? There are a lot about.
N Can you recommend one?
W 'Yes, You Can!' is very popular. 'How to Succeed in Business' is another. If I were you, Nicole, I would put your plans on hold for now. I wouldn't do anything until you yourself feel more confident that it's going to work. But that's just my advice.
P Has that been any help, Nicole?
N Yes, it has. Thank you.
P And so on to the next caller who is …

12.3

What kind of person do you think you have to be to be successful?

Speaker 1
Determined. Determined and ambitious. Erm, yes, you've got to have a single thing in your mind and you've got to be determined to go for it.

Speaker 2
I think you need to be confident, erm enthusiastic, and energetic.

Speaker 3
I think you have to be quite confident, and er perhaps quite lucky, too.

Speaker 4
I think you have to be very determined. Erm, you have to be confident. You have to not be afraid of disappointment. Erm, can't think of anything else.

Speaker 5
Flexible, and I think you need to be, have a sense of humour, erm I think you need to know exactly what you want to achieve, I think you need to have a sense of priorities.

Speaker 6
Hard-working, dedicated, erm, someone who can get on with people, yes, a good people manager, person manager, and focused, and that's about it.

Speaker 7
I think you need to be ambitious, you have to have a lot of belief in yourself, erm you have to do something that you enjoy, so you've got the enthusiasm for it, erm and that's about it.

Speaker 8
Single-minded, I think. You have to want it more than anything else, you have to want success in whatever field you're in. Erm, and I think you have to be obsessed and you have to stay obsessed. I think single-mindedness is the … is the most important thing.

Speaker 9
To be successful in anything, not any particular, not one particular business or field or anything …? Erm oh my goodness! Erm very driven. Very motivated and very determined to succeed. Erm, I think you have to believe really passionately in whatever it is you're doing or whatever you're trying to succeed at … and you have to believe that it's going to work and you believe that you've got a really great idea, and just keep going, keep trying keep going. What else, what else can I say?

12.4

Speaker 1
I suppose a big achievement for me personally was when I passed my maths GCSE. I didn't actually take the exam until I was forty and I'd always failed terribly at maths at school and been bottom of the class but when I when my children started secondary school I found that I couldn't help them with their maths so I

decided to take the matter in hand and so I went to evening classes with my friend and passed my maths GCSE in a year, which I was very proud of.

Speaker 2
Something I found very hard to do originally was to stand up in front of lots of people, erm talk to them, in a in a comfortable way. Erm, it actually took me quite a long time to do that once I started my job. In the end I suppose it was really a matter of practising and doing it erm often enough, preparing myself for doing it. Erm, that took quite a long time to start with. I had to make sure that I had all my notes very carefully prepared and I rehearsed it. I used to stand in front of a mirror or record myself on video. And that was quite time-consuming but I think in the end it worked and … It doesn't it doesn't really worry me too much any more. I still feel a little bit nervous before I stand up in front of people but as soon as I'm there in front of them and I've started it feels quite natural and er I'm not unhappy about it any more.

Speaker 3
The thing I'm think I'm most proud of achieving is passing my driving test because I passed it when I was very young and I had to overcome a total loss of confidence in driving. That was because on my second test I had a very bad experience where the driving examiner grabbed the wheel from me and we almost collided with a bus. So when I eventually passed my test it was a really great sense of achievement because I felt that I had really been able to achieve something which I had thought I would never be able to achieve.

Pronunciation

Unit 1

1 Read these questions. Which words do you think will be stressed? Follow the example.

   a <u>What's</u> your <u>name</u>?
   b Where were you born?
   c What do you do?
   d What does your father do?
   e How many jobs have you had?
   f How many languages can you speak?
   g Do you like your boss?
   h What are your plans?

2 **1.4** Listen and check your ideas.

3 What kind of words were stressed? What kind of words were not stressed?

4 Listen again and repeat. Be careful about weak forms.

Unit 2

1 When we speak, we divide what we say into 'chunks' and we stress the important words (nouns, verbs, adjectives, etc.). In each chunk one word is more important than any of the others, depending on the context. We give this word the strongest stress.

   a Read these conversations. Which word do you think will be most stressed in B's replies?
   1 A What are you doing on Saturday?
     B I'm having a <u>party</u> on Saturday.
   2 A When are you having a party?
     B I'm having a party on Saturday.
   3 A How are things between you and Peter?
     B We're getting married next month.
   4 A When are you getting married?
     B We're getting married next month.
   5 A I saw a red car parked outside your house last night.
     B My brother's staying with us at the moment.
   6 A Who's your brother staying with?
     B My brother's staying with us at the moment.

   b **2.10** Listen and check your ideas.

   c Which word do you think will be most stressed in each of these chunks?
   1 / I'm having a party on Saturday. / You will come, / won't you? /
   2 / We're going to the theatre. / Do you fancy coming? /
   3 / We're getting married next month. / We'd like to invite you to the wedding. /

4 / My brother's staying with us at the moment. / Would you like to meet him? /
5 / I've got two tickets for the theatre. / Do you want to come? /

   d **2.11** Listen and check your ideas.

2 When you accept invitations, it is polite to sound enthusiastic.

   a **2.12** Listen to these expressions. Which speaker sounds enthusiastic in each pair?
   1 a b
   2 a b
   3 a b

   b **2.13** Listen and repeat.

Unit 3

1 a Which syllables do you think will be stressed in these expressions?
   1 I agree.
   2 That's true.
   3 You're right there.

   b **3.5** Listen and check your ideas. Then listen again and repeat.

2 a Which syllables do you think will have the main stress in B's replies, and why?
   1 A I think the government is doing a good job.
     B I don't.
   2 A I was worried when I heard the news.
     B I wasn't.
   3 A I didn't agree with what he said.
     B I did.
   4 A I'm not surprised.
     B I am.

   b **3.6** Listen and check your ideas. Then listen again and repeat the replies.

3 a **3.7** Listen to these expressions. Notice how some words are linked together.

   1 So do I.
   2 So was I.
   3 Neither did I.
   4 Neither am I.

   b Listen again and repeat.

c Use the examples to help you work out the rules of pronunciation. Match sentence beginnings **1–4** with endings **a–d**.

1 When a word ends in a consonant sound (like /z/) and the next word begins with a vowel sound (like /aɪ/) …

2 When a word ends in a vowel sound and the next word begins with a consonant sound …

3 When a word ends in the letter *r* and the next word begins with a consonant sound …

4 When a word ends in the letter *r* and the next word begins with a vowel sound …

  a … we pronounce the letter *r*.

  b … the words run together and sound like one word.

  c … we don't pronounce the letter *r*.

  d … the words don't run together.

d How are these expressions pronounced? Mark the links.

1 I don't agree.

2 Neither do I.

3 So have I.

4 So will I.

e **3.8** Listen and check your ideas. Then listen again and repeat.

Unit 4

1 **4.5** Listen to these expressions. How are the words in **bold** pronounced in natural speech?

a **Would you** mind helping me with this chair please?

b **Could you** put that over there please?

c **Can't you** forget I told you?

2 Intonation is very important when you make a request. If you use the wrong intonation, your request can sound like an order.

a **4.6** You are going to hear three requests. Which speaker sounds polite, a or b?

1 a b

2 a b

3 a b

b **4.7** Listen and repeat. Make sure you sound polite!

Could you carry this upstairs?

Unit 5

1 a **5.4** Listen. Which letters are not pronounced?

1 what do

2 had to

3 can't go

4 not true

5 I don't think

6 not something

7 difficult to

b Complete this general rule of pronunciation.

When a word ends in *t* or *d* it is not usually pronounced if the next word begins with _____

2 a **5.5** Listen to these expressions. Tick (✓) the sentences where the letter in **bold** is pronounced.

1 a What would you sa**y**?

    b I'd sa**y** it's a good idea.

    c I'd sa**y** they were stupid.

2 a I don't kno**w**.

    b I don't kno**w** what I think.

    c I don't kno**w** if it's a good idea.

3 a Is that you**r** opinion?

    b Is that you**r** view?

    c Is that what most people you**r** age think?

b Choose the correct alternative to complete the rule.

y, *w* and *r* are pronounced when the next word begins with a *consonant sound / vowel sound*.

3 a Mark any unpronounced letters (╱) and indicate linking between words (‿) in these expressions. Follow the example.

1 Wha̸t do you think about this idea?

2 It's difficult to say.

3 I'm not sure.

4 It's not something I've really thought about.

5 I'd say it's a stupid idea.

6 Do you have an opinion on military service?

b **5.6** Listen and check your ideas.

c Listen again and repeat.

Unit 6

1 a `6.6` Listen to these expressions. Are the speakers happy to give their permission or not? Write ✓ or ✗.

1 All right.
2 All right.
3 Yeah.
4 Yeah.
5 OK.
6 OK.

b `6.7` Listen and repeat. Make sure you sound happy to give your permission.

2 a Which syllables do you think will be stressed in these expressions? Which syllables do you think will carry the main stress? Follow the example.

1 <u>Go</u> a<u>head</u>.
2 Of course.
3 Sure.
4 No problem.
5 I don't mind at all.

b `6.8` Listen and check your ideas.

c Listen again and repeat. Remember that to sound happy to give permission you should start high on the first stressed syllable, go higher on the main stressed syllable, and then fall.

Go ahead.

If there is only one syllable, start high and fall.

Sure.

3 `6.9` You are going to hear eight requests for permission. Respond to them using the expressions in **1a** and **2a** in the same order. Sound happy!

Unit 7

1 a Read these expressions. Cross out (╱) any letters which you think are not pronounced, and indicate any linking between words (‿). Follow the example.

1 I'm not so keen on that idea.

2 That's a good idea.

3 That's not a bad idea.

4 I'm not so sure about that.

b Which syllables do you think are stressed? Which are the main stressed syllables?

c `7.6` Listen and check your ideas.

d Listen again and repeat.

2 If you think that someone's suggestion is good, you need to sound enthusiastic in your response.

a `7.7` Listen to these expressions said in two different ways. Which version sounds enthusiastic, and which sounds unenthusiastic? Write **E** or **U**.

1 Yeah!	a	b
2 Great!	a	b
3 Fantastic!	a	b
4 Brilliant!	a	b
5 Absolutely!	a	b

b `7.8` Listen and repeat. Sound enthusiastic!

3 `7.9` You are going to hear some suggestions. Respond to them using any of the expressions in **1a** and **2a**. Make sure you use the right intonation.

Unit 8

1 a `8.9` Listen to the strong and weak forms of these prepositions. You will hear the strong form first, and then the weak form.

at   for   from   to   of

b Will the speakers use the strong form or the weak form of the prepositions in **bold** in these expressions? Write **S** or **W**.

1 Thank you **for** calling.
2 What type of holiday are you looking **for**?
3 Who would you like to speak **to**?
4 I'd like **to** speak to the manager, please.
5 I'm afraid Miss Smith is **at** a conference today.
6 What's he looking **at**?
7 Where did you get our number **from**?
8 I got it **from** Yellow Pages.
9 How many copies **of** our brochure would you like?
10 What does the accommodation consist **of**?

c `8.10` Listen and check your ideas.

d Match sentence beginnings 1 and 2 with their endings A and B to give you the rules of pronunciation.

1 We use the strong forms of these prepositions when …
2 We use the weak forms of these prepositions when …
A … they are the last word in the sentence.
B … they are not the last word in the sentence.

2 a `8.11` Listen to these eight expressions. Which words are stressed most in each one?

1 Can I help you?
2 Who's calling, / please?
3 I'll put you through.
4 Just a moment.
5 Let me take your details.
6 I didn't quite catch that.
7 Shall I send it to you?
8 I'll put one in the post to you today.

b Listen again and repeat.

Unit 9

1 a **9.5** Listen to these expressions. Which are the main stressed syllables in each one?

1 What's the matter?
2 Why are you crying?
3 What are you doing out of bed at this time of night?
4 Why didn't you tell me you had problems?
5 Why aren't you in bed?
6 What on earth are you doing?

b Listen again. Choose the correct alternative to complete this rule about intonation in *Wh-* questions.

▨ Intonation in *Wh-* questions usually goes *up/down*.

c Listen again and repeat.

2 The word *that* has a strong form /ðæt/ and a weak form /ðət/.

a **9.6** Listen to these expressions. Do the speakers use the strong form or the weak form of *that*?

1 The main reason was that they were green.
2 That isn't a good reason.

b Do you think the speaker will use the strong form or the weak form of *that* in these expressions? Write **S** or **W**.

1 That's no excuse.
2 Another reason was that I forgot.
3 I lost the instructions that you gave me.
4 That's why.
5 Don't give me that old excuse.

c **9.7** Listen and check your ideas. Then repeat the sentences after the tape.

Unit 10

1 a Read these two short conversations. Which syllables do you think will be especially stressed in B's responses?

1 A So you're going to Italy. Lucky you!
  B I'm not going for a holiday. I'm going there on business.
2 A Is that the Grand Hotel?
  B No. This isn't the Grand Hotel. It's the Hilton Hotel.

b **10.4** Listen and check your ideas. Why do the speakers use strong stress on these words?

c Listen again and repeat.

2 a **10.5** Read these details. Then answer the questions, correcting the information you hear. Listen to the example first.

Sam Kennedy
16, Smith Avenue
Forest Hill
3131 Victoria
Australia
Tel. no. 9877 5291
Date of Birth 14/1/80

Example
Your surname is Smith. Is that right?
No, it isn't Smith. It's Kennedy.

b **10.6** Listen to the whole conversation.

Unit 11

1 a **11.7** Read and listen to what the speakers say. What do you think their next sentence will be? Choose A or B.

1

There's something I've got to tell you.

A I'm getting married next month.
B I can't go on holiday with you after all.

2

You know that tape you lent me?

A I think it's really good.
B I've lost it.

3

You know your new green shirt?

A Louise thinks it's really cool.
B I'm afraid I burnt it while I was ironing it.

b **11.8** Listen and check your ideas.

c **11.9** Listen and repeat these expressions for introducing bad news.

2 a Read these expressions. Which syllables do you think will be stressed? Which syllables do you think will carry the main stress?

1 I'm really sorry.
2 I'm so sorry.
3 I'm ever so sorry.

b **11.10** Listen and check your ideas.

c **11.11** Now listen to two speakers saying the same expressions. Which speaker sounds more sorry in each pair, a or b?

1 a b
2 a b
3 a b

d **11.12** Listen again and repeat.

Unit 2 — Skills p.19

Answers

1 Women are better at hearing sounds.

2 Women are better at hearing a song and being able to sing it back.

3 Men don't recognize voices easily. Women are better at working out who is on the phone before the person says who they are.

4 Women have more developed intuition than men.

5 Women have a far better memory for faces than men.

6 Girls are better at writing and spelling than boys at an early age. As boys get older the difference evens out.

7 Men have better spacial awareness than women.

8 Women are good at direction if they've been to a place once, but not if they haven't.

9 Men aren't happy getting too close.

10 Men hear the tap but they are able to ignore it. But a dripping tap drives a woman crazy!

Unit 3 — Language in action p.33

CHAIRPERSON

Details
In the meeting your job will be to …
• introduce people
• ask people to speak, and keep the discussion going
• keep the meeting orderly and to time
• give a final summary.

Preparation tasks
• Find out what roles the others have chosen.
• Prepare some prompt questions for each item on the agenda.
• Decide approximately how long you want to spend on each topic.
• Have a notebook ready to record the main points of the discussion.

Unit 6 — Language in action p.63

Student B

Situation 1
You are renting a room in someone's flat. You moved in last week. Ask permission to do the following:
• have a party to celebrate your birthday
• have a friend to stay overnight in your room from time to time
• keep a pet in your room.

If they refuse permission, try to persuade them to change their mind.

Situation 2
You are a very strict boss. An employee is going to ask your permission to do the following:
• take three days off
• make a phone call to another country
• come in late tomorrow.

You can decide whether or not to give permission, but if you do, don't agree immediately. Student A will need to persuade you.

Unit 4 — Grammar extra p.40

Unit 2 ━━━━━━━━━━━━━━━━━━━━━━ Language in action p.23

Student A

Invite other students to do the things in blue.

Monday

Tennis 7.00 p.m.
((Get a partner!))

Tuesday

Favourite TV programme this
evening – don't miss it!

Wednesday

No plans

Thursday

Stay in!

Friday

Don't go out! Always too tired

Saturday

Morning – go shopping
for clothes – not alone!
Afternoon – no plans (going out
this evening)
Evening – Lucy's birthday party.

Sunday

Morning – jogging as usual
Afternoon – invite some people
home for lunch
Evening – no plans

notes

Unit 4 ━━━━━━━━━━━━━━━━━━━━━━ Language in action p.43

Student B

Situation 1

Student A is going away on a business trip. Student A will ask you to lend them three things, and to do two things for them. You can agree to their requests or you can refuse them. If you refuse, be polite! (Give an excuse!)

Situation 2

You are going to another country on a business trip. Decide which country you are going to.

Ask Student A to lend you
- their mobile phone
- their lap-top computer
- their … phrase book

Ask Student A to
- teach you a few useful … phrases before you go
- pick you up from the airport

If Student A does not want to help you, try to find another Student A who can.

Unit 8 ━━━━━━━━━━━━━━
Language in action   p.83

Student A

1 Someone has told you about a company called The World of Adventure, which organizes activity holidays in unusual places. Phone the company, find out as much as you can about the holidays and ask to be sent more information.

2 You work for the Globe Arts Centre. Answer your partner's questions about the event in this advertisement and respond to their requests.

ACOUSTIC AFRICA

FIVE EVENINGS OF AFRICAN MUSIC

THE FIRST SUNDAYS IN THE MONTH
APRIL – AUGUST AT 8.30 PM

AT

THE GLOBE ARTS CENTRE

PROGRAMME INCLUDES ARTISTS FROM

ZIMBABWE · MADAGASCAR · TANZANIA

NIGERIA · RWANDA · SUDAN

TICKETS £10

Student B

Invite other students to do the things in blue.

Monday
Important exam tomorrow - revise!

Tuesday
No plans this evening - go out? NOT the cinema.

Wednesday
Sister's for dinner

Thursday
No plans

Friday
John's party 9.00 p.m. - find someone to go with.

Saturday
No plans!

Sunday
Morning - clean the flat
Afternoon - no plans
Evening - get someone to come and watch a video (rent it)

notes

16-year-old student

Details
- You were hoping to work in the PZM offices after leaving school.
- You are disappointed about the closure, but you are optimistic about the future.
- You think you will be able to find work.

Questions to think about
- What job did you expect to do?
- What are your future plans?
- Where else could you work?

27-year-old factory worker

Details
- You have worked for PZM since you left school.
- You are shocked by the closure news.
- You don't want to leave the town and you are pessimistic about the future.

Questions to think about
- What is your job?
- Are you well paid?
- How has this news affected you?
- Why do you want to stay?
- How do you see your own future?

35-year-old office worker

Details
- You have worked part-time for PZM since your 4-year-old child was born.
- For various reasons, you cannot leave the area.
- You are very dependent on PZM.

Questions to think about
- What is your job?
- Who looks after your child while you are at work?
- Why can't you leave?
- In what ways are you dependent?

56-year-old manager

Details
- You have always worked for PZM.
- The closure news has taken you by surprise.
- You think PZM dominated the town for too long.

Questions to think about
- How long have you worked for PZM?
- How do feel about your own personal situation?
- How could the town possibly benefit from the closure?

Student B

1 You have heard about a series of monthly concerts of African music that are being held at your local arts centre, the Globe. Phone the Centre and find out as much as you can about the concerts and ask to be sent more information.

2 You work for this holiday company, World of Adventure, which organizes activity holidays in unusual places. Answer your partner's questions about the company and respond to their requests.

World of adventure

Mountaineering, Cycling, Trekking holidays in

ANTARCTICA · NEPAL · INDIA · VIETNAM · SOUTH AMERICA · AUSTRALIA

SPECIAL HOLIDAYS FOR 20–30s and over 40s

Free Colour brochure

Representative of PZM

Details
- It is your role to defend the closure decision.
- You work for PZM and live in the town.

Questions to think about
- How will you explain the need for PZM to close?
- How will you personally be affected by the closure?

Property developer

Details
- You represent the building firm which is buying the PZM site.
- You hope to attract other firms to the town.

Questions to think about
- What plans does your company have for the site?
- What kind of firms do you want to attract?

Unit 2 Language in action p.23

Student C

Invite other students to do the things in blue.

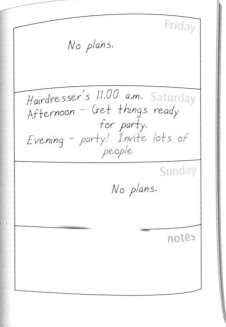

Monday
Dentist 6.00 p.m.

Tuesday
Great film on at cinema! Ask someone to come!

Wednesday
George visiting from America – ask some people round for a drink to meet him.

Thursday
No plans

Friday
No plans.

Saturday
Hairdresser's 11.00 a.m.
Afternoon - Get things ready for party.
Evening - party! Invite lots of people

Sunday
No plans.

notes

Unit 11 Language in action p.113

Student B

Spend a few minutes preparing what you will say in Situation 2 before you start the role play.

Situation 1

You have just come back from holiday. Student A has been staying in your flat to 'look after things' while you were away. Student A will start the conversation.

Situation 2

You are renting a room in your friend's flat. While Student A was out of town last night you had a party. You did not ask Student A's permission. Start the conversation with Student A. Explain how the following things happened and apologize.

- There is a cigarette burn on the sofa.
- There is a stain on the carpet.
- There are several broken plates.
- There are one or two damaged CDs.

Unit 9 Language in action p.93

Student A

Motorist

You parked illegally for a few minutes to buy something from the chemist's. You are furious that your car is being taken away. Explain why you parked your car here and ask why the police are being so unreasonable. Do everything you can to persuade the police officer not to remove your car.

Doctor in hospital

Find out how the patient was hurt. They have cuts and bruises all over their body and both legs are broken. Be prepared to explain what you have done to the patient and what is going to happen next. (Ideas: legs in plaster/stay in hospital for … weeks)

Shop detective in supermarket

It is your job to catch people stealing from the supermarket. Interview the customer. Find out as much personal information from them as you can. Explain the normal procedure in shoplifting cases like this.

Unit 10 Language in action p.103

Student A

Situation 1

A customer phones you to check whether information they have about a holiday home is correct. This is the correct up-to-date information about St Martin. Correct any wrong information and give correct up-to-date details.

St Martin (Burgundy)
1 km from centre of village
for 2 adults + 2 children
Facilities include
Colour TV • Fridge and freezer
Telephone • Washing machine
Sorry, no pets
Available April–October only
Price €385 per week

Student D

Invite other students to do the things in blue.

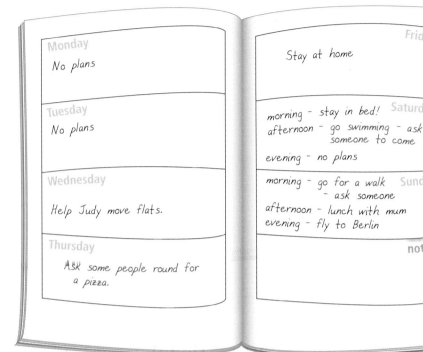

Monday
No plans

Tuesday
No plans

Wednesday
Help Judy move flats.

Thursday
Ask some people round for a pizza.

Friday
Stay at home

Saturday
morning - stay in bed!
afternoon - go swimming - ask someone to come
evening - no plans

Sunday
morning - go for a walk - ask someone
afternoon - lunch with mum
evening - fly to Berlin

notes

Choose one of these roles, but don't tell the others in your group.

- Someone who is very shy.
- Someone who talks about themself all the time.
- Someone who only has one subject of conversation.
- Someone who has just come back after several years living in another country.
- Someone who is bored and can't stop yawning.
- Someone who is very inquisitive about other people.
- Someone who refuses to give straight answers to questions.
- Someone who talks to everyone as if they were children.
- Someone who has just had some good news and can't stop thinking about it.
- Someone who has just had some bad news and can't stop thinking about it.

Student B

Police officer
It is the policy of the police to remove all cars parked illegally. There are no exceptions to this strict rule. Explain patiently and politely to the motorist why the car has to be removed.

Patient in hospital
You have ended up in hospital after doing something rather careless. You don't really want to tell anyone else exactly how the accident happened. Ask the doctor to explain what is going to happen to you from now on.

Shoplifter in supermarket
This is the first time you have stolen anything from a shop. In this case you put a small packet of biscuits in your pocket without thinking. Explain to the detective that you are getting more and more forgetful – think of a good reason for this.

Student B

Situation 2
A customer phones you to check whether information they have about your fast food leaflet is right. This is the correct up-to-date information about Pronto Pizza. Correct any wrong information and give correct up-to-date details.

PRONTO PIZZA
TAKE AWAY AND FREE DELIVERY
Free delivery – in the city and 5 miles outside
10% DISCOUNT FOR TAKE AWAY
OPENING TIMES
6.00 p.m. – 12 midnight
SUNDAY– FRIDAY
3.00 p.m.– 3.00 a.m.
SATURDAY

Group B

2 Write brief notes about the island of Eigg in answer to these questions. Then check your answers with the other students in your group.

a How many people live on the island?
b Where is it? How far is it from the mainland?
c What language do the islanders speak?
d What are the main problems for the islanders?
e What important change has happened recently? What effect has this had?
f How often does the ferry service operate?

Desirable island, wet, cold, windy. No electricity, plenty of sheep. No longer for sale.

The sixty-three inhabitants of the island of Eigg, which lies 12 miles off the north-west coast of Scotland, are celebrating a new era. They have just bought the island for £1.5m, and with it their freedom.

5 £1m of the money needed to buy the island came from a businesswoman who prefers to remain anonymous. The rest came from private donations from around the world.

The sale marks the end of a ten-year fight between the Gaelic-speaking islanders and a succession of millionaire owners. Relations between the two groups had always been bad. None of the owners had ever come to live on
10 the island, and all had promised to invest money, which they never did.

It is for this reason that Eigg, inhabited since the Stone Age, still has no mains electricity, mains gas or even a rubbish dump.

But now there will be many changes. The islanders plan to improve the infrastructure of Eigg and encourage 'green' tourism. The area has 430 different
15 plants and 130 species of birds and is already popular with nature lovers.

New businesses are starting up, new families are arriving and old ones are returning. It's clear that Eigg is going to have a bright future. Eigg's newest resident is Grace Fergusson, 19, who left her job at 'Burger King' in Edinburgh to open a cafe on the island. Later this year Robert Melohn, 28, whose father
20 is the local doctor, will move his software business to the island. In the autumn another local boy, 19-year-old Colin Carr, will give up farming on the Scottish mainland and return to tend sheep on Eigg.

Eigg has good transport links with the mainland. In summer a daily ferry service links the island with the small town of Mallaig. In winter the service
25 runs three times a week.

Close up

1.5 What other things can be *anonymous*?

1.14 What is the opposite of *encourage*? What is the structure after *encourage* and its opposite?

1.14 What is *green tourism*? What other things can be *green*?

3 In your group, answer these questions.
a Why do you think the businesswoman donated money?
b Why do you think the previous owners bought the island, but never lived there and didn't invest in it?
c Why do you think old families are returning and new families are arriving?

4 Decide on four or five key facts about the island.

Turn back to p.46, Information exchange.

Top 10 annoying noises

1 NOISY NEIGHBOURS
2 BUILDING SITES
3 PUBS AND RESTAURANTS
4 NOISY PARTIES
5 CAR ALARMS
6 ROAD WORKS
7 BARKING DOGS
8 TRAFFIC NOISE
9 RADIOS OR PERSONAL STEREOS IN PUBLIC PLACES
10 AEROPLANES

OXFORD
UNIVERSITY PRESS

Great Clarendon Street, Oxford OX2 6DP

Oxford University Press is a department of the University of Oxford. It furthers the University's objective of excellence in research, scholarship, and education by publishing worldwide in

Oxford New York

Athens Auckland Bangkok Bogotá Buenos Aires Calcutta Cape Town Chennai Dar es Salaam Delhi Florence Hong Kong Istanbul Karachi Kuala Lumpur Madrid Melbourne Mexico City Mumbai Nairobi Paris São Paulo Singapore Taipei Tokyo Toronto Warsaw

with associated companies in Berlin Ibadan

Oxford and Oxford English are registered trade marks of Oxford University Press in the UK and in certain other countries

Acknowledgements

The authors and publisher are very grateful to the following for their professional expertise and valuable comments and feedback on the material as it was written: Jan Borsbey, Brian Brennan, Jane Hann, Felicity Harwood, Bernie Hayden, Marek Herda, Jane Hudson, Sue Inkster, Amanda Jeffries, Magdalena Junkieles, David Massey, Nick Sheard, Ruth Swan.

The authors would like to thank everybody who contributed to the recordings, with a special thanks to Heather Barton, Jo Ruffell, Becky Haines, Lisa Foster.

The authors and publisher are grateful to the following for permission to reproduce the following extracts and adaptations of copyright material: Curtis Brown on behalf of the author for article by Barry Norman: 'Elizabeth', copyright © Barry Norman 1998, from The Radio Times, 3–9 October 1998. Express Newspapers for article by Mike Ward: 'The Ice Sculptor', from Express on Sunday, 11 January 1998. Focus Magazine for articles by Janet Fricker: 'Why Laughter is the Best Medicine' from Focus, May 1993; by Jerome Burne: 'So You Want to be a Success' from Focus, June 1994; and 'Sun, Sea and Roof!' from Focus, September 1997. The Guardian for articles by Peter Carty: 'New Job: Safari Park Worker', copyright © Peter Carty 1995, first published in The Guardian 13 December 1995; John Mullan: 'Letters@last' from The Guardian 7 September 1998; copyright © The Guardian 1998; and by Owen Bowcott: 'Irish Isle Smiles Through the Rain to Lure Visitors' from The Guardian 24 August 1993, copyright © The Guardian 1993. Harper Collins Publishers Ltd for extract from Simon Mayo's Confessions by Simon Mayo (Marshall Pickering, 1991). Independent Newspapers for articles by Miles Kington: 'Taxi Etiquette, The Vastness of the Universe and Other Issues That Divide Humanity' from The Independent, 8 May 1998; and by Hester Lacey: 'Still With The Beatles' from The Independent on Sunday, 13 September 1998. Music Sales Ltd for Where Have all the Cowboys Gone? Words and Music by Paula Cole © 1996 Hing Face Music/Famous Music Corporation, USA. All Rights Reserved. International Copyright Secured. The Observer for article by Michael Palin: 'And Now for Somewhere Completely Different'

copyright © Michael Palin 1992, first published in The Observer October 1992. Penguin Books Ltd for 'Brain Sex Test' from Brain Sex: The Real Difference Between Men and Women by Anne Moir and David Jessel (Michael Joseph, 1989), copyright © Anne Moir and David Jessel 1989. Helena Pozniak for extract from her article 'The Year of Living Dangerously' from The Independent, 12 March 1999. The Radio Times for articles 'The Smile of the Shark' from The Radio Times 20–26 February 1999; and by Emma Norman: 'Amistad' from The Radio Times 13–19 March 1999. Transworld Publishers Ltd for extract from Notes from a Small Island by Bill Bryson, (Black Swan, 1995, a division of Transworld Publishers Ltd), copyright © Bill Bryson 1995. All rights reserved.

Although every effort has been made to trace and contact copyright holders before publication, this has not always been possible. We apologize for any apparent infringement of copyright and if notified, the publisher will be pleased to rectify any errors or omissions at the earliest opportunity.

The publisher would like to thank the following for their kind permission to reproduce photographs and other copyright material: Action-Plus p.116 (G.Kirk); The Advertising Archives p.18; AKG, London p.38 (Wright Brothers); The Bridgeman Art Library p.6 (Pieter Brueghel the Younger (c. 1564–1638), A Wedding Feast, Johnny van Haeften Gallery, London; George Brooks pp.28–9; Bubbles Photo Library p.16 (driving licence/J.Woodcock), p.54 & p.60 (children/J.Woodcock), p.56 (wedding/G.du Feu), pp.118–9 (death of parent/I.West); Camera Press p.21 (Femina); Colorific/Black Star p.59 (1951 joyride/Ralph Crane), Corbis p.40 (Tory Island fishermen/P.Turnley), p.62 (T.Aruzza), p.99 (waste incineration plant/H.A.Jahn), p.99 (classical building/J.Sohm; ChromoSohm Inc.), pp.118–9 (boy in car/J.Cooke); Corbis Sygma pp.38–9 (Breitling Orbiter 3), p.44 (Toyota worker/Sion/Touhig), p.70 (Tom Hanks/ N.Ephron), p.74 & p.77 (angry motorist/T.Markow), p.109 (The Spice Girls), p.111 (exhibition/Y.Forestier), p.114 (athlete/D.Giry); Devon News Ltd p.96 (couple); Courtesy of Flamingo, HarperCollins Publishers: Andrea Barrett, The Voyage of the Narwhal, 1999 p.112; Frank Spooner Pictures p.22 (rattlesnake/Gamma/Liaison/Sander), p.93 (soldiers/ Gamma/ Liaison/E.Adams), p.96 (cave interior/Gamma/ F.Reglain), p.114 (Children's Parliament/Gamma/G.Brassignac), (beauty competition/Gamma/Bernstein) Courtesy of Andrew Hayton and Longleat Safari Park p.24 (with elephant), p.30; © Hundertwasser Architekturprojekt p.98 (4 photos Rogner-Bad Blumau); Impact Photos p.56 (standing woman/ J.A.Jafferji); Katz Pictures p.48 (aid worker/S.Lehman), (bus travel/B.Trueba), (rafting/J.Warburton-Lee), p.93 (policeman/ A.Moore), p.118 (beauty competition/V.Winship/IPG); The Kobal Collection p.66 (©1998 Universal City Studios Productions, Inc); Magnum Photos pp.8–9 (all pictures except aerial view/M Parr), p.53 (soldiers/P.Marlow); National Motor Museum, Beaulieu p.59 (car rally); Courtesy of Panasonic p.81; Photonica p.84 & p.90 (people leaning on railing/C.Gray), p.90 (mother and child/P.McDonough), (woman with ball/C.Gray), (fancy dress/G.Cunnick); Pictorial Press p.108 (The Beatles 1963/Combi Press), p.109 (George Michael/R.Lewis), (Joan Baez, Madonna, U2/J.Mayer), (Elvis), (The Supremes/Combi Press), (Rolling Stones/PP), p.112 (Joni Mitchell/J.Mayer), ('Elizabeth' 1999/©Polygram); Pictures Colour Library p.16 (Cherry Blossom festival), p.44 (island with hut), p.50 (Warsaw), pp.68–9 (moorland background), p.68 (York Minster), p.69 (street), p.94 & p.99 (Hundertwasser, coloured apartments), p.95 (Sydney), p.97, p.100, p.101 (villa with balconies); Planet Earth Pictures/ Space Frontiers p.34 & p.38 (astronaut on the moon), p.44 & p.51 (aerial view of island/L.Murray), p.90 (giraffes/J.Scott); Redferns p.104 & p.108 (Beatles fans/Michael Ochs Archives), p.108 (man with headphones/A.Redfern), p.120 (violinists/ O.Noel); Rex Features p.9 (aerial view), p.22 (wife-carrying festival/Lehtikuva/SoileKallio), p.70 (Billy Connolly/ J.Makey), (Eddie Murphy/P.Brooker), (Woody Allen), p.94 (coach interior/M.Hill), p.110 (S.Wood), p.111 (The Globe/G.Allen/The Times), p.111 (cinema/J.Sutton-Hibbert), p.114 & p.123 (walking dogs); Robert Harding Picture Library p.34 (train), p.50 (Bieszczady region), pp.68–9 (village/A.Woolfitt), p.69 (industrial town/A.Woolfitt), p.123 (market); Royal Geographical Society, London p.38 (Tenzing on Summit of Mt Everest 29/5/53 /©Hillary), (Scott finding Amundsen's tent); Science Photo Library p.84 (black eye/M.Dohrn); Still Moving Picture Library p.12 (restaurant/ K.Paterson), p.46 (island of Eigg/G.Summers); Tate Gallery, London p.29 (© Carl André Equivalent VIII, 1966 ©VAGA, New York/DACS, London 2000); © Tiger Television Ltd 1991

p.107 (Mr Bean); Tony Stone Images p.4 (theatre signs/S.& N. Geary), (couple driving/P.Correz), (woman eating/A.Booher), (snowboarders/M.Timo), (woman reading/S.McComb), (man listening to music/J.Millar), (couple shopping/E.Larrayadieu), p.12 (cinema/C.Slattery), (theatres/ S.&N.Geary), (opera house/M.Loken), (nightclub/ P.Chesley), p.14 (carnival/A.Diesendruck), (patchwork/ Z.Kaluzny), (barbecue/P.Redman), (father on beach/ E.Bernager), (cyclists/ L.Monneret), p.16 (couple with flowers/D.Bosler), (family Christmas/Kaluzny/Thatcher), (birthday/L.Monneret), (graduation/A.Sacks), p.19 (A.Aspinall), p.22 (carnival/A.Diesendruck), p.24 (grape-picking/C.Ehlers), (executives around a table/F.Herholdt), (office building/A.Errington), p.34 (camels/P.Chesley), (Ayers Rock/D.Austen), p.44 (business meeting/C.Gupton), (crowded beach/G.Allison), (woman at computer/T.May), (Greek restaurant/S.Huber), p.48 (consulting books/ D.Joel), p.49 (T.Flach), p.52 (J.Passmore), p.53 (children/ C.Bissell), (backpackers/B.Torrez), (vacuuming/I.Shaw), p.54 (cowboy/D.Rosenberg), p.64 & p.71 (frowning/ J.Bradley), p.71 (laughing/C.Bissell), (crying/N.Reeve), (winking/N.Dolding), (yawning/P.Gentieu), (smiling/ K.Fisher), (giggling/B.Yee), p.73 (car traffic/J.Pobereskin), (bus traffic/P.Harris), p.77 (airport check-in/C.Bissell), (tourists/C.Gupton), pp78–9 (P.Gentieu), p.80 (open plan office/B.Ayres), p.83 (H.Sitton), p.84 (red card/B.Thomas), (woman on phone/J.Bradley), p.93 (teacher/W.Eastep), p.94 (thatched cottage/P.Cade), (hotel/C.Condina), (block of flats/C.Thomaidis), p.95 (Eiffel Tower/J.Lamb) (Stonehenge D...ildun/I.Sitton), (Statue of Liberty/ Rohan), (Taj Mahal/C.Haigh), p.99 (Bilbao/O.Strewe), (office buildings Docklands/R.A.Butcher), p.101 (villa with pool/A.Smith), (castle/H.P.Merten), p.102 (S.Norfolk), p.104 (man eating/J.Polollio), (couple with pizza/ S.Werner), (Japan fast food/M.Blank), (street stall/ L.Bobbe), p.106 (Rajasthan face decoration/P.Harris), (tattoo/D.Day), p.107 (yellow house/G.Benson), p.112 (shark/T.Flach), p.114 (violinist/M.York), p.119 (schoolboy /A.Sacks), p.120 (exam/P.Cutler); Topham Picturepoint p.34 (traffic 1960), p.36 (B.Curtis/Press Association); Trip p.35 (shepherd/H.Rogers), p.56 (portrait red dress/J.Okwesa), p.69 (colliery/J.Ellard), p.69 (beach/D.Houghton), p.94 (canal boats/R.Langfield), (bungalow/M.Lee), (tent/ D.Pluth), (hut/T.Bognar), p.111 (Her Majesty's Theatre/ A.Tovy)

Researched illustrations: © Glen Baxter from The Collected Blurtings of Glen Baxter, Little, Brown & Co, 1993, p.64 (I can't be absolutely certain...); Punch Ltd pp.64–5 (four cartoons along bottom of page)

Illustrations by: Asa Andersson pp.7, 39, 61, 71, 90; David Axtell p.76; Kathy Baxendale pp.12, 62, 81; Francis Blake pp.15, 67, 59, 87, 115; Wendy Blundell pp.20, 27 (gym), 45, 77, 93; Stephan Chabluk p.27; Emma Dodd pp.26, 43, 91; Mark Duffin pp.103, 157, 158; Mike Flanagan p.68; Jonathan Gibbs p.57; Madeleine Hardie pp.17, 60, 70; Sarah Jones pp.41, 74, 122; Satoshi Kambayashi p.73; Debbie Lush pp.23, 40, 63, 121; Kevin O'Keefe p.13; Dettmer Otto pp.20, 42, 83, 88, 113; Debbie Ryder pp.11, 31, 47, 51, 86; David Semple pp.10, 21, 85, 117; Steve Roberts pp.72, 92

Commissioned photography by: Mark Mason Photography p.47 (menu), p.53 (clipboard), p.67 (year planner), p.112 (book)

Location photography by: Rob Judges p.80 (desk top), p.123 (group of students, with special thanks to The Swan School of English, Oxford); Maggy Milner p.24 (stacking shelves/working on building site), p.84 (man getting into car), p.93 (mother and daughter)